THE

BOOK

EDITED BY KARL CORYAT

Backbeat
Books

SAN FRANCISCO

Published by Backbeat Books

600 Harrison Street, San Francisco, CA 94107

www.backbeatbooks.com

Email: books@musicplayer.com

An imprint of Music Player Network

United Entertainment Media, Inc.

Publishers of *Keyboard, Bass Player,* and *Guitar Player* magazines

Distributed to the book trade in the U.S. and Canada by
Publishers Group West, 1700 Fourth St., Berkeley, CA 94710

Distributed to the music trade in the U.S. and Canada by Hal Leonard Publishing, P.O. Box 13819, Milwaukee, WI 53213

Cover Design: Rich Leeds

Interior Design: Paul Haggard

Production Editor: Jan Hughes

Library of Congress Cataloging in Publication Data:
The bass player book / edited by Karl Coryat.
       p.   cm.
       Periodical articles from Bass player.
       Includes bibliographical references (p. ****).
       ISBN 0-87930-573-8
       1. Bass guitar. 2. Double bass. I. Coryat, Karl. II. Bass player.
ML1015.B35B37 1999
787.87—dc21   99-22675
                                    CIP

Printed in the United States of America
02 03 04 05 06   8 7 6 5 4

THE BASS PLAYER BOOK

Acknowledgments

This book would not have been possible without the generous and loyal support of the BASS PLAYER readers. In addition to being a wellspring of ideas, our readers have diligently kept us focused on the nuts-and-bolts needs of bassists everywhere. I'd like to thank BASS PLAYER's godfather and my first publishing mentor, former *Guitar Player* editor Tom Wheeler, who in just a few weeks turned a couple of fledgling editors into journalism professionals and gave BASS PLAYER a strong sense of purpose. Founding BP Editor Jim Roberts had a huge impact on this book—not only through his story assignments but through his years of guidance on editorial voice and stylistic matters. (He wrote a mighty fine Foreword as well.) When Richard Johnston took over as BP Editor in 1997, he taught us how the magazine's text could be tighter and more straightforward, and in editing this book I put the articles through my new RJ-style editorial sieve—as a result the material has been condensed by probably 20 or 30 pages without losing an ounce of meaning. Our illustrious Advisory Board has always been a guiding force and contributed greatly to this book's Musical Bibliography (page 208). Finally I'd like to thank the writers of all the material in this book as well as the rest of the BASS PLAYER staff. You're a great group, and with your help the future of the magazine—and our instrument—looks awfully bright.

About The Editor

Karl Coryat has been a BASS PLAYER editor since the magazine's 1989 inception. He served as its chief Editor from the January '97 through January '98 issues, and in October '98 became Editor of BASS PLAYER ONLINE (**www.bassplayer.com**). Along the way he has played bass in numerous San Francisco Bay Area bands and built a project recording studio, where he honed his skills not only as a bassist but also a record producer. He graduated from the University of California at Berkeley, where he tutored writing and led writing workshops at the school's Student Learning Center.

Part One: **Playing The Bass**

Part Two: **Equipment**

Part Three: **Innovators**

CONTENTS

Foreword

Are bass players born … or made?

It depends. When I interviewed Steve Rodby in 1987, he told me this: "I remember watching *Captain Kangaroo* when I was about three years old. I saw this guy with a string bass, and my heart skipped a beat. Then he started to play it, and I heard the sound. I couldn't get over it—I became completely convinced this was the instrument for me." Steve clearly has the "bass gene." For some other bassists, learning to love the low end is more an evolution than an epiphany. Paul McCartney, for one, has admitted that "none of us wanted to be the bass player" in the Beatles, and says he got "lumbered" with the job. Before long, though, Paul learned to love his new instrument. (To read all about it, see page 170.)

Whether you were born with the right DNA or had the bass thrust upon you, you need lots of information to become a truly good bass player. You should acquire a solid grounding in a variety of techniques, a good sense of time, an understanding of music theory, substantial knowledge about gear, and something else, too—something that's a little harder to capture in a musical example or write down on a page.

That "something else" is inspiration. As you learn how to play bass, you should seek inspiration in the work of the great players who preceded you and then channel that inspiration through your own playing. At first this can sound like mere imitation—even the most radical innovators admit they once copied their heroes note for note. But as you learn more about music (and more about yourself), all of that information and inspiration will come together within you and become the source of your own individual style. As Charlie Haden once said, "The sound that happens *inside* you is the sound that should come to your instrument." And when you hear that sound coming from your bass—whether you're the next Jaco or just a guy in a bar band—there's nothing like it.

In 1989, when I was asked to be the first Editor of BASS PLAYER, one of the goals I set was to make sure BP was filled not only with information but inspiration. There would be lessons on scales and song forms, there would be articles on buying basses and tweaking amps, and there would be lots of "nuts & bolts" about how bass lines had been composed, played, and recorded. But there would also be, I hoped, a healthy dose of inspiration in every issue— the kind that would help our readers on every level and in every style to become better and more distinctive players. And some of those readers, in turn, would go on to inspire the next generation of bass players.

Karl Coryat has done a great job of culling the best from BP's first ten years to create this volume. I hope you will refer to it often, and I hope you'll find the information you need to become a better bass player—and some of the inspiration, too.

—*Jim Roberts*
Group Publisher, the MFI Music Group

Jazz legend Ray Brown
in his early years

Introduction

Welcome to the BASS PLAYER family—what jazz legend Milt Hinton has called "the Brotherhood of the Bass." There's something special about this instrument. People get attracted to voice, guitar, and other lead instruments because of their centerstage glamour, and the drums beckon those who like the idea of banging things and making lots of noise. But the bass has a different appeal. Perhaps for you it all started at a concert with a single ultra-deep note that resonated your body cavity, causing a euphoric tingling that rose up your spinal column and made you say, "I want to do *that!*" Before you knew it you were in a music store plucking the open strings of basses hanging on a wall. You plugged one into a big amp, and *BOOM!*—you were hooked on the low end for good. Years from now you might be at a ball game listening to the National Anthem—but instead of singing along, you'll find yourself humming a bass line, reharmonizing the tune on the spot. Then you'll *know* you're a bass player.

BASS PLAYER magazine began regular publication in 1990, and I've had the pleasure of working on every single issue. All along I've been struck by a few common themes in artist interviews and columns. Again and again people refer to bass as the glue that bonds rhythm, harmony, and melody—the thing that ties a whole song together. They talk about the power of a bass line—how hanging on one note can radically alter a tune's harmony and create suspense, or how *not* playing can create a conspicuous void and draw attention elsewhere (or focus listeners on the bass when it returns). They mention that the best bass lines are the simplest ones, those that serve no other function than just to make the song sound great. And with very few exceptions, every bass player I've met has a warm, laid-back personality that fits perfectly with the instrument's supportive, unifying role.

How to Use This Book

THE BASS PLAYER BOOK has three main parts: Playing The Bass, Equipment, and Innovators. They shouldn't necessarily be read in that order, cover-to-cover—Parts One and Two each start with beginner information and progress toward material for the more advanced bassist, so read a little from one part and then jump to the other. Rich Appleman's Beginning Theory For Bassists (page 34) contains information necessary to understand Mike Hiland's Rock & Roll Basics (page 54)—so even if music theory interests you about as much as your shampoo's ingredients list, don't skip it. You'll be surprised how often the material comes up throughout your bass-playing career. And even if you have no desire to play country (page 77) or Latin music (page 84), understanding as many different musical styles as

Fig. 1: Schematic diagram of an acoustic bass

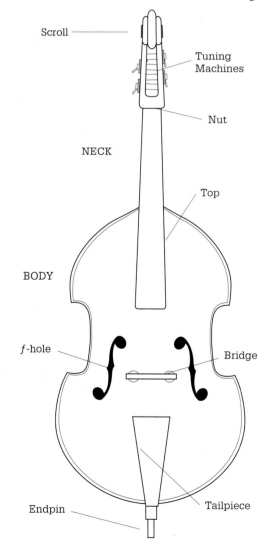

Scroll

Tuning Machines

Nut

NECK

Top

BODY

ƒ-hole

Bridge

Tailpiece

Endpin

possible can only enhance and broaden your general understanding of the bass. (And you never know when a tumbao groove will come in handy.)

Every bassist uses gear. Part Two takes you from buying an instrument to hooking up a full amp system, choosing effects, and recording. Plus there's a photo essay on the most notable electric basses ever designed.

Part Three contains stories on seven bassists who forever changed the way the instrument was played. You'll find these artists' words inspiring no matter where you are in the learning process. Revisit these pieces often—you'll likely get more out of them as your playing skills and experience progress.

The Rock-Bottom Bass Essentials

The acoustic-upright bass has a centuries-old tradition, but the electric bass is relatively new: Leo Fender designed the first truly practical version in 1951, basing it more on the electric guitar than the acoustic bass. The basic electric-bass design incorporates *frets*—strips of metal set into the fingerboard at the various note positions. (This is why Fender called his first electric bass the Precision.) Like the violin, the acoustic bass doesn't have frets, and you learn through experience and ear training where each note is located on the neck. Electric basses are also made without frets; fretless basses have a distinctly throaty, growling sound, but they're much harder to play in tune.

Figures 1 and 2 show the parts of an acoustic and electric bass, respectively. An acoustic bass produces sound mechanically, through the resonance of its hollow body and the vibrations of its top. (It can be electronically amplified as well; see page 134.) An electric bass, on the other hand, produces almost no sound on its own and depends on *pickups*, which are essentially wire-wrapped magnets, to generate a small electric current that's then amplified and sent to loudspeakers.

The strings of a 4-string bass are traditionally tuned *E, A, D,* and *G,* from low to high. 5-string electrics usually add a *B* string on the bottom, although a configuration called "tenor bass" adds a *C* string on the top. Modern 6-string electrics are tuned *BEADGC.* (There are 5- and 6-string acoustic basses, too, but these are rare.) Fig. 3 shows the notes at the various fingering positions of a 4-string. Notice that at the 5th-fret position the note is the same as the next higher open (non-fretted) string. The note names also start repeating when you move across the neck by two strings and up the neck by two frets. These important concepts will become clearer as you read through the first few articles in Part One: Playing The Bass.

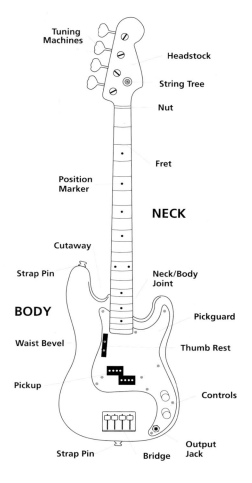

Fig. 2: Electric bass

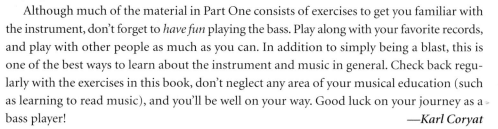

Fig. 3

Although much of the material in Part One consists of exercises to get you familiar with the instrument, don't forget to *have fun* playing the bass. Play along with your favorite records, and play with other people as much as you can. In addition to simply being a blast, this is one of the best ways to learn about the instrument and music in general. Check back regularly with the exercises in this book, don't neglect any area of your musical education (such as learning to read music), and you'll be well on your way. Good luck on your journey as a bass player!

—*Karl Coryat*

PART ONE

PLAYING THE BASS

Starting Out On Electric Bass

By Dave LaRue

You've decided you want to play the electric bass. What's next? Throughout your development as a musician, making informed decisions will help you progress and avoid the pitfalls that could slow you down or even discourage you from playing altogether. Let's start by looking at the equipment you'll need.

The most important decision you will have to make is which instrument to buy. A bass that plays well and sounds good will make practicing and playing much more enjoyable, which will encourage you to play more often—and you'll become a better player in less time. I've always thought it ironic that established players have basses that play like butter, while most students, not knowing any better, struggle with instruments that are better suited for archery.

Here are a few things to keep in mind when shopping for your first bass. (There's more information in the section titled How To Buy An Electric Bass on page 110.)

Research. Most stores don't carry all brands. Look around, pick up literature, read magazines, and ask questions. Try to see and play as many basses as possible. Prices on the same instrument will vary from store to store, so look for the best deal.

Neck and fingerboard. If you buy a bass with a bolt-on neck, be sure the bolts are tight and the neck heel fits *tightly* into the body's neck pocket. This prevents the neck from shifting, keeping the action and tuning more consistent. Check the neck for obvious dips or twists by looking down the fingerboard's surface and edges.

Fingerboards come in several types of wood, the most common being light-colored maple and dark brown rosewood. Rosewood tends to sound warmer than maple, which is a harder wood and therefore sounds brighter. The feel is different, too, since maple boards are often sprayed with a tough, slick finish. Experiment to see which you prefer.

Pickups. The two most common pickup designs are the "P" (Fender Precision Bass-style), a split pickup with the lower half offset from the upper half, and the "J" (Fender Jazz Bass-style), which is narrow and bar-shaped. A common pickup arrangement is the PJ setup: a P pickup mounted near the neck and a J pickup mounted near the bridge. This configuration offers lots of tone flexibility. In addition, virtually all pickup manufacturers make direct replacement P and J pickups that you can easily install if you later want to upgrade your electronics. Whatever you decide, be sure you understand what all the controls on the bass do, and make sure both pickups work.

When you've finally selected and purchased a bass, ask the salesperson for a complete setup, which should include string height, intonation, pickup height, and neck adjustments. The initial setup should be free; after that, expect to pay $30 to $60 plus string cost for this essential service.

Amplifiers. There are many good-quality, inexpensive amplifiers on the market. You should probably start with an amp in the 50- to 75-watt range, equipped with a 15" speaker. Such an amp is portable and should cover most of the situations you'll find yourself in for a while, from practicing at home to playing with a small group.

You'll need to get a couple other items that are standard equipment for serious musicians.

Metronome. Always remember that a bassist is, first and foremost, a member of the rhythm section. A crucial part of your job is keeping good, solid time. For this reason, you should work with an electronic metronome from day one.

Many types of metronomes are available in various price ranges. Initially you won't need one with a lot of frills. If you can get a unit with an output jack, you'll be able to practice late at night by plugging into your amp and using headphones.

By the way, a drum machine can make a great "metronome." For now don't worry about fancy features; find one that's easy to use.

Tuning aid. It's important to keep your bass tuned properly and to begin training your ears right from the start. Tuning your instrument is the first step toward those goals. As a beginner you may need some guidance in learning to tune your bass—but once you understand the concept, all you'll need is something that can generate a reference note. If you have a piano or keyboard at home, that will suffice—or you can purchase a tuning fork or pitch pipe at any music store. Be careful to stay in the correct register when using any of these tuning methods.

You can also use an electronic tuner; there are many good ones available at reasonable prices. There's a problem, though: Tuners do the work for you, so you don't get any valuable ear-training practice when you tune up with one of these units. For that reason I

Sting with the Police
in the early '80s

recommend starting with a pitch pipe or tuning fork. Tuning from a reference note encourages you to develop your sense of pitch, and in no time you'll be tuning up (or down) to your favorite albums and stealing licks from all the great bass players.

First Lessons

Today's bassist must know several playing techniques (fingerstyle, pickstyle, thumbstyle, etc.) and be able to improvise parts that are creative and rhythmically powerful. This takes time—but a good teacher and a solid practice routine will help you improve quickly.

Selecting an instructor. If you have some innate musical ability (most of us do), you can figure out quite a bit on your own right from the start. This can be gratifying—but it's also a way to acquire bad habits that will limit your development. To avoid that, you need a teacher. Find out who teaches bass in your area. Ask other musicians, go to local music stores, and check ads in the local papers. Once you've found some possibilities, set up meetings so you can get background information and ask a few questions.

I recommend studying with a teacher who is a bass player, not a guitarist who teaches bass. Bass and guitar techniques—especially picking-hand techniques—are quite different. A bass player will also be more comfortable with the bass clef, more familiar with bass method books and the bass repertoire, and more aware of the bass players currently on the scene.

Find a teacher who can teach you to play with your fingers. Although using your fingers is not necessarily preferable to playing with a pick, I've found it's much easier for a finger-style player to adapt to using a pick than it is for a pick player to learn fingerstyle. Your teacher also should be capable of playing and teaching thumbstyle technique (slap and pop). Be sure you'll be learning how to work with a metronome and how to read music.

Fortunately these days there's a great number of bass method books, play-along tapes, and instructional videos on the market, so try to familiarize yourself with as many of these as possible, and find out which ones each instructor uses.

Once you've gotten a good start on technique basics, you may want to move on to (or add) an instructor who is well versed in music theory and improvisation. Mastering theory fundamentals will enable you to progress quickly; instead of learning only one song a week at your lesson, you'll be able to pick up five a day at home. (For an introduction see Beginning Theory For Bassists on page 34.)

Practicing. The most important aspect of learning to play is making a commitment to practice regularly. *There is no substitute.* Owning the best gear and studying with the world's greatest musicians will not, by themselves, improve your playing. However, playing your instrument as often as possible will definitely make you a better player—and the more time you devote to practicing, the faster you'll improve.

As you start establishing a practice routine, keep in mind the following: First, no matter what you're playing—whether it's a Top-40 tune or a Mel Bay exercise—play it as well as you can. Be critical of all aspects of your playing: fingering, timing, plucking, excess finger noise, etc. If you play things slowly at first, your execution will be better when you increase the tempo. Second, work hardest on perfecting the things that give you the most trouble. All of us have strengths and weaknesses; I have students who are incredibly gifted physically but cannot understand musical concepts. If there were a Bass Olympics, these players would win gold medals—but they'll never get a gig with a band. I also have students where the reverse is true: good ideas, poor execution. Always try to exploit your strong points and improve your weak ones.

When you're starting out, play every day. Bass is a physical instrument, and developing and strengthening your hand muscles is essential to your playing. Try to establish a weekly routine and stick to it. Strive to be consistent—but if you miss a day, don't be too hard on yourself. Playing music should always be fun.

Work with your teacher on what you need to accomplish each day and each week. Setting goals will enable you to see how fast you're progressing. Also, be sure to prepare for each lesson. Learning music is a cumulative process, and your teacher won't be able to give you new material if you haven't mastered the old.

As you practice each day, try to keep an open mind about the materials you're using. Some aspects of your lesson may seem irrelevant—but if you have a good instructor, there is a reason for everything you've been assigned and a benefit to be derived from each assignment. Those of us who teach are not looking for ways to torture our students—although it may look like it sometimes. As you begin developing a relationship with your teacher, remember that you're the boss. If you have questions, ask them. If you're dissatisfied with your teacher, change. A lousy student-teacher relationship is bad for everyone.

Last, don't be afraid to strike out on your own. Look for ideas everywhere. Listen to and learn from all the great bassists. When you find a piece of music that particularly interests you, bring it to your lesson and work on it with your instructor. You'll be surprised how much your teacher appreciates and benefits from your initiative.

The Plucking Hand

Both students and instructors often place too little emphasis on the correct usage and development of the plucking hand (which for simplicity I'll call the right hand). Here are some exercises that will help you with "standard" right-hand technique—i.e., two-finger alternation. While no technique works in every situation, and there's an exception to every rule, these exercises will build the facility and flexibility you'll need to deal with most situations.

Begin by lightly anchoring your thumb on top of the pickup. If your bass has two pickups, use the one closer to the bridge. Playing near the bridge gives you better attack and note definition, and the strings are less likely to rattle against the frets. (Later you may want to play some or all of the time on the neck pickup, which provides a rounder tone but requires cleaner technique.) Pluck a few notes in different locations and listen to the sounds you get.

Once you've positioned your hand comfortably, allow your wrist to move freely as you reach for the higher strings. Keep your index and middle fingers straight (but not rigid), and pluck over the top of each string. Don't pull or pluck from underneath the strings. Avoid curling your fingers; use your thumb as a pivot point and move your arm. Your index and middle fingers should look about the same—straight—regardless of which string you're playing.

To build right-hand speed, you must be able to use both fingers equally well. Begin with Ex. 1, always alternating your fingers. The first time you play the exercise, start with your index finger; then play it again starting with the middle finger. Apply these same techniques to Ex. 2. Playing each of these exercises several times a day will help train your right hand—and before long, alternate plucking will be automatic. (Rich Appleman's Beginning Theory For Bassists article on page 34 explains music-reading fundamentals.)

When playing scales and licks, bassists often play runs consisting of three notes per string. This results in slightly more complicated plucking patterns. Ex. 3 alternates plucking in groups of three; although it may feel unnatural at first (the tendency is to "rake" the strings when coming down), it will become natural with repetition.

Practice these exercises *slowly*, and be sure to use a metronome. (A setting of 66–72 beats per minute is good to start.) This will improve your timing and enable you to check your progress. When you can play through each exercise without a mistake, move the metronome up a notch.

The Fretting Hand

Playing electric bass requires strength and flexibility in the fretting (left) hand. First, let's

Ex. 1

Ex. 2

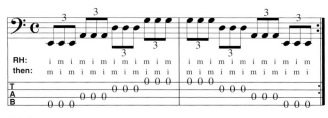

Ex. 3

cover basic hand positions, starting with the placement of the thumb behind the neck. The thumb is used as a guide and a pivot point, and it should always be able to move freely. Don't put a lot of pressure on your thumb; the force that pushes the strings down should come primarily from the other fingers, with the thumb providing balance and a reference point. Try to keep your thumb in the center of the neck, roughly opposite your middle finger. No matter what you see on MTV, don't hang your thumb over the top of the neck—your wrist should be able to move freely, giving your fingers easy access to all the strings.

Try to keep your fingers arched, somewhat perpendicular to the strings, and always play on your fingertips. To do this it's essential that you keep your palm off the neck: There should always be space between the lower edge of the fingerboard and your hand. When playing a note, put your fingertip in the forward (toward the bridge) part of the space between the frets. Put it close to the next fret, but not actually on top of it; this is usually the best-sounding and least noisy spot.

An important consideration in building speed is economy of motion. As you practice, be sure your fingers are not flying way off the neck. The farther a finger has to travel, the more time it takes to get to each note, thereby slowing down your playing. Each finger should stay in position, close to the fingerboard, anticipating the next note to be played. Watch many of the best players in action—even if you're hearing a flurry of notes, it often looks like their fingers are hardly moving.

Ex. 4, "the spider," was shown to me by one of my teachers years ago, and I still use it to warm up every day. It's very good for practicing position shifts as well as for building strength. Start with your index finger on the 1st fret of the *E* string, and using one finger per fret, play

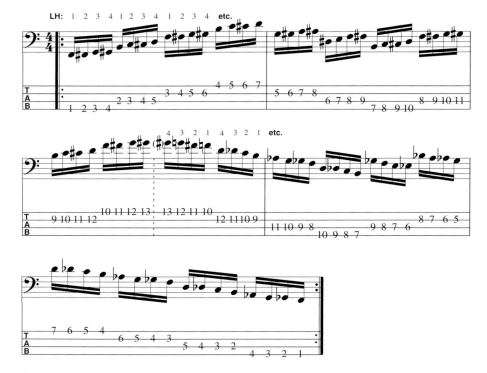

Ex. 4

1–2–3–4 (*F* to *A*♭ chromatically). Move up a fret and a string (to the 2nd-fret *B* on the *A* string) and repeat. Continue moving up a fret and a string each time, until you reach the 13th-fret *G*♯ on the *G* string. Then, using your pinkie as a guide, reverse the exercise, playing 4–3–2–1 and going down one string and one fret at a time, eventually returning to low *F*. You'll find that smoothly playing 4–3–2–1 requires more practice than playing 1–2–3–4. Starting with your pinkie is not as natural a movement, but repetition will improve your execution and strengthen your 3rd and 4th fingers. Remember to alternate your picking fingers when playing any exercise, and use a metronome to keep time and to check your progress.

Ex. 5

Ex. 5 is a workout for the weakest fingers, the 3rd and 4th. Substitute various combinations here: 1–4, 2–4, 1–3, 2–3, etc.

While you're working through these exercises, it's important not to get hung up practicing exercises and not devoting enough time to learning and playing *music*. Try to find a good balance; spend part of your practice time working on your technique, but be sure to spend as much or more time increasing your knowledge. That can come in the form of learning a new rock tune or a classical piece, or just studying some music theory.

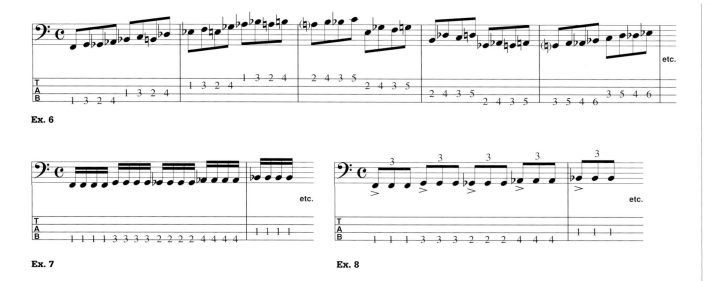

Ex. 6

Ex. 7   **Ex. 8**

Now let's expand on the spider exercise. Ex. 6 is a repeating pattern of 1–3–2–4, starting on low *F* and playing the pattern across all four strings. After you've done that (ending with the *G* string), move the pattern up a fret and play *down* the strings—that is, move your 1st finger to the 2nd-fret *A* on the *G* string, play 1–3–2–4, and then move down to the *D* string. This will build your endurance and get you accustomed to each area of the fingerboard. Next, move over to the 3rd-fret *G* on the *E* string and play up the strings, and so on. You can move in this fashion all the way up the neck (in time with a metronome, without stopping, of course). As you become comfortable, gradually increase the tempo and go on to new combinations, including ones that begin with different fingers. (1–4–2–3, 2–1–3–4, and 3–4–2–1 should provide you with a lot of laughs!)

Bringing Both Hands Together

Let's get your right hand a little more involved and work on alternate picking techniques, which will build your right-hand endurance. Ex. 7 moves up the neck in the same way as Ex. 9, but now we'll pick four 16th-notes for each left-hand finger. The secret to keeping this up for a long time lies in relaxing your right arm and hand; as soon as you begin to tense up or dig in too hard, you'll feel your chops start to fade. Start slowly and try to play for as long as you comfortably can. As your endurance increases, push up the tempo. To work on different feels and meters, play this exercise in triplets with three notes per finger (Ex. 8), and if you're in a daring mood, try groups of five notes per beat (Ex. 9).

The Major Scale

In order for us to begin "speaking" the complex language of music, we must first learn the

Ex. 9

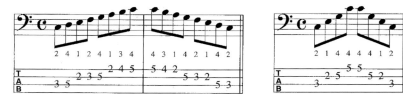

Ex. 10　　　　　　　　　　　　　　　　　**Ex. 11**

Ex. 12　　　　　　　　　　　　　　　　　**Ex. 13**

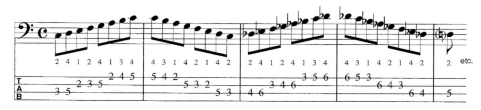

Ex. 14

Ex. 15

Ex. 16　　　　　　　　　　　　　　　　　**Ex. 17**

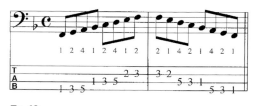

Ex. 18　　　　　　　　　　　　　　　　　**Ex. 19**

basic "words" and "phrases" (which we can think of as notes and patterns) that comprise this language. Virtually all the music you'll be playing will have a key center or centers and an associated scale that consists of all the notes in that key. The most common scale is the *major scale*, which contains all the notes of a particular major key. (Read more about scales and keys in Beginning Theory For Bassists on page 34.) Let's begin establishing your musical vocabulary with a study of major scales.

Learning an electric-bass scale in all keys is easy. Unlike keyboard or horn players, we can learn one scale fingering and—*voilà!*—we know that scale in every key. What's tricky is that we must be able to play the same scale several ways, using different fingering patterns in different positions. To facilitate learning the various scales I'll refer to them from their starting points. The first scale you'll learn is the 2–3 major scale—the "2–3" means you'll start fingering with your 2nd finger on the 3rd (*A*) string. The 2–4 scale starts with your 2nd finger on the 4th (*E*) string, the 1–3 with your 1st finger on the 3rd (*A*) string, and so on. Ex. 10 is the 2–3 *C* major scale pattern. Once you've learned it, you can use the same pattern starting on any other note to play the major scale in that key.

Ex. 11 is a 2–3 major *arpeggio*. An arpeggio is a "broken" chord: The notes are played one at a time rather than together. Since many bass lines are derived from arpeggios, you should begin incorporating them into your vocabulary right away. The arpeggio of a major triad (a chord made up of three notes) consists of the 1st, 3rd, and 5th notes of the major scale.

Examples 12 and 13 are the 2–4 major scale and arpeggio, respectively. As you can see, the patterns are identical to the 2–3 fingerings but in a different key: *G* major. Move this pattern around, playing different major scales and arpeggios. Notice that you can play the same key in different positions; for example, you can play in the key of *C* starting on the 3rd fret of the *A* string or the 8th fret of the *E* string.

Once you've become comfortable with these scales and arpeggios, you can use them to develop your musicianship. For Ex. 14, play the 2–3 major scale up the neck in half-steps, without stopping, and say the name of each new key *out loud* as you go. This will help you learn the fingerboard, and it will also make you think ahead, improving your focus and concentration. To challenge yourself use the "flat" names (e.g., *B♭* instead of *A♯*) when naming the keys. After playing the 2–3 scales up the neck, apply this exercise to the 2–3 arpeggio (Ex. 15) and then the 2–4 scale and arpeggio. As always, use a metronome to work on your time and to check your progress as you increase the tempo.

More Difficult Major-Scale Fingerings

The 1–3 scale (Ex. 16) and arpeggio (Ex. 17) are more difficult because you need to either stretch, pivot your hand, or actually shift positions—but they're good basic fingerings because of their symmetry and extended range. As you begin to develop solo lines and fills, you'll find this fingering is readily adaptable to a variety of melodic "shapes," especially those that span more than one octave.

Once you've become familiar with the 1–3 fingerings, try to apply them in situations where you have been using 2nd-finger positionings. This will force you to view the fingerboard in a slightly different fashion, and it may enable you to find some interesting melodic variations. The 1–4 scale and arpeggio (Examples 18 and 19) are identical to the 1–3 but start on the *E* string instead of the *A*, and they cover a different set of keys as a result.

The 4–3 and 4–4 scales and arpeggios (Examples 20 through 23) can be somewhat tricky. Although they aren't that common, there are instances where one can be the best fingering

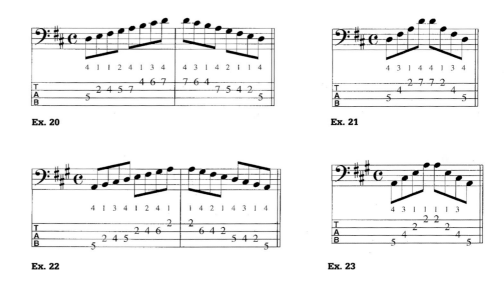

Ex. 20

Ex. 21

Ex. 22

Ex. 23

for a certain passage, so get familiar with them. The 4th-finger scales and arpeggios are the first ones we've encountered where the *E*- and *A*-string fingerings are not identical. You can play the 4–4 scale the same way as the 4–3, but I've included both options so you can see all the possibilities and stay in one position whenever possible.

When shifting positions on the 4–3 scale, remember to move your 1st finger by a whole-step (two frets); do this smoothly and with as little string noise as possible. You'll use this type of shift more often when you begin playing longer, extended lines. The 4–3 arpeggio introduces an even larger shift; since the first three notes are all in position, you can "ignore" them and focus on your target note, the high octave. This is a difficult move, but it becomes easier with practice.

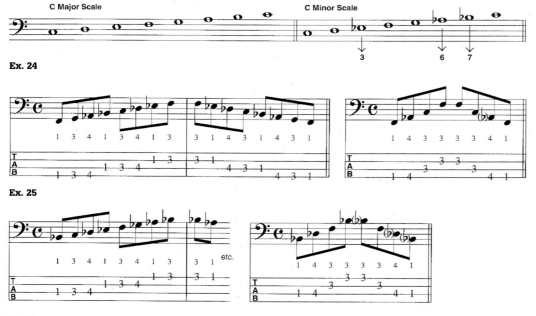

Ex. 24

Ex. 25

Ex. 26

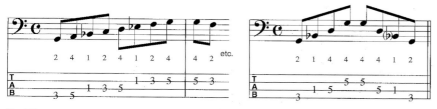

Ex. 27

The Minor Scale

Let's move on to minor scales. First you need to get acquainted with the "minor sound." You know that a major chord consists of the 1st, 3rd, and 5th notes of the major scale; in the key of *C*, for example, a *C*-major chord is made up of *C*, *E*, and *G*. (If you have access to a keyboard or guitar, you might want to start pounding out these chords. You can play them on your bass, but they'll sound a little muddy.) A *C* minor chord is built by simply lowering the 3rd (*E* in the key of *C*) one half-step to *E*♭. Many people describe major chords as sounding "bright" or "happy"; I think you'll agree the *C* minor chord (*C*, *E*♭, and *G*) sounds "darker" than *C* major.

Writing and playing in minor keys presents problems we don't encounter in major keys. Mainly, there are several different minor scales, which composers often interchange freely within their music. So as not to get ahead of ourselves, let's learn about them one at a time.

The most common minor scale is the *natural minor*. (The natural minor scale sounds the same as something called the *Aeolian mode*, but don't worry about that for now.) Compared to the major scale, the natural minor is constructed with a lowered 3rd (as in the minor chord), a lowered 6th, and a lowered 7th. Therefore the notes of the *C* natural-minor scale are *C*, *D*, *E*♭, *F*, *G*, *A*♭, and *B*♭ (Ex. 24).

Learning this scale's fingerings should clarify the differences between major and natural minor. As with the major-scale fingerings we've worked with, each natural minor scale is labeled according to the finger and string you start on. Since we've done so much work with major scales and arpeggios, I've included all the fingerings for the natural-minor scale we'll be using (Examples 25 through 30). As you practice the minor scales and arpeggios, play each up the neck in half-steps, naming the keys as you go in order to maximize your fingerboard fluency.

If you do a little exploring with natural-minor scales, you'll notice the *A* natural minor scale contains no sharps or flats; consequently it has the same key signature as *C* major. These two keys are said to be *relative* to each other; *A* minor is the relative minor of *C* major, and *C* major is the relative major of *A* minor. You should be able to identify any key's relative major or minor. It's actually quite easy to do. To find a major key's relative minor, play to the 6th degree of the major scale—that note gives you the root of the relative minor. For instance, the 6th degree of *D* major is *B*, so we know *B* minor is the relative minor of *D* major. To find the relative major of a minor key, play to the 3rd degree in the minor scale; this tells us *F* major is relative to *D* minor.

As you study this concept you'll notice how often relative majors and minors are used together in songs. They can be interchanged easily; experiment with substituting one scale for its relative when playing a fill or a solo. For a fill over *D* minor, for instance, try using something based around *F* major. This will get you away from starting every lick on the root, which tends to sound boring.

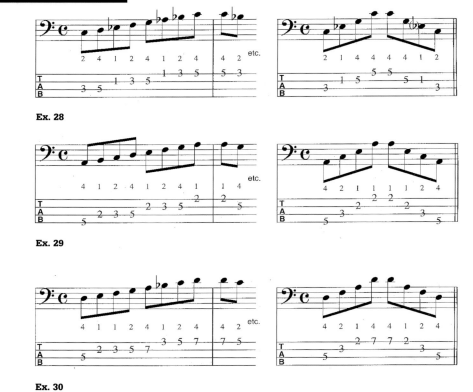

Ex. 28

Ex. 29

Ex. 30

Let's close out our study by looking at two more varieties of the minor scale: the *melodic minor* and *harmonic minor*. You won't encounter these as often as natural minor, but they present interesting sounds you might want to incorporate into your playing and writing.

The melodic minor scale differs from natural minor in that it uses the non-flatted 6th and 7th from the major scale. (Some people call this a raised 6th and 7th when talking in minor terms.) The melodic minor formula, in relation to the major scale, is: 1, 2, ♭3, 4, 5, 6, and 7—although traditionally the descending form of the scale uses the same notes as the natural minor (Ex. 31). When the notes are the same whether ascending or descending, the melodic minor scale is sometimes called the *jazz melodic* minor scale (Ex. 32).

The harmonic minor scale formula is 1, 2, ♭3, 4, 5, ♭6, and 7 (Ex. 33). The interval between the flatted 6th and the non-flatted 7th—an augmented second—makes for some interesting sounds. Examples 34 through 39 illustrate fingering possibilities for these minor scales. Practice them with a metronome, in all the different keys, etc.—you know what to do.

The Big Picture

I'll close with some overall concepts, some of which I've already touched on:

1. Don't get bogged down in the technical end of playing. Even though most of these exercises have been technique-oriented, don't take this to mean working only on technique will enable you to play good music—or, more important, to *create* good music.

2. Divide your practice time so you cover many facets of music. As a beginner you need to spend a lot of time on technique, because you must learn to physically play the instrument. Once you've developed some facility, however, start covering other areas, such as ear training. (For instance, when you're in the car try figuring out bass lines and chord

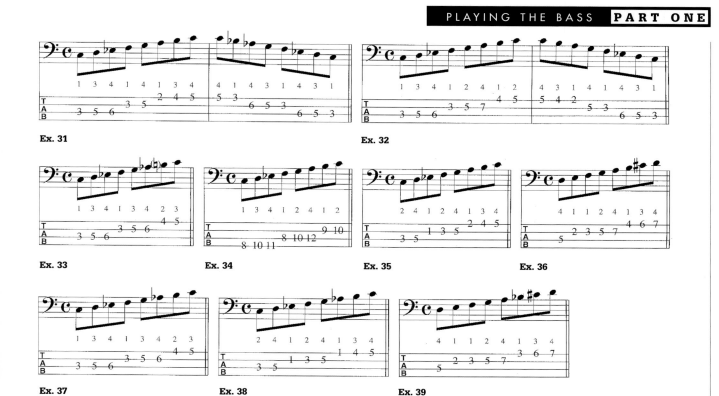

Ex. 31   Ex. 32

Ex. 33   Ex. 34   Ex. 35   Ex. 36

Ex. 37   Ex. 38   Ex. 39

progressions off the radio.) Theory and improvisation, reading, recording techniques—everything is important.

3. Force yourself to improve every day. That may not sound easy, but it is. If you can do one thing better each day—whether it's reading one more measure of a Bach cello suite or perfectly executing something one metronome mark higher—you've improved. It would be even better if you could transcribe one more measure of a Jaco solo or get comfortable playing in another odd meter. Leave time in each practice session (more and more time as you improve) for fun and experimentation. Improvise on a new scale or over an unfamiliar chord progression, or experiment with different polyrhythms.

4. Record yourself as much as possible. This is the best way to determine your weak spots. Even if you tape yourself playing only exercises, you can learn a lot about your playing. Experiment with your sound, check for string noise and fret buzz, and—most important—make sure you're playing in time. (Always record your metronome or drum machine so you have a timing reference on playback.) Record different feels and figures, such as pumping straight eighths and syncopated funk lines, and see how accurate you can make them. If you have a drum machine, write some bass lines around the kick-drum patterns and see if you can be right on with them. Make your lines feel good.

5. Write as much original music as possible, whether it's bass lines, songs, or fragments of either. You don't have to finish a line or song all at once; some composers are happy to write four new bars per day. When you're writing something that's truly new to you, it can be great for your ears and your technique. And when you hear something in your head, try to let your ears lead you to it (yes, you can use your bass as well), and don't fall back on what you'd usually play. You might spend a lot of time playing this new idea over and over as you try to work it out—but it will make you a physically better player as well as a more creative one.

6. Combine transcribing and writing. When I hear one of the greats play something really cool, especially if it includes a technique I'm working on (like some perverted slap method), I learn it note-for-note and then try to write something of my own that incorporates a version of that idea.

In the final analysis, no one can teach you to play music creatively. Those of us who teach can only provide students with the tools and perhaps offer some insight into the creative process. Playing music requires much more than technique, and the dedication and inspiration have to come from inside you.

Proper Positioning

By Ed Friedland

Let's discuss the ergonomic considerations pertaining to the biomechanical interface with a low-frequency vibrational output device … in other words, the right way to hold the bass. This may seem intuitive—you know, strap it on and play—but improper playing position can lead to a variety of physical problems, including tendinitis, carpal-tunnel syndrome, and the dreaded "bass player's back." I'm not trying to scare you off, but you should be aware of the potential for problems. Fortunately they're easy to avoid.

The most common problem I see is a player trying to look like the guys on MTV, with the bass hanging down near the knees. While this may look cool and "rock & roll," it reduces your mobility on the instrument and forces an extreme left-wrist bend, which can lead to big problems down the road. The other side of the coin is the "fusion geek" posture, in which the bass hangs just below the jawbone. This position gives you clear access to the upper frets for soloing, but it creates a sharp bend in the *right* wrist, which also spells trouble. The proper position can be found somewhere between these two extremes.

To find the most comfortable position to play the bass, stand up with your shoulders relaxed and your arms at your sides. Bend your left elbow so your hand comes up into playing position. Now extend your right arm in front of you at a little below shoulder height, with your hand hanging down naturally; then bend your elbow and bring your hand straight in toward your body, keeping your shoulder relaxed. This is the most tension-free position—adjust your strap so the bass hangs at this height. You can alter the height a little in either direction based on your preference.

Next comes hand position. Take your left thumb and plant it in the middle of the back

Ex. 1

of the neck, as if you're giving a thumbprint. Let your fingers rest on the strings. Sometimes you will play on the tips of your fingers, and sometimes you will use more of the pads. Keep your fingers open, and avoid contact between your palm and the bass neck. Remember to keep your thumb low on the back of the neck; when it peeks over the top, your fingers cramp up and you lose your ability to stretch. (See Figures 1 and 2.)

For the right hand, start with your thumb resting on a pickup. Keep your fingers naturally hanging down across the strings. Grab the *E* string with your index finger first, and pluck across the top of the string with a slight inward motion. Do the same with your middle finger, and alternate the two. Now go to the *A* string; use the same movement here, but pay attention to how your finger comes to rest against the *E* string at the end of your stroke. This is what you want: The *E* string is muted with a finger, so it won't ring when you don't want it to. Switching to the *D* string, drop the thumb to the *E*; this keeps the *E* muted and helps to maintain a consistent angle of attack on the *D* string. Your finger will come to rest against the *A* string at the end of the stroke, muting it. Finally, when moving across to the *G* string, you have two muting choices. One method is to drop the thumb onto the *A* string and lean it against the *E* so you're muting both strings. Another is to keep your thumb on the *E* string and let your ring finger rest against the *A*. (Fig. 3 shows how this technique can be used on a 5- or 6-string.) This may seem a little harder than the first method, but both techniques feel more natural after you practice them.

Now let's get both hands working together. Ex. 1 is a mechanical warmup that will get your hands accustomed to playing the bass. Play slowly, paying attention to the quality of sound you're producing. Let your notes ring, and go for consistency of volume and tone. Notice how your left hand feels: is it relaxed or tight? If it's tight, relax the grip between your thumb and the back of the neck.

Play this exercise every day, and within two weeks you will see major changes taking place in your hands. Remember to practice with focus, to pay attention to the details, and to have fun!

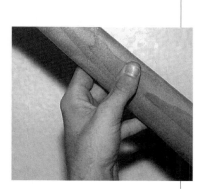

Fig. 1

Fig. 2

Fig. 3

Learning From Yourself

By Victor Wooten

Learning is valuable—we all know that. But like any skill or talent, it can be practiced and refined to an art. Most of us have never spent much time thinking about the art of learning, because when it's time to learn something new we usually look to be taught by someone else. Most of our teaching comes from an outside source; rarely do we approach something new by going inside of ourselves. Although it may seem strange, this actually may be the best, most thorough way to learn.

Don't get me wrong—having a teacher can be wonderful and necessary, and it can definitely speed up the learning process. I'm not saying learning from others is the wrong way to learn—but even when an idea is brought to you from another person, you still must bring it into your inner recesses for it to be truly learned, refined, and personalized. It has to become *your* truth before you can learn it completely.

People often ask me to show them how to play a particular pattern or lick. I don't mind

showing them—but I enjoy it more when they've already tried to figure it out for themselves. Just think: If you figure out something on your own, you'll probably do it the way that suits you best. Then when you finally learn how someone else does it, you'll have *two* ways of doing it. Both are equally valuable.

It also works in the other direction: People sometimes show me easier ways of playing my own licks. These people have taken *my* way and brought it deep within themselves, until it came out *their* way. Again, both methods are equally valuable.

Think of all the great inventors throughout time—they came up with ideas that didn't exist before them. They would not have been able to accomplish this had they listened only to outside sources. Similarly, there are inside sources just waiting for you to ask them for their help.

The more you do this "inner" learning, the better you get at it. Your brain will get into the habit of producing instead of waiting to receive. Eventually you might be able to hear a musical passage and immediately know how to reproduce it—and you'll personalize it, with your own touch, without even trying. This is the key to being original. All of your favorite musicians—Marcus Miller, Geddy Lee, John Patitucci, and all the rest—have spent a tremendous amount of time sitting down by themselves in order to sound the way they do. That's the key to their sound, and it's also the key to their success.

Most animals possess this kind of knowledge, but among humans it has become almost a lost art. I remember many years ago being fascinated by my dog; she would get sick, go outside, eat some grass (which would usually make her throw up), and then she would be all better. Who taught her this? Not me. It's the same "person" who teaches a caterpillar to become a butterfly—and that "person" lies deep within us all. We all have this ability, and it can be practiced.

So if you're looking for a teacher, don't just sit there idling—practice, practice, practice until you find one, and then keep practicing. If you already have a teacher, listen closely to what he or she has to say, because you may discover directions you wouldn't have thought of on your own. But remember always to take any teachings deep within yourself to see if they match your individual truth. Then go practice some more.

To all of you teachers out there, I'd like to offer this challenge: Ponder what I have said here, and if it makes any sense to you, teach it to your students. Don't worry—it won't encourage them to stay home. In fact, you might find it will actually bring you *more* students.

Music will take on a whole new meaning when you hear it through your own ears. Go inside and see what is there to learn. Go inside, my friend. Go inside.

Phil Lesh, formerly with the Grateful Dead

Producer Steve Rodby
and Michael Manring
look over a chart for
Manring's *Drastic
Measures* CD

Beginning Theory For Bassists

By Rich Appleman

One of a bassist's most valuable tools is the ability to read music. Along with the ability to read comes an understanding of basic music theory, also an invaluable skill. Music notation and music-theory terminology comprise the standard written and spoken languages musicians use to communicate ideas—so whether you're striving to be a first-call session player or are content to rock out in your garage, understanding these concepts will pay off again and again throughout your life as a musician.

We'll be learning and using the standard music-notation system. Although there are other ways to notate music, this is the most widely accepted method. There's no mystery to reading music, and you'll discover that you learn faster as your reading improves. But as you learn, remember that it's the player who brings written music to life. Without the

understanding and skill to read and play the written notes, there would be no sound—
and without the sound of the pitches there would be no music.

Reading The Bass Clef

Music is written on a *staff*, which consists of five lines and four spaces (Ex. 1). A *clef* is a symbol, placed at the beginning of each staff, that designates which pitches correspond to the

Ex. 1

Ex. 2

Ex. 3

Ex. 4

lines and spaces of the staff. There are several kinds of clefs; we're interested in the *bass clef*, also known as the *F clef*. It's called the *F clef* because the staff line between the two dots corresponds to the note *F* below middle *C*. The *grand staff* consists of the bass-clef staff and the treble-clef staff together; middle *C* falls right between the two staves, hence its name (Ex. 2).

We'll continue to discuss clefs and staves, but first I'd like to introduce the *musical alphabet*: seven letters (*A, B, C, D, E, F,* and *G*) that name the notes or pitches used to write music. Of course, music ranges a lot further than seven notes, so we use the musical alphabet in a circular fashion; that is, the next note after *G* is *A*, then come *B, C,* and so on. Ex. 3 shows the musical alphabet on the staff in the bass clef. Notice that the notes go from the bottom of the staff to the top and occupy every line and space in an alternating fashion. It's important to memorize the location of each note. It may help if you remember that the notes in the spaces (from bottom to top) stand for "All Cows Eat Grass," and that the notes on the lines stand for "Good Boys Do Fine Always." Sometimes it's necessary to extend the staff to accommodate notes either above or below it; for this, we use *ledger lines* (Ex. 4).

Now let's put everything together. Ex. 5 shows the notes on a 4-string bass, up to the 12th fret of the *G* string. The four open strings—*E, A, D,* and *G*—are indicated by the filled-in

Ex. 5

notes. For practice, write down the names of a few notes and try locating them on the staff. Then write some notes on the staff and name them.

Time Signatures & Rhythms

Since good bass playing establishes a solid foundation for the music, it's important to begin thinking about rhythms right away. A great bassist once told me that in the 1940s, musicians were more interested in the bass keeping time than playing pitches, since bass back then was usually more felt than heard (due to primitive equipment and recording techniques). Things are quite different today—but keeping good time should still be one of your primary concerns.

The *time signature*, placed on the staff after the clef (Ex. 6), defines the music's rhythm and the values of the notes within that rhythm. For now we'll concern ourselves only with the simplest time signature, *common time*, often represented by the letter C (Ex. 7).

In order to understand what common time is, we need to understand one more concept: the *measure*. Measures, which are also commonly called *bars*, are bite-size sections of music separated on the staff by *bar lines* (Ex. 8). In common time, one measure contains four beats. If we think of a measure as a pie, we see that four beats equals the whole pie; therefore, we call a note that is four beats long a *whole-note*. Similarly, a note that is two beats long is called a *half-note*, and so on down to *32nd-notes* and *64th-notes*. On the staff each of these note values is represented by a different note symbol (Fig. 1). Eighth-notes, 16th-notes, and the smaller notes are usually written with *flags* if they are alone, or they may be ganged together with *beams* (Ex. 9). In either case, the individual notes' time values are the same.

Measure division	Name of note	Symbol	Number of beats note gets (common time)
◯	Whole-note	𝅝	4
◯	Half-note	𝅗𝅥	2
◯	Quarter-Note	𝅘𝅥	1
◯	Eighth-note	𝅘𝅥𝅮	1/2
◯	16th-note	𝅘𝅥𝅯	1/4

Fig. 1

Ex. 6

Ex. 7

Ex. 8

Ex. 9

Ex. 10

Ex. 10 reviews the material covered so far. All the notes are the open strings *E, A, D,* and *G.* Practice the exercise slowly. Some hints:

1. Concentrate on reading the notes. Memorize the name of each line or space, and listen to each note's sound. It's not unusual to relate certain pitches to certain colors; I've always thought *A* sounded "red," for example.

2. The sound quality (timbre) should be pleasing to your ear. Try to emulate the sound of a bassist you enjoy. Experiment getting different sounds with your fingers, a pick, or a bow if you're playing an upright.

3. Keep accurate time. Establish a steady pulse and groove. Playing with a drum machine or metronome is helpful and fun, but be aware that you should also learn to groove by yourself—so do some practicing alone as well.

Half-Steps & Whole Steps: Building Blocks Of Tonal Music

A half-step is the *interval*, or distance, between two notes that are next to each other in pitch. It's easy to hear half-steps on a fretted instrument like an electric bass; if you move up the neck by one fret, you've gone up a half-step. (On a keyboard, going up by one key, including the black ones, is a half-step.) A whole-step is simply two half-steps—two frets or two keys. The electric bass and the keyboard are *equal-tempered* instruments, meaning the semitones (another term for half-steps) between any two adjacent frets or keys are equal. If you play a fretless or upright bass, you need to practice equal-tempered intonation very carefully, using your ear, open-string notes, and reference points on the neck.

For purposes of illustration, Fig. 2 shows the notes as they are laid out on a keyboard. The white keys correspond to the notes of the musical alphabet (sometimes called *natural* notes). The black key above any natural note is called a *sharp*, designated in notation by the ♯ symbol; for example, the black key above C is C♯, and the black key above D is D♯. Therefore, anytime a note has a ♯ next to it, it means the natural note should be raised by a half-step. The black key below any natural note is a *flat*, designated by the ♭ symbol, which lowers the natural note by one half-step. Therefore, the black key below A is A♭, and the black key below B is B♭. The symbols ♭ and ♯ are called *accidentals*, and if no accidental precedes a note, that note is assumed to be natural.

Fig. 2

Ex. 11 shows a bass-clef staff with accidentals. Anytime an accidental is used, it applies to all notes with the same name within that measure; after a bar line, the previous accidentals are canceled. If a sharped or flatted note returns to natural within the measure, it must be preceded by a natural sign (♮).

Ex. 11

Ex. 12

Two little twists to the system: You might have noticed that there are no black keys between B and C, or between E and F. The intervals between those notes are called *natural half-steps*. Also, many notes can sound the same but have different names—C♯ and D♭, for example. These pairs of notes are called *enharmonics*. For now, suffice it to say an enharmonic name for C♯ is D♭.

Ex. 12 shows two *chromatic scales*—scales containing all the half-steps—that you should practice on your bass and memorize. When you're familiar with them, play, sing, and memorize the chromatic scales starting on all the different pitches. Play up and down to the same-named pitch—E to E, F to F, etc. Use both fretted and open strings. Begin slowly, and play with a metronome or drum machine.

The Major Scale

One of the most important concepts in our musical language is the *major scale*. It's vital for playing, writing, hearing, and understanding most forms of Western music. Let's take a close look.

Most standard scales are a succession of seven notes in a fixed order. The major scale contains all seven letters of the musical alphabet, and it always begins and ends on the same note. This note is called the *tonic*, and it defines the name of the scale. For instance, a *G* major scale begins and ends on *G*, the tonic note in the key of *G*.

Let's build a major scale using the building blocks you learned earlier: the half-step and whole-step. The major-scale formula is whole-step, whole-step, half-step, whole-step, whole-step, whole-step, half-step. In other words, a major scale consists of two successive whole-tones, followed by a semitone, then three whole-tones, and finally another semitone. The various notes in a scale are called *scale degrees*; the tonic is the 1st scale degree, the scale's 2nd note is the 2nd degree (often called simply the 2nd), and so on. Look at the three major scales in Ex. 13; note that in the *C* major scale, the natural half-steps *E–F* and *B–C* fall conveniently at the right spots. In the *F* major scale, though, we must flat the *B* (lower it by a half-step) to create the semitone between the 3rd and 4th scale degrees, and in the *G* major scale we need to sharp the *F* to create the whole-step needed between the 6th and 7th degrees.

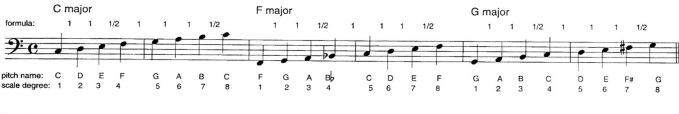

Ex. 13

Ex. 14

Notice that the *F♯* provides the half-step to end the scale at *G*.

Another way to look at scales is to think of *tetrachords*. A tetrachord is a series of just four notes; the formula for a major tetrachord is whole-step, whole-step, half-step. Ex. 14 shows two major tetrachords separated by a whole-step; combined, they form a complete major scale. Breaking a larger scale into two smaller four-note scales makes it easier to play, hear, and sing.

Now let's shift gears and discuss a different time signature: 3/4. Earlier you learned about common time, in which one measure gets four beats. In 3/4 time, each measure gets three beats. This changes the way the music is counted; instead of *one* two three four, *one* two three four, we count *one* two three, *one* two three. In any time signature, the top number indicates how many beats are in each measure, and the bottom number designates what type of note gets one beat or one count. For instance, a measure in 3/4 contains three quarter-notes, a measure in 3/8 contains three eighth-notes, and so on (Ex. 15). By now it

Ex. 15

Ex. 16

should be easy to understand why common time is also written as the time signature 4/4: A measure in common time contains four quarter-notes.

Let's construct a major scale in 3/4 time. Ex. 16 shows the B♭ major scale. Play it slowly, counting out "*one* two three, *one* two three" and accenting each measure's first note to emphasize the rhythm. For homework, write out the following major scales in 3/4, using Ex. 16 as a guide: *C, F, E♭, Ab, D♭, G♭, B, E, A, D,* and *G.* For extra credit try the enharmonic equivalents of the flatted scales: *D♯, G♯, C♯,* and *F♯.* Then try to figure out fingerings for playing the scales, starting on different fingers and places on the neck. You'll be surprised how many ways there are to play the major scale!

Key Signatures

If you did your homework, you should now have 15 major scales built on the following pitches: *C, F, B♭, E♭, A♭, D♭, G♭, C♭, G, D, A, E, B, F♯,* and *C♯.* Each of these scales should have the same order of half-steps and whole-steps, and they should sound similar when you play or sing them. The sequence of steps between the notes (whole-whole-half-whole-whole-whole-half) creates the characteristic sound of the major scale.

All the notes in a major scale are said to be in the *key* defined by the tonic, or first note, of the scale. A key, when assigned to a piece of music, provides a "home base" to the series of notes and indicates which notes should be flatted or sharped. In the key of *C* major, for instance, all the notes in the piece correspond to the notes of the *C* major scale, unless indicated otherwise. For now we'll discuss only major keys.

Ex. 17 shows the 15 major *key signatures* that correspond to the scales you built for homework. A key signature, placed between the clef and time signature, designates the notes that need to be flatted or sharped in order to produce the sound of that key. For example, to play in the key of *G* major you need to include *F♯* in the key signature; for the major key of *F* you need to include *B♭.* The key signature places accidental symbols (♯ and ♭) on the lines

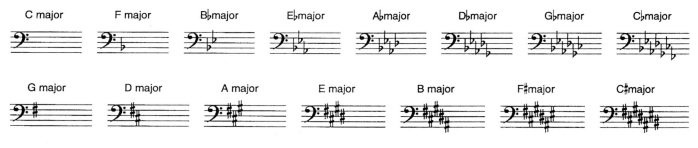

Ex. 17

Ex. 18

and spaces they affect; a note is natural if nothing is placed on that particular line or space. The accidentals that make up a key signature are always placed in the same order and on the same lines or spaces; therefore you should memorize the key signatures by writing them out on a musical staff as part of your practice routine. (Remember, music is like a language— and the more you speak, write, and listen to a language, the quicker you will learn to express yourself fluently.) A few things to keep in mind:

• All the notes sharped or flatted by a key signature are affected, even if they are in different octaves and therefore don't fall on the same line or space as the key-signature accidental. In Ex. 18 *every* note is flatted. (If you want to play that low E♭, you'll need to detune or use a 5-string.)

• Traditional key signatures don't mix sharps and flats, even though both sharps and flats may be used in the music itself. Ex. 19 should sound familiar—especially if you watch too much TV. (If you're puzzled by the rhythmic notation, that's okay; we'll learn about those little dots later.)

• If a piece of music has no key signature, either it's in the key of *C* major or the key signature has been intentionally omitted to make it easier to read.

Rests, Dots & Ties

Remember the pie chart? One whole-note = four beats, one half-note = two beats, and so on. Like notes, rests are characters that represent musical time values—except they desig-

Ex. 19

nate *silence* instead of sound. Whole-rests, half-rests, quarter-rests, etc., are equal in duration to the notes they replace (Ex. 20). As you listen to and play music, think about how important the rests are; the absence of sound is just as important as the sound itself. Why? Because continuous sound exhausts (or bores) the listener. It's like the balance between space and color in a painting, or between textures and flavors in a fine meal. Sometimes it's what you leave out that really makes music happen—especially when you're the bass player.

Still another concept that relates to time is the *dot*. A dot after a note or rest adds half

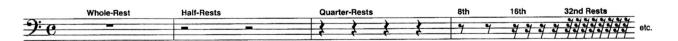

Ex. 20

again the value of that note or rest. For example, in common time (4/4) a half-note gets two beats—so a dotted half-note gets three beats. A quarter-note gets one beat, so a dotted quarter-note gets one-and-a-half beats, and so on (Ex. 21). It helps to associate the dot with

Ex. 21

Ex. 22

Ex. 23

the number three, since a dotted note always lasts for three subdivisions of that note. (A dotted eighth-note lasts for three 16th-notes, for instance.) You may need to spend some time working with dotted notes and rests to get a good feel for them.

You can even double-dot notes and rests, which adds half *again* the value of the dotted note. Associate the double-dot with the number seven, since a double-dotted note always lasts for seven *sub*-subdivisions. For example, a double-dotted half-note gets seven eighth-notes (three-and-a-half quarter-notes), and a double-dotted quarter-note gets seven 16ths (three-and-a-half eighths). Double dots aren't used extensively, but you will see them.

One more common written device you'll see is the *tie*. A tie is a curved line connecting two or more notes that have the same pitch (Ex. 22). A tie simply means you don't re-attack the note; rather, you let it sustain for the full combined time value of all the notes involved. For instance, a half-note and a quarter-note tied together sound the same as a dotted half-note. Ties are used where using dots would be awkward or impossible—for example, across a bar line. You'll also see notes of different pitches "tied" together. In this case the tie is called a *slur*; it means the pitch changes but the note isn't re-attacked, for example when you're sliding up the neck from one note to another.

Ex. 23 combines a few of the concepts you've learned so far. For homework, practice this exercise and then come up with similar lines, using what you know about scales, key signatures, time signatures, rests, dots, and ties. Also, take some of your favorite bass lines and try to *transpose* them (change their keys).

The Circle Of Fifths

The circle of fifths (Fig. 3) plays a big part in the construction of chord progressions. Studying the circle is also an excellent way to learn, understand, and remember the key signatures of major scales. The circle of fifths looks something like a clock, with all 12 notes of the chromatic scale represented on the "face" at some point, and each "hour" representing a key signature. (For now we'll talk only about major keys.)

As we go clockwise around the circle we find that each key is in the 5th musical-alphabet position relative to the previous key. For example, if we consider the key of C (at 12 o'clock) to be at the 1st position of the musical alphabet, the 2nd position would be D, the 3rd would be E, the 4th would be F, and the 5th would be G—which is the key right after C on the circle of fifths. Similarly, it's easy to see that the 5th position from G is D, once you remember that the musical alphabet repeats from A after G. We say that G is a "fifth" higher than *C*, and that *D* is a fifth above *G*.

The circle of fifths gets a little more complicated after *B*, since the fifth above *B* is not *F* but *F#*. Every fifth we've looked at so far is equivalent to seven half-steps up the chromatic scale, and seven half-steps up from *B* is *F#*. Likewise, the fifth above *F#* is *C#* (or *Db*). Eventually we come back to the starting point, *C*.

The circle is also directly related to key signatures. As we go clockwise around the circle, each key adds one sharp to the key signature; as we go counter-clockwise, each key adds one flat. Notice that at the six o'clock position we have both *F#* (six sharps) and *Gb* (six flats); these keys are enharmonic equivalents—they're simply different ways to write the same sound.

I've also included the keys of *C#* and *Cb* on the circle. As you know from your major-scale studies, all the notes in these keys are sharped or flatted, respectively. You may be asked to play and read in these keys—although most people prefer to use *Db* or *B*, their enharmonic equivalents.

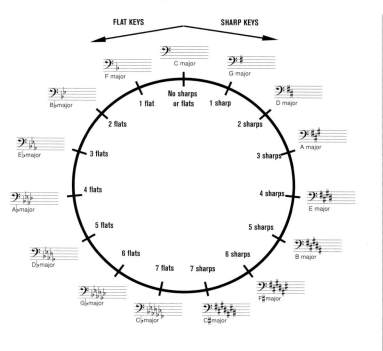

Fig. 3

Memorize the circle and strive to understand just how it works. Make a copy for your wall, music stand, manuscript book, etc.; if the various keys sound like certain colors to you, color-code them. It's helpful to have a sentence or slogan (a mnemonic) to help you remember the order of the keys as you go around the circle; I've always used these:

Sharps: *Go Down And Eat Breakfast F#ast C#harlie*

Flats: *Fat Bboys Ebat Abpple Dbumplings Gbreedily Cbharlie*

When you practice, play all of the major scales around the circle of fifths. Ex. 24 demonstrates how to add sharps while moving clockwise around the circle; Ex. 25 shows how to add flats while moving counterclockwise. (By the way, you might come across the term *circle of fourths* or *cycle of fourths*; this is the same as the circle of fifths only in the opposite direction, since moving one position counterclockwise around the circle of fifths means going up a fourth.) Remember, when you add sharps you go *forward* five letters in the musical alphabet, and when you add flats you go *backward* five letters. This will become clearer

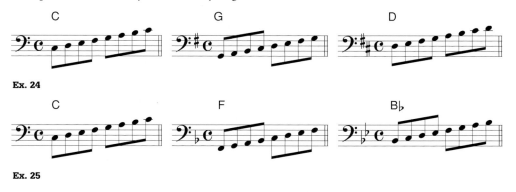

Ex. 24

Ex. 25

as we move on to intervals in just a moment; for now, it's enough to realize that keys adjacent to each other on the circle are closely related. Practice going around the circle both

ways, starting at different spots for a variety of sounds and fingerings. And listen carefully to what you're hearing!

Major Intervals

We touched on the concept of intervals earlier; an interval is often described as the distance between two pitches. Bear in mind, though, that the two tones making up an interval can be sounded together as a chord or double-stop (fretting and playing two notes together). If you can hear and play intervals fluently on your bass, you will be on your way to developing *relative pitch*, which will pay serious musical dividends as your musical career progresses.

Let's first talk about measuring intervals from a major scale's tonic or root notes, both ascending and descending. As you've already seen, many musical concepts are organized in concise, structured systems—and intervals are no exception.

Ex. 26 shows the names of the intervals in a *C* major scale. Intervals are named according to the number of musical-alphabet letter names between the two notes, including the first and last notes. For example, the interval between *C* and *E* is a third, because there are three musical-alphabet letter names inclusively between them (*C*, *D*, and *E*). Likewise, the interval between *C* and *F* is a fourth, the one between *C* and *A* is a sixth, and the one between *C* and *C* is an eighth (usually called an *octave*). If there is no distance between two notes, the interval is called a *perfect unison*. You probably won't play perfect unisons very often on your bass, but we have the term because when two or more instruments are playing the same notes in the same octave, together they form a perfect unison. A perfect unison is sometimes called a *prime* or *prime unison*.

| Unison (Prime) | Major Second | Major Third | Perfect Fourth |

| Perfect Fifth | Major Sixth | Major Seventh | Perfect Octave |

Ex. 26

Intervals larger than an octave are called *compound intervals* and continue with the same numbering system; for example, an octave plus a second equals a ninth (with nine notes between them inclusively), an octave plus a third equals a tenth, and so on. Memorize the interval-naming system, and play and sing all the intervals that make up the major scale in the different keys. The better you memorize the sounds and names of these major intervals, the better you'll be prepared for other types of intervals.

Interval Inversion

As you know, there are more notes than just those in the major scale—so there are more intervals than just the major ones. Fortunately the interval-naming system allows us to describe all the intervals, whether they're in the major scale or not. For that reason we put in front of interval names such terms as *major*, *minor*, *perfect*, *augmented*, and *diminished*.

Before we discuss what those words mean, you need to understand interval *inversion*. When you invert an interval you switch the two notes; the lower note (the tonic) moves up an octave and therefore becomes the higher note. Ex. 27 shows the inversions of all the major

Opposite: Paul McCartney with his left-handed Hofner

intervals. We're still using the *C* major scale with *C* as the reference tonic note, but the other scale notes are now lower than the tonic—so you have to measure the intervals as you go

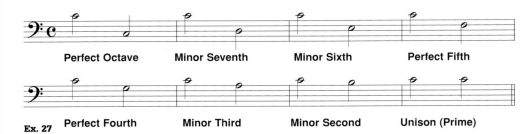

Perfect Octave   Minor Seventh   Minor Sixth   Perfect Fifth

Ex. 27   Perfect Fourth   Minor Third   Minor Second   Unison (Prime)

down the scale. The intervals that were the major second, major third, major sixth, and major seventh are now called the *minor seventh*, *minor sixth*, *minor third*, and *minor second* respectively. The perfect intervals (unison, fourth, fifth, and octave) remain "perfect" either way.

If you measure all of these intervals in terms of half-steps or semitones—frets on a bass or keys on a piano—you'll find the minor intervals are one semitone (fret or key) smaller than the major intervals. Likewise, you'll find the major intervals are one semitone larger than the minor intervals.

In the major second, major third, major sixth, and major seventh, the higher note must be in the major scale of the lower note. You'll notice that in these intervals, the lower note is *not* in the major scale of the higher note.

If you find all of this somewhat confusing, that's because it is! Take your time, read the intervals slowly, play, sing, and listen. Find these intervals in popular songs. (The first interval I learned was the perfect fifth at the beginning of "Twinkle Twinkle Little Star.") Ask friends, other musicians, and teachers. It's all part of the language of music!

Now on to Ex. 28, which brings together everything we've learned about interval inversion. Here are the general rules:
• When a second is inverted, it becomes a seventh.
• When a third is inverted, it becomes a sixth.
• When a fourth is inverted, it becomes a fifth.
• When a fifth is inverted, it becomes a fourth.
• When a sixth is inverted, it becomes a third.
• When a seventh is inverted, it becomes a second.
• When a major interval gets inverted, it becomes a minor interval.
• When a perfect interval is inverted, it remains perfect.
• If you add the numbers in the names of two inverted intervals, the total always equals nine. (Try to figure out why that is.)

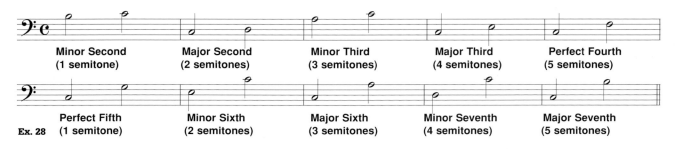

Minor Second   Major Second   Minor Third   Major Third   Perfect Fourth
(1 semitone)   (2 semitones)   (3 semitones)   (4 semitones)   (5 semitones)

Ex. 28   Perfect Fifth   Minor Sixth   Major Sixth   Minor Seventh   Major Seventh
(1 semitone)   (2 semitones)   (3 semitones)   (4 semitones)   (5 semitones)

A terrific ear-training game is to pick a key, randomly hit notes in the key, and then try to name the interval relative to the tonic of the key. As you get better, you can start playing notes *not* in the key—which conveniently leads us to our next topic.

Augmented & Diminished Intervals

Simply put, an *augmented* interval is any major, perfect, or prime interval that's raised by one semitone (Ex. 29). A *diminished* interval is any minor or perfect interval that's lowered by one semitone (Ex. 30). You'll notice I didn't include minor intervals with those that can be augmented, because if you raise a minor interval a half-step, it becomes—yes—major. (You have to raise a minor interval a whole-step to make it augmented.) Likewise I didn't mention diminished major intervals, because if you lower a major interval a half-step, it becomes minor. (You must lower a major interval a whole-step for it to become

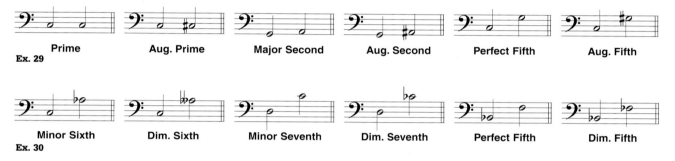

| Prime | Aug. Prime | Major Second | Aug. Second | Perfect Fifth | Aug. Fifth |

Ex. 29

| Minor Sixth | Dim. Sixth | Minor Seventh | Dim. Seventh | Perfect Fifth | Dim. Fifth |

Ex. 30

diminished.) Also, prime or unison intervals cannot be diminished, because once you lower a pitch in a prime interval you then have to measure from the lower pitch—so a diminished prime unison becomes a minor second.

Fig. 4 is a chart that will help you determine the "quality" of intervals and figure out how diminished and augmented intervals work. Here's how it works: If an interval is major or minor, use the left side of the chart. With each half-step you add to the interval, go up one level; that tells you the type of the new interval. Likewise, go down the chart as you subtract half-steps. If the interval is perfect, use the right side of the chart in the same manner. You won't see many double- and triple-augmented or diminished intervals, but they do exist. You should also know there are such things as double flats and double sharps; they aren't common, but they will come into play here. Finally, remember enharmonics—two notes that sound the same but have different names? They're sometimes mentioned when dealing with augmented and diminished intervals.

DOUBLE-AUGMENTED	
AUGMENTED	
MAJOR	PERFECT
MINOR	DIMINISHED
DIMINISHED	DOUBLE-DIMINISHED
DOUBLE-DIMINISHED	TRIPLE-DIMINISHED

Fig. 4

Earlier I mentioned compound intervals—those larger than an octave. You can also think of these as smaller intervals expanded by the number of letters in our musical alphabet (seven). A second expanded equals a ninth, a third expanded equals a tenth, and so on (Ex. 31). The labels "major," "minor," "augmented," and "diminished" are continued in the

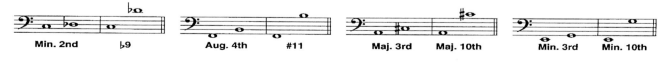

| Min. 2nd | ♭9 | Aug. 4th | #11 | Maj. 3rd | Maj. 10th | Min. 3rd | Min. 10th |

Ex. 31

compound intervals; a minor ninth is often called a ♭9, an augmented eleventh a ♯11, a minor thirteenth a ♭13, etc. These expanded intervals sound great on the bass because there's room for the two notes to breathe. To hear what I mean, check out Stanley Clarke's "Bass Folk Song #3" on *Live 1976–1977*. And while you're at it, name the intervals pictured on the cover of Stanley's *School Days*.

When you combine enharmonics, interval names, compound intervals, and chord progressions, things can get pretty tricky. For instance, there's such a thing as an augmented third; you don't see it often because, for instance, the *C*-to-*E♯* interval sounds the same as the *C*-to-*F* interval, a perfect fourth. Just keep in mind there are valid compositional and notational reasons for spelling some intervals in ways that may seem awkward. To learn more, check out traditional theory, composition, or counterpoint books.

The Tritone

One last topic for our crash course in music theory. So far we've covered all the intervals that make up the octave except for one: the *tritone*, also called the augmented fourth, the ♯4, the diminished fifth, and the ♭5. This interesting interval is simply a perfect fifth that's been lowered by a semitone, or a perfect fourth raised by a semitone. The tritone consists of three whole-steps (hence its name), and it also equals six half-steps. It can be found within a major scale as the interval between the 4th and 7th scale degrees (Ex. 32); every major scale has a tritone between the 4th and 7th scale tones. Also notice that the 4th and 7th scale degrees are a half-step from the scale's 3rd and root (tonic) respectively. These are the only half-steps in a major scale; listen as you use them, because playing them can be the best way to define the tonal center or to bring out the color of your music. (On the other hand if you want the tonality to be vague, stay away from them.)

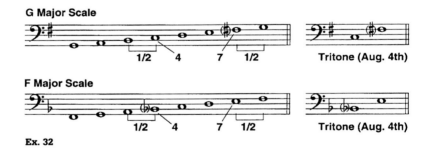

G Major Scale

1/2   4   7   1/2   Tritone (Aug. 4th)

F Major Scale

1/2   4   7   1/2   Tritone (Aug. 4th)

Ex. 32

Major keys that are a tritone away from each other have interchangeable 4th and 7th scale degrees, and these keys are always found directly opposite each other on the circle of fifths. For example, the major keys of *A* and *E♭* are a tritone apart, and their 4th and 7th scale degrees, *D* and *G♯* (or *A♭*), are interchangeable. The same is true for *C* and *F♯* major, whose 4th and 7th scale notes are *F* and *B* (or *C♭*). Play or write a few major scales that are a tritone apart and notice how the 4th and 7th scale degrees are interchangeable.

Another look at the tritone reveals that it splits the octave in half. Remember the chromatic scale? If you divide the 12 half-steps equally, you get six half-steps or three whole-tones—a tritone.

Let's get away from the math for a moment and discuss the tritone's sound. A late-medieval nickname for the tritone was *diabolus in musica*, because it was considered a dangerous and awkward interval. (I have even heard that the three tines of the devil's pitchfork signify the three whole-steps in a tritone.) We no longer think of the tritone as evil, but it is distinctive. Play, sing, and listen to the tritone to get a feel for how it sounds and how it can be used musically, try to find it in melodies and bass lines you know, and try to write some new bass lines that incorporate the tritone.

Don't Stop Learning

The material in this brief survey should give you a good start reading and writing music and understanding its concepts—but there's a lot more. I encourage you to continue expanding your knowledge of music theory, preferably with the guidance of a private teacher. There's no end to the depth you can take your understanding of music—and believe me, everything you learn will make you a better, more rounded musician.

George Porter Jr. of
the Meters

Grooving On The Grid:
How To Improve Your Sense Of Time

By Ed Friedland

We bassists have the unique responsibility of bridging music's melodic and rhythmic aspects. While the pitches we play must support the harmonic content, *when* we play them is equally important. Playing rhythm is a manifestation of your time-keeping ability—and if your sense of time is undeveloped or underdeveloped, your rhythm won't be very accurate.

Playing rhythm involves breaking the steady flow of time into specific measuring units. (This might sound like a math lesson, but don't be scared.) These units may vary in length according to the style or demands of the music, but they all must line up to the time grid; this means all rhythms must exist within the tempo of the piece of music. (We're talking about meat-and-potatoes, groove-oriented bass playing here, not free-form expressionism.) Consider "the grid," my concept of the rhythmic hierarchy. To keep this manageable we'll discuss only note values as long as whole-notes and as short as 16th-note triplets—but be aware that this information applies to longer and shorter notes, too.

Ex. 1 shows the rhythmic hierarchy. Notice how all the rhythmic activity levels are connected. Four 16th-notes take up the same space on the time grid as two eighth-notes or the three notes in an eighth-note triplet. This means the amount of space for any rhythmic grouping is set and non-negotiable. Four 16th-notes get as much space as they get—no more, no less.

Playing these different rhythmic levels can be challenging, because the shorter the rhythmic values the more opportunities you have to get off track. But there's an old saying: "The faster you play, the slower you count." In other words, if you're playing lots of short notes you should count *longer* time values, both to prevent losing the pulse and to maintain a strong groove. For example, if you're playing 16th-notes you could count eighth-notes—but that really isn't slow enough to keep the feel *grounded*. We want the groove to come from a deeper place. So in this case I recommend you count half-notes (Ex. 2). In order to do that, you'll need to function on several rhythmic levels at once—something drummers do all the time. (Is this starting to make sense?)

Play some of your cool, busy slap licks—but instead of tapping your foot on every quarter-note, tap it on every half-note. Tapping slower removes the anxiety of having to play at a fast tempo, and it relaxes you. It also helps anchor the 16th-notes to the time grid, which makes them easier to play. This will take some getting used to, but once you settle into it you'll find that your 16th-notes feel more relaxed—so your grooves fall into the pocket, big time!

Our goals are to be able to recognize rhythms when they're written, to play them accurately, and to make them groove. The way to accomplish this is to *internalize* rhythm. If the rhythm comes from inside you, you'll always be able to call upon it. What's the best way to internalize rhythm? Sing! Singing is the most direct route from the inner musician to the outside world. Jazz players have a saying: "If you can't sing it, you can't play it." I would alter that to say, "If you can't sing it, you don't own it." Ownership means you understand something so well it's a part of you. You don't have to think about how you blink your eyes or

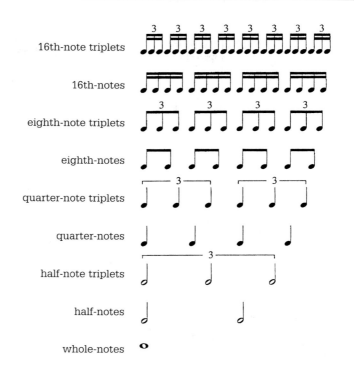

Ex. 1: The rhythmic hierarchy. Each level has four beats, but they become subdivided as you go up.

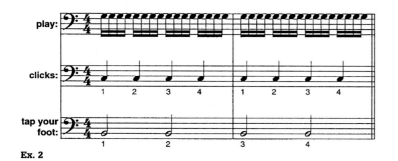

Ex. 2

breathe—and playing rhythms can be just as easy. Sing them until you can *feel* the groove in your body.

Say It—Don't Spray It

Here's a series of exercises that give syllables to common rhythmic patterns. This idea is centuries old, stemming from the classical Indian tradition of rhythmic *solfège*. Before tabla students are allowed to learn the drum, they spend years vocally learning the rhythmic language of the music they will play. This approach ensures that once the mechanics of the instrument are mastered, the music will come from inside the musician. As bass players this is our goal as well.

Let's work with two levels of the rhythmic hierarchy that are common in music: the 16th-note and the eighth-note triplet. The syllables will help you internalize the rhythms' feel, and they'll also give you a "tag" to help you remember what they look like. We often see a rhythm and figure it out, only to have to figure it out again the next time it shows up—so giving these rhythms "tags" helps you remember them visually.

It's important to realize how many rhythms you already know just from listening to modern music. The 16th-note, for example, is very common in rock, funk, Latin, jazz, and pop, so the sounds of 16th-note rhythms are deeply embedded in your musical consciousness. However, it's common for people to play such rhythms unevenly. Instead of aligning them with the rhythmic grid, they're sprayed wildly around the bar like water spewing from a runaway garden hose.

Sing the rhythms in Ex. 3 with a metronome clicking quarter-notes. Keep in mind it's unimportant how well you sing; since this is a purely rhythmic exercise you can just speak them. The syllables in parentheses are rests that need to be inserted in order to capture the groove. Feel the 16th-note pulse continuing through the rests on beats *two* and *four*—or, if you're having trouble with that, fill them in silently with "dig-a-chik-a." When you've played through all of the phrases in Ex. 3, loop them into one eight-bar exercise. Stay focused on the groove!

The triplet is the underlying rhythmic element of jazz, blues, hip-hop, and many other styles. It's also the essence of swing. The swing feel is a broken-up triplet rhythm (Ex. 4).

Since eighth- and 16th-notes are divisible by two, they can be imagined as little square

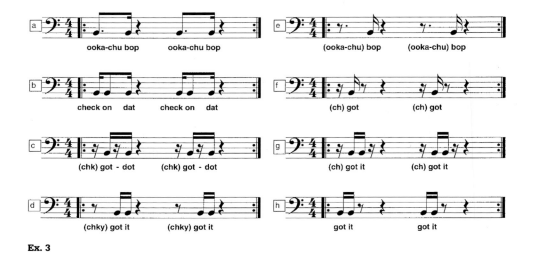

Ex. 3

Ex. 4

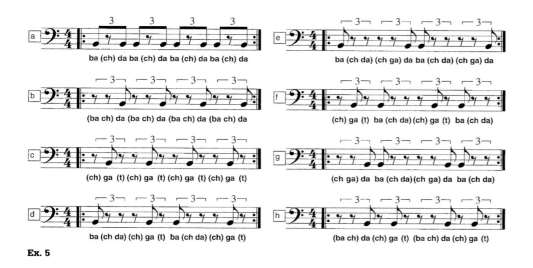

a — ba (ch) da ba (ch) da ba (ch) da ba (ch) da

e — ba (ch ga) (ch ga) da ba (ch da) (ch ga) da

b — (ba ch) da (ba ch) da (ba ch) da (ba ch) da

f — (ch) ga (t) ba (ch da) (ch) ga (t) ba (ch da)

c — (ch) ga (t) (ch) ga (t) (ch) ga (t) (ch) ga (t)

g — (ch ga) da ba (ch da) (ch ga) da ba (ch da)

d — ba (ch da) (ch) ga (t) ba (ch da) (ch) ga (t)

h — (ba ch) da (ch) ga (t) (ba ch) da (ch) ga (t)

Ex. 5

boxes that rotate in time. A triplet, however, is round and wave-like; it can be imagined as a circle containing an equilateral triangle (Fig. 1). With each beat of the triplet, the circle rotates an equal distance. Triplets are also very flexible; they can be stretched and compacted. This is why two jazz drummers can play the same exact rhythm and still sound different— each interprets the triplet his own way. For the sake of clarity, we'll go for an even, relaxed, flowing triplet that sits in the middle of the beat. Ex. 5 is a series of rhythmic patterns based on triplets. Sing the rest syllables but accent the ones that are to be played; this will give you a better feel for the triplet. Remember: It's just as important to groove when playing rests as it is when playing notes.

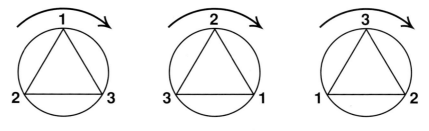

Fig. 1

Go With The Flow

Practicing these exercises with the metronome and without your instrument will solidify your internal connection to the grid. Rhythm is generated by the seamless meshing of our internal clock with the gears of the ever-moving time continuum. Like the inside of a fine pocket watch, time and rhythm exist in a synchronous unity. Each level of rhythmic activity exists on its own plane, yet it's simultaneously linked to every other rhythmic plane as well. Take rhythm inside, and your bass playing will groove with the flow of the universe. Peace.

ZZ Top's Dusty Hill
and Billy Gibbons

Rock & Roll Basics

By Mike Hiland

Rock bass playing is a lot more than just pounding an eighth-note pulse on the root of the chord. To fully understand many of the ideas and concepts of rock bass playing, you need to get some theory under your belt. You should have read Beginning Theory For Bassists (page 34), as much of the material I'll be covering assumes you understand music-theory fundamentals. As a rock bassist you should try to get an understanding of rock & roll harmony that you can use in real-life situations.

The Major Scale

Ex. 1 shows the major scale. There is a major scale for all 12 notes. Start on any note and play this same series of intervals, and you'll be playing the major scale based on the first note. Use Fig. 1 to help you visualize the major-scale fingerboard pattern. It's very important to be able to find and play all 12 major scales at any time.

C Major Scale

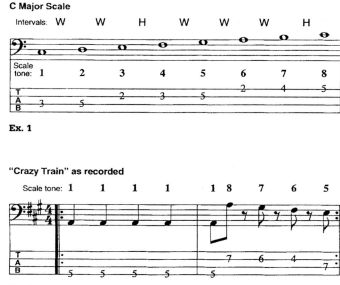

Ex. 1

(Numbers = Scale Tones)

Fig. 1

"Crazy Train" as recorded

Ex. 2

The major scale sounds happy—so sometimes it does not lend itself to rock bass playing. Most of the major-scale notes work fine, but there are a couple that often sound just *too* happy. Here's a good rule to follow when playing notes from the major scale: *Beware of the 3rd and 7th scale tones.* If the guitar player is crushing a power chord and you play that pretty-sounding major 7th, you may have to duck to avoid flying objects! There is, however, one fine example of a bass line that uses all of the major-scale notes (including the 7th) and *still* manages to sound very cool: "Crazy Train," from Ozzy Osbourne's first solo album, *Blizzard of Oz* [Jet]. During the verses Bob Daisley walks down the major scale under a rocking guitar riff (Ex. 2)—and it works amazingly well.

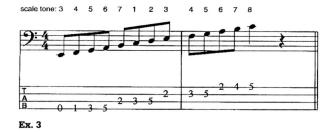

Ex. 3

There are seven notes in a major scale (eight if you include the octave). When you play those seven notes, or any of those notes in any other register, you're still playing within the scale. The *C* major scale consists of the notes *C, D, E, F, G, A, B,* and *C,* so every *E* you can find on your bass is in the *C* major scale, as is every *D* and every *G.* If this is true, isn't it a good idea to be able to play the *C* major scale in all fingerboard positions, from the lowest note to the highest? You bet! If you know where all of a scale's notes are, it makes the hunt for the right ones that much easier. Here's how you do it: Write down the notes in the *C* major scale. Now, in a position covering the first five frets, play every note in the scale, starting with the lowest in that position and ending at the highest. In Ex. 3 the lowest note is open *E* and the highest is *C* at the 5th fret on the *G* string. Repeat this in the other positions,

scale tone: 5 6 7 1 2 3 4 5   6 7 8 2

Ex. 4

scale tone: 6 7 1 2 3 4 5 6   7 8 2 3

Ex. 5

scale tone: 7 1 2 3 4 5 6 7   8 2 3 4

Ex. 6

scale tone: 1 2 3 4 5 6 7 8   2 3 4 5

Ex. 7

scale tone: 3 4 5 6 7 1 2 3   4 5 6 7 8

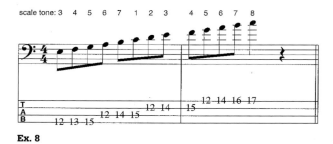

Ex. 8

as shown in Examples 4 through 8. Then try Ex. 9: Play up the notes in one position (as in Ex. 3) and down the notes in the next position (as in Ex. 4). Repeat this for the other positions as well, ultimately connecting all of the positions into one long, fretboard-covering major scale. You should learn all 12 major scales this way; I've started the *D*-major scale for you in Ex. 10. When you have mastered the major scale, move on.

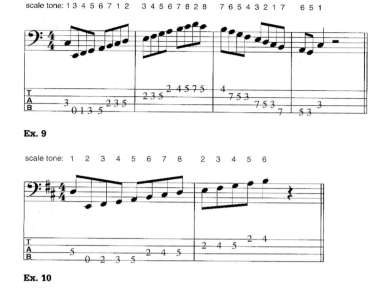

Ex. 9

Ex. 10

Bigger & Flatter 7ths

Earlier I mentioned that the 3rd and 7th major-scale notes usually sound pretty weak in rock. Now we're going to correct part of that problem. Instead of using the major 7th, which is found one half-step below the octave (or root), we'll flat that note—that is, lower it by a half-step. Now it's called a "♭7" (or dominant 7th), and it's found one whole-step below the octave or root. Ex. 11 shows the *C* major scale with the lowered 7th; Fig. 2 is the fingerboard pattern.

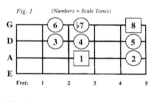

Fig. 1   *(Numbers = Scale Tones)*

Fig. 2

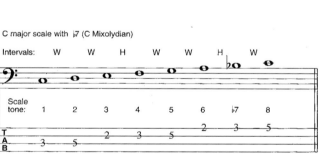

Ex. 11

If you know some theory, you may know this scale is called the Mixolydian mode. But we rock bassists don't have a lot of use for the modes. Just think about it this way: When you flat the 7th tone of the scale, you imply the dominant 7th—a common sound in blues and R&B, which is where most rock & roll comes from. Even though the guitar player or keyboardist may not be playing a dominant-7 chord, if you play that ♭7 the dominant-7 sound is implied in the overall sound of the band. This usually makes a song sound a little *meaner*. When you're developing a bass line and someone asks for a tougher sound, ask yourself if you're using the ♭7—it works most of the time.

Watch what happens when you incorporate the ♭7 into a simple bass line: Ex. 12 is just an eighth-note pulse in *A*; Ex. 13 is that same part with the ♭7 (*G*) incorporated to add some

Scale tone: 1 1 1 1 1 1 1 1   1 1 1 1 1 1 1 1

Ex. 12

Scale tone: 1 1 1 1 1 ♭7 1 ♭7   1 1 1 ♭7 1 ♭7 1 ♭7

Ex. 13

Scale tone: 3 4 5 6 ♭7 1 2 3   4 5 6 ♭7 8

Ex. 14

Scale tone: 5 6 ♭7 1 2 3 4 5   6 ♭7 8 2

Ex. 15

toughness and movement. Of course, it gets more complex when you start changing rhythms and adding other notes—but a lot happens when you just occasionally use the ♭7.

Naturally, you need to be able to locate the ♭7 anywhere on the fingerboard, in all keys. Ex. 14 and Ex. 15 correspond to Ex. 3 and Ex. 4, with the ♭7 replacing the major 7th. (I'll leave it to you to learn all of the other positions and keys.)

Major-Scale Bass Lines

If you want to better understand what you're playing, you need to understand how to use scales in the context of songs, arrangements, and specific parts. Therefore you need to be able to analyze bass lines and see how they relate to scales, which will reveal why certain notes are used in certain places. You've already learned the first step, believe it or not. By learning scales all over the fingerboard, you have begun to learn which note is the root, the 2nd, the 3rd, etc., for any given scale. This will help you identify a bass line's individual notes relative to a specific scale, and thus you'll be able to understand why that bass line works the way it does.

For now, let's assume that for whatever chord you are playing under, the root of the chord is also the root of the scale from which you're taking notes. This isn't always the case, but you aren't playing through chord changes just yet—only bass lines against a single chord. Ex. 16's notes are taken from the *C* major pentatonic scale, which consists of the 1st, 2nd,

Ex. 16

3rd, 5th, and 6th major-scale tones (1–2–3–5–6). This type of walking pattern is found in many early rock & roll bass lines *à la* Elvis and Jerry Lee Lewis, and I'm sure it will sound familiar as soon as you play it. You can also find this kind of line in latter-day rockabilly tunes, like Queen's "Crazy Little Thing Called Love" and the Stray Cats' "Rock This Town," and in numerous blues songs. Examples 17 and 18 illustrate a couple of other major pen-

Ex. 17

Ex. 18

tatonic bass lines; notice the scale tones associated with the notes in each bass line. Look at each note and determine what scale tone it is. The more you're able to hear how the different scale tones sound, the easier it will be to choose good notes when you're developing your own lines.

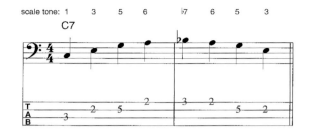

Ex. 19

Ex. 20

Ex. 21

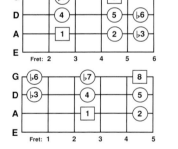

Fig. 3

Examples 19 through 21 are Mixolydian-based lines and are more bluesy and R&B-sounding. (That ♭7 really makes a difference!) Experiment with all six of these lines in different keys, and see if you know any other songs that have similar bass parts. If you find some, analyze them by scale tone to see what's going on.

The "Metal Scale"

Since the late '60s the world has been blessed with some great hard rock and heavy metal bands: Led Zeppelin, Black Sabbath, Deep Purple, Van Halen, Metallica—the list goes on and on. One significant element in the sound of metal is the minor scale. It sounds much "sadder" than the major scale, and when you blast it through a wall of blazing Marshalls and thundering SVTs, it gets downright ugly. So if you're into making heavy music, get familiar with the minor scale.

In major-scale terms the natural minor scale (also known as the "pure minor" or simply "minor" scale) has a lowered 3rd, 6th, and 7th, so it consists of the tones 1–2–♭3–4–5–♭6–♭7–8. Fig. 3 shows two minor-scale fretboard diagrams in the key of *C*; Ex. 22 shows how the *C* minor scale is written musically. One easy way to learn the minor scale is first to play a major scale and then the minor scale in that key. At this point you should learn all 12 minor scales in all positions, using all strings, just as you did with the major scale.

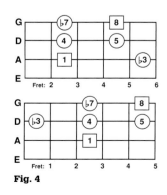

Fig. 4

Ex. 22

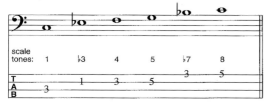

Ex. 23

The minor scale can be trimmed down to a minor pentatonic scale consisting of the 1st, ♭3rd, 4th, 5th, and ♭7th. In fact, the minor pentatonic is probably the most commonly used scale in heavy metal and hard rock bass playing. Fig. 4 shows two minor-pentatonic fretboard diagrams; Ex. 23 is the written notation. As you learn the minor pentatonic, notice the shape created by the fingering—it's often called "the box pattern."

A side note before we get into some lines that use the minor pentatonic: As you know, rock & roll is "guitar music." It's usually written on the electric guitar, and the licks and riffs usually feature the guitar. Because the guitar is so dominant, we bass players usually end up playing the same riffs the guitar plays. Or, we may be relegated to simply pumping the root AC/DC-style. A third approach involves rhythmically playing the root and adding a few notes to create rhythm-section movement. Obviously there are other approaches, but I'll limit it to these three for now.

In the following examples, note the use of the scale tones in each bass line. You'll notice that the most commonly used pentatonic scale tones are the 1st, ♭3rd, 5th, and ♭7th. ("P" indicates a passing tone, which is a note that isn't part of this scale.) Ex. 24 is a bass riff in

Ex. 24

the style of John Deacon of Queen. Under a chord progression, such a riff would probably be too busy—but on its own or in unison with the guitar, it becomes very cool. Ex. 25 is another riff that may be played in unison with the guitar.

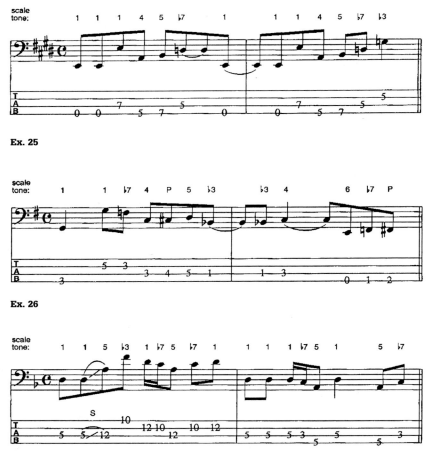

Ex. 25

Ex. 26

Ex. 27

Ex. 26 is right out of the Geezer Butler school of heavy metal playing. The guitar could play some chord progression that seems unrelated—but as long as it's based around the *G minor* pentatonic scale, this bass line would probably work. Check out "Lady Evil," from Black Sabbath's *Heaven and Hell* [Warner Bros.], to see what I mean. Ex. 27 might also work this way, or it might work in unison with a guitar part.

Ex. 28 shows how you might vary what would normally be a straight eighth-note root pulse in *A*. By pedaling off the 5th and ♭7th scale tones (see below), this type of bass line turns a pulse into a driving groove. Ex. 29 is similar.

Listen to some of your favorite tunes to see where the minor pentatonic scale is used— it shouldn't be hard to find. For a start, check out Roger Glover's pentatonic fill-fest in the verses of Deep Purple's classic "Smoke on the Water" [*Machine Head*, Warner Bros.].

Pedal Power

One common technique that helps the bass line drive the band a little harder, or to "toughen up" a groove, is known as *pedaling*. This approach can do more than just help a line's overall feel—it can open up numerous possibilities for fills and other embellishments. Pedaling means continually alternating between a low "pedal tone" and the other notes in the bass line. (The term comes from the bass pedals on church organs.)

Let's consider pedaling in the key of *A*. One way to pedal on the root would be to play

Ex. 28

Ex. 29

an *A* and then another note (or notes), and then another *A* followed by a fourth note. Then you'd repeat this pattern. Ex. 30 is a good exercise for learning this technique. Notice how the open *A* is played between the other Mixolydian notes?

Examples 30 through 33 demonstrate different ways to practice pedaling through the scales. (This will work for any scale, by the way.) Examples 34 and 35 show you how to pedal on the 5th instead of the root. Pedaling on the 5th works really well when you want to make your part sound meaner and more driving; it's especially effective in the key of *A* because you get to use the lowest note on the 4-string bass (open *E*) as the pedal tone. (If you're playing in the key of *G*, don't be afraid to detune your *E* string to *D* so you can pedal on the 5th of *G*.) Learn these exercises the way they're written, and then try your own variations.

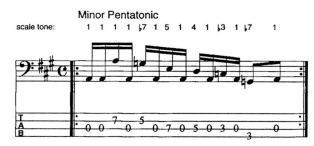

Ex. 30

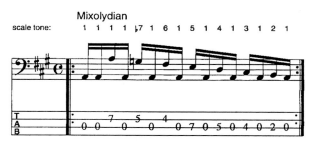

Ex. 31

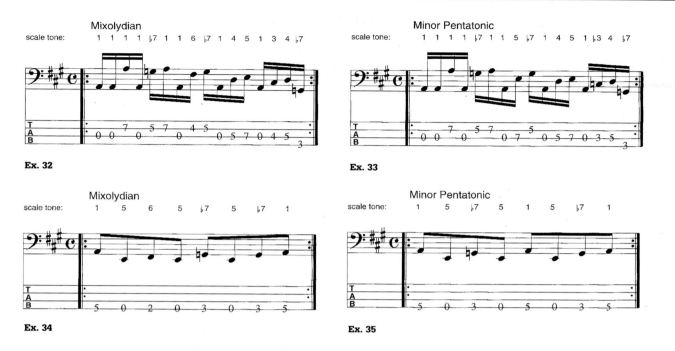

Ex. 32

Ex. 33

Ex. 34

Ex. 35

Try mixing up the order of the scale tones, and listen to what each resulting lick sounds like. Then try adding some other scale tones and passing tones and see what happens.

Since most rock songs are played in keys that correspond to the open bass strings, there's a world of pedaling opportunities for the bass player. Still, it's also a good idea to practice pedaling in all the other keys. Examples 36 and 37 will get you used to the idea of pedaling on the 5th in non-open-string keys. With a little practice you should have no problem pedaling in any key.

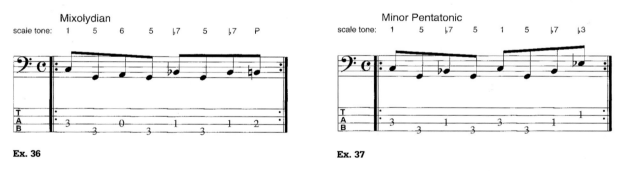

Ex. 36

Ex. 37

The Dropped D

Earlier I mentioned detuning your *E* string to *D* when playing in the key of *G*. Besides opening up pedaling possibilities, "*D*-tuning" just sounds cool and can have some *heavy* results, since the tone of any note you play on a detuned *E* string (especially open *D*) is much fatter.

There are two ways to get a dropped tuning: simply tuning your *E* string down to *D* with the tuning machine, or using a device called a Hipshot XTender. The Hipshot, which you install on your bass to replace the *E*-string tuner, has a lever that drops the string's tuning; when you flip the lever back, the string returns to *E*.

When you tune that low string down to *D*, your fingering patterns suddenly change. For

Opposite: Metallica's Jason

Newsted in his home studio

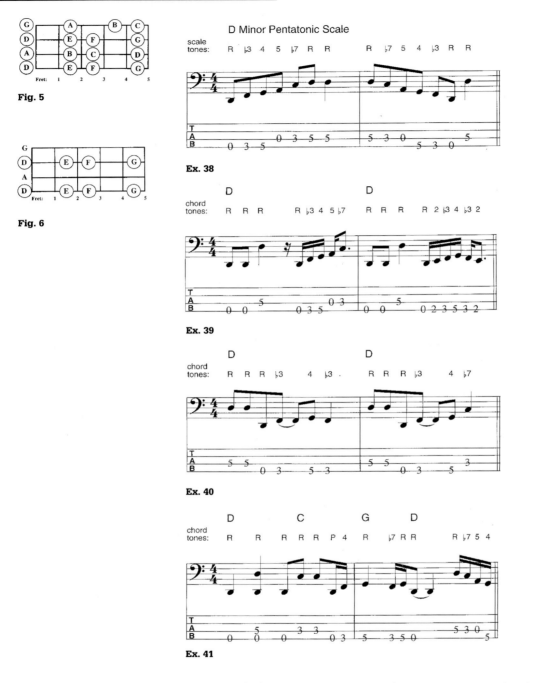

Fig. 5

Fig. 6

Ex. 38

Ex. 39

Ex. 40

Ex. 41

some people this is a major crisis, but fear not—you can solve the mystery of the moving notes. Fig. 5 shows where all the notes can be found in the area covering the first five frets. Starting with open *D*, notice that *E* is now at the 2nd fret, *F* is at the 3rd, and *G* is at the 5th. The notes have simply moved up the fingerboard by two frets, or one whole-step. As you'll discover, this provides some interesting and unusual fingering patterns. (The notes on the other three strings, of course, haven't changed.)

Ex. 38 shows where the *D* minor pentatonic scale can be played in that area of the fingerboard. Pay particular attention to the new relationships between the scale tones; things have changed a bit, making some intervals easier to play and others more difficult.

Ex. 42

Ex. 43

Experiment with this and other *D* scales by playing them farther up the neck—you'll find that some positions call for unusual left-hand stretches. With a little practice, you'll learn how to make these new fingering patterns work for you.

Examples 39 through 41 show how you might use this new tuning in bass lines. I've referred to the notes as "chord tones"; when there are chord changes over a bass line, it's often easier to think of each bass note relative to the chord that's occurring at that particular moment. For example in Ex. 41, when the chord changes to *C* in bar 1, the note you play is also *C*, the chord's root—so I've indicated that note with an "R" for "root." (We'll talk more about this system, so if it's confusing, don't worry about it for now.) Ex. 42 shows how to use a *D* tuning in songs written in the key of *G*, with the open *D* the 5th of the *G* chord. (The ♭7, *F*, works well, too.)

When you're playing in a dropped tuning, notice the *D* string's fat tone. Also, because of the reduced tension, the string feels slightly more "floppy" or "spongy" than the others—so you may have to adjust your plucking to control the tone. Experiment a little and you'll find a technique that suits your playing style.

One last thing: It's important to understand how octaves work in this new tuning. Fig. 6 illustrates the concept in diagram form; Ex. 43 is a line using a root-5th-octave pattern to get your fingers used to it. If you find it's a tight squeeze to get into position for octaves like this, practice running octaves from the open *D* strings (you have two now!) all the way up to the 12th fret and back down.

Analyzing Bass Lines

It's common for beginning students to be so amazed by a new "killer riff" that they have a tough time trying to figure it out for themselves. This allows them to cop the tried-and-true "I don't have a good enough ear" excuse for not being able to get the riff right. While ear training does take time to develop, don't sell yourself short. Most rock & roll riffs consist of notes from a few basic scales—and if you can find the scale a particular riff belongs to, you're

Based on A minor pentatonic

Ex. 44

Based on A minor pentatonic

Ex. 45

Based on E minor pentatonic

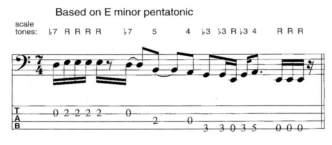

Ex. 46

Based on E minor pentatonic

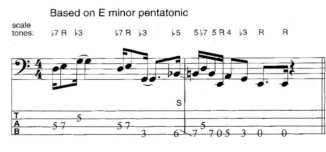

Ex. 47

well on your way to being able to cop *any* riff. Figuring out new riffs is simple: Just identify the scale, and then figure out which scale tones are being used.

Now, a certain amount of ear training is required in order to distinguish between the notes and determine which scale you're hearing. To improve your ear, you need to cop songs and riffs off records as much as possible—without the aid of written music or tablature! The more you try to figure out songs and riffs on your own, the better your ear will become. It's also very helpful to hook up with a teacher who can help you develop a better sense of pitch.

Led Zeppelin and Deep Purple used the same pentatonic scales 20 years ago that most hard-rock bands are using today. Don't believe me? Well, the examples on the previous page may sound familiar. Ex. 44 is a very simple Pearl Jam-style riff; as you can see, it's pentatonic. Ex. 45 goes back to the Led Zep heyday; again, it's all pentatonic, with the addition of the ♭5. It's common to use the ♭5 when playing otherwise pentatonic patterns, as it makes for a very cool passing tone between the 4th and 5th scale tones. Ex. 46 is one of the coolest riffs I've heard in a long time; it uses the minor pentatonic scale and is played in 7/4 time. (In case you don't know, this means you count seven beats per measure instead of the usual four.) Ex. 47 is an "Aerosmithy" riff you might find on *Get a Grip*. Notice again the use of the ♭5 as a passing tone leading up to the 5th. That ♭5–5–♭7 figure is a very bluesy lick that adds lots of swagger.

We've touched on the Mixolydian mode in a few places; recall it sounds identical to the major scale but with a flatted 7th. The tricky thing about the Mixolydian is identifying it when you're learning a riff. After all, if the riff uses primarily the root, 4th, 5th, and ♭7th, how do you know whether it's Mixolydian or pentatonic? The first clue is the use of the 3rd. Ask yourself whether it's a major (natural) 3rd or a minor (flat) 3rd. If it's a ♮3, you can be pretty confident the riff is Mixolydian-based; if it's a ♭3 you should probably assume it's based on the minor pentatonic (unless, of course, a ♮3 appears and blows that theory). Another giveaway is the use of the 6th. The major 6th is in the Mixolydian mode; the minor pentatonic scale does not use the 6th. So if you find a major 6th, you can assume the riff is Mixolydian. If you find a minor 6th, it's probably built from a minor scale—not a minor pentatonic but a natural minor (1–2–♭3–4–5–♭6–♭7).

What if the riff doesn't use the 3rd or 6th scale tones? In that case, try playing the ♮3 and ♭3 in the context of the song to see if one sounds more "right" than the other. When you have limited information available, you have to test the water a bit to find out what works with the rest of the band. There are no sure-fire answers in some cases—you just have to experiment. And listen.

We know the minor pentatonic scale contains the root, ♭3rd, 4th, 5th, and ♭7th—but that doesn't necessarily mean pentatonic bass lines use *only* those five scale tones. Still, when you're analyzing pentatonic lines, first try to identify the notes that belong in the scale; then look for non-pentatonic notes. That way you can be sure the bass line is, in fact, built on the pentatonic scale. (For simplicity I'm using "pentatonic" to refer to the minor pentatonic scale—but remember there are other types of pentatonic scales.)

Sometimes the boundary between Mixolydian and pentatonic bass lines can get blurry, because some of the same scale tones (root, 4th, 5th, and ♭7th) are shared by both. The key is to identify as many scale tones as you can—then you can figure out how to think about the other notes. Ex. 48 is reminiscent of an old Led Zeppelin riff; as you can see, it

Ex. 48

E Pentatonic bass line

Ex. 49

uses all five *A* pentatonic scale tones and nothing else. This makes it easy to identify as a pentatonic line. Sometimes you'll get lucky and all of the notes will fall right into the scale; sometimes you'll need to do a little more work.

In Examples 49 through 51 things start to get more sticky; in addition to the pentatonic scale tones you'll notice some non-pentatonic notes. Ex. 49 is based on the *E* pentatonic scale but also uses the major 2nd and major 3rd scale tones. When I encounter parts like this, I tend to look at all of the notes as a unit; in most cases the majority of notes fall within a certain scale, so that's how I can tell which scale the line is built upon. In this case, starting on beat *three* we come right down the pentatonic scale (root, ♭7, 5, 4, ♭3); this strongly suggests that the line is pentatonic, with the non-pentatonic notes (the 2nd and 3rd) acting as passing tones to help make it more melodic (and bluesy).

Ex. 50 is a fairly straightforward pentatonic line, but notice the major 7th (*G♯*). As I said at the outset, the major 7th is usually too weak for rock & roll, so it functions best as a passing tone—and that's exactly what it's doing here. All of the notes are pentatonic scale tones except for that wimpy major 7th, which is just acting as a bridge between the ♭7th and the root.

A Pentatonic bass line

Ex. 50

Ex. 51 once again harkens back to the mighty Led Zeppelin catalog. Bar 1 is totally pentatonic, while bar 2 borrows the major 3rd to create the appropriate melody. No big deal—it's basically a pentatonic line, despite that major 3rd.

Another way to tell if a riff is pentatonic-based is to see how it sounds when modified to be strictly pentatonic (using only those five scale tones). It won't sound like the same part, but all the notes should sound like they belong. If one sounds out of place, it's probably time to consider another scale.

A Pentatonic bass line

Ex. 51

It's Only Rock & Roll

Remember, there's no "secret scale" only MTV gods can understand. If you hear a cool rock & roll riff, chances are it's just pentatonic or Mixolydian—so just grab your axe, find the appropriate scale, and knock it out! Work out as many bass lines as you can; it's absolutely the best way to improve your ear and get a handle on what works in rock bass. That way when your band starts to work up a new song, you'll find the perfect part—probably using the same roots, ♭7's, 5ths, octaves, pedal tones, and scales you've heard all your life. Only now you'll *understand* how they work.

Legendary blues
bassist J.W. Williams

Blues Essentials:
15 Lines You Must Know

By Gregory Isola

IF you join a band that covers anything from swing standards or skankin' ska to '50s oldies or Led Zeppelin, you must be able to *play the blues*. And if you're not yet in a band, there's no shorter road to gigsville than the Blue Highway. The ability to nail down chorus after chorus of 12-bar, three-chord jamming is the hallmark of the working bassist, so let's dig into some classic blue grooves.

A note about the music: The vast majority of blues and blues-based tunes incorporate just three chords: the I, IV, and V. (In the key of G, these would be G, C, and D.) Most of the following examples are one- or two-bar excerpts based on a song's I chord; it's up to you to continue these lines across the IV and the V. In many cases this is as simple as moving the I chord's root note up one string (toward your feet) to hit the IV, and then over two frets (toward your bridge) for the V. Of course, you should always be on the lookout for other, smoother, more interesting ways to traverse the changes.

Walk The Walk

Let's get to it: Ex. 1 is *the* blues bass line. This major-scale-based beauty was developed in the 1930s at the dawn of the swing era and became ubiquitous during the heyday of jump blues (from the late '40s through the early '50s). Still widely used today, it's appropriate beneath almost any jump or swing groove. Those quarter-notes can be played straight (as written), doubled up and played as straight eighth-notes, or played as swing eighths. Ex. 2 shows the most common variation; notice how much more "bluesy" things get with the simple addition of the flatted 7th (in this case, F♮) on beat *one* of bar 2.

Examples 3 through 5 present a trio of boogie-woogie lines derived from early piano-blues grooves. Ex. 3, the most basic of the bunch, has a nice rolling feel due to those eighth-notes in beat *four* as well as the momentum they carry into the quarter-note root on beat *one*. The keys that drive Ex. 4, a popular mid-tempo groover, are the quick 4ths (D♮'s) in beat *three* and that ♯4th (D♯) passing tone in beat *four*. Guitar great Albert King based many of his classic tunes on grooves similar to Ex. 3 and Ex. 4. Ex. 5 is a brisk line with a distinctly jazzy feel. Jumping *down* to the major 3rd on beat *two* and then climbing back up to the root is a jazz-approved move that imparts a real uptown vibe to a song's low end. This line, too, works with quarters, straight eighths, or swing eighths.

Dance The Blues

We've all heard Ex. 6 a thousand times, but it's still worth a close look. Most effective when played as a shuffle, this line provides groundwork for a variety of upbeat blues grooves. Strive for clear, even articulation and a pumping, bouncy feel. Variation: Play the final, beat-*four* eighths as an eighth-note triplet. This is very effective for punctuating a chord change—especially if the third note of the triplet becomes a passing tone into the next chord.

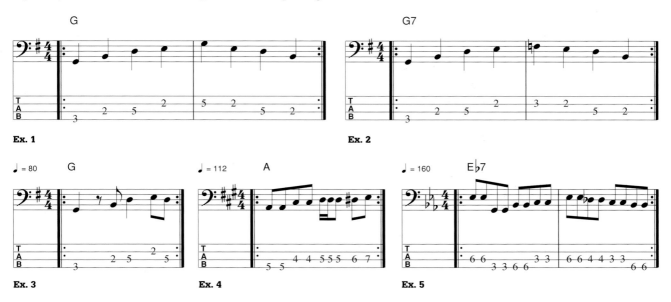

Ex. 1

Ex. 2

Ex. 3

Ex. 4

Ex. 5

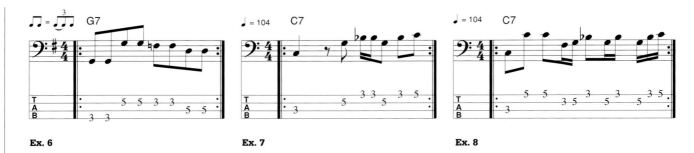

Ex. 6   **Ex. 7**   **Ex. 8**

In the late '50s and early '60s, many popular blues artists put a dancefloor-savvy spin on the root–octave–♭7th–5th sequence from Ex. 6, injecting this old standby with slippery rhythms and funky attitude. Ex. 7 and Ex. 8 are groovy examples of the kind of thing you'll often hear under the highly danceable R&B instrumentals of guitarist Freddie King and harmonica player Junior Wells. Notice how hard these riffs work the 5th and ♭7th across beats *two* and *three*, even though they always dedicate the downbeat to the root and end the measure with the octave. This approach reached its apex with Jerry Jemmott's incredible work alongside B.B. King and sax great King Curtis.

Take It Slow

Every blues bassist needs to have a pocketful of slow blues grooves. Tommy Shannon is one of this arena's greats; Ex. 9 is a line Shannon might have played on a slow 12/8 blues with Stevie Ray Vaughan. Dotted quarter-notes on beats *one* and *three* establish the line's dominant flavor by nailing the chord's root and ♭7th, and that chromatic walkup to the 5th in beat *four* is a great tension-builder. It really sets up the whole band to come crashing down on the subsequent downbeat.

Ex. 10 is a slow-blues classic. This heavy, 6/8 *E*-string groove can anchor everything from Texas slow-burn to '60s-style rock-blues. Hit bar 1's root and ♭7th hard, and consider some wobbly finger vibrato to enhance the line's plodding, psychedelic vibe. If this crawling pace leaves you a bit *too* dazed and confused, take the tempo up to a smooth 60 BPM, and you've got one of B.B. King's favorite slow grooves. Variation: Play the dotted quarters as quarter/eighth figures. Sure, less is more—but sometimes a few additional notes can keep things from dragging too much.

Get Minor

Few things get guitarists going like a mid-tempo minor blues. Ex. 11 is a rolling, syncopated line perfect for those late-night, Chicago-style jams. Notice that this line actually skirts the ♭3rd, which would outline the minor tonality; let your ears be the judge, of course, but know that it's often perfectly acceptable to let the horn players or the guitarist define a tune's

Ex. 9   **Ex. 10**

Ex. 11　　　　　　　　　　　　　　　　　　　　**Ex. 12**

tonality. Windy City guitar giants Otis Rush and Buddy Guy can ride a minor line like this 'til the cows come home. Examples 3 and 11 both work well with Albert King's legendary "Crosscut Saw" groove (with Duck Dunn on bass).

Speaking of Duck Dunn, the Man from Memphis owns one of the all-time great minor blues grooves: the stone-simple, root–♭3rd–4th figure that fuels the timeless Booker T. & the M.G.'s chestnut "Green Onions" (Ex. 12). For another prime example of this classic line, check out Chicago harp-man Charlie Musselwhite's raucous version of Sonny Boy Williamson's "Help Me," with Bob Anderson on bass. Advice: Lay back, lock in with the kick, and really land on that ♭3rd (*C*) in beat *three*.

Funk It Up

Ex. 13 outlines the I–IV change across bars 4 and 5 of a gritty soul stomper. The masterful Chuck Rainey spun out sweaty grooves like this beneath many a classic by Aretha Franklin, King Curtis, and Donnie Hathaway. Don't gloss over those ghosted 16ths at the end of beat *two*—they really bring the line to life—and pay close attention to the varying rhythms from

Chic, with guitarist Nile Rodgers and bassist Bernard Edwards

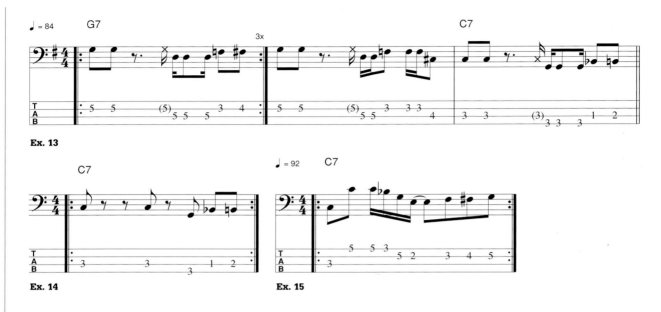

Ex. 13

Ex. 14

Ex. 15

one beat to the next (especially that killer 16th–eighth–16th figure in beat *three*). The key to nailing the change is that C♯ in beat *four*, the true-blue flatted 5th of the G chord, which just happens to lead chromatically into the root (C♮) of the IV. Very cool.

Ex. 14 is pure gut-bucket funk. This stuttering groove has roots in early-'60s Chicago—dig Howlin' Wolf's supremely funky "300 Pounds of Joy," with Buddy Guy on bass!—but it works equally well beneath chicken-scratch rhythm guitar or hard-edged metalloid blues. No laying back here; punch those eighth-note roots with everything you've got. Variation: Swap the ♮7th passing tone in beat *four* for another low 5th, and you're on your way to the greasy Louisiana grind of Slim Harpo's swamp-blues classic "Got Love If You Want It," or the take-no-prisoners charge of John Mayall & the Bluesbreakers' "Steppin' Out" (with John McVie on bass).

Rock The Blues

Ex. 15 revisits our old friend, the root–octave–♭7th–5th figure. This time, though, we're filtering Ex. 3's basic box pattern through Led Zeppelin's infectious strain of riff-rock. Really emphasize the major 3rd (*E*, tied across beats *two* and *three*) that begins the dramatic walk up to the 5th (*G*). Variation: Play that final, eighth-note 5th as two 16ths—the first as written, and the second an octave lower—thereby surrounding the upcoming, downbeat root. Many imitators followed, but few even came close to Zep's mighty, blues-based bombast. Jimmy Page gets all the credit—but it's John Paul Jones's bass thunder that makes these righteous riffs *rock*.

Buy The Blues

Any decent blues collection contains a healthy dose of classic bass lines. At first, hunt for discs that feature a wide variety of artists and span several decades. Next, focus on your favorite tracks, noting their similarities and differences. Once you've settled on a few favorite artists and styles, head back to the record mart and begin building your own blues bass collection. Two particular compilations that contain many of the lines cited here are *Legends of Guitar—Electric Blues, Vol. 1* [Rhino] and *Essential Blues, Vols. 1 & 2* [House of Blues].

Dave Pomeroy with his
Fleishman electric upright

Country Bass: The Song Is King

By Dave Pomeroy

When I moved to Nashville in 1977, I learned early on that in country music, fast licks and soloing chops are nowhere near as important as the ability to create a simple groove the whole band can lean on. It's not that technique and harmonic knowledge aren't important to good country bass playing—they absolutely are. It's just that a different set of priorities are at work: focusing on economy and creating solid, supportive lines with good tone and most important, a good feel—that magical, mysterious element that's hard to measure but is most noticeable by its absence. The songwriting quality and the emotional commitment of the great country vocalists are the primary reasons for the music's success over the years—and if you pay close attention to the words, you're heading in the right direction.

The vast majority of Nashville sessions use number charts (see page 80). This musical-shorthand system enables musicians to quickly write an easily transposable chord chart based on traditional diatonic harmony, and it allows room for collaborative head arrangements. If you're serious about country music you'll need to learn how to use the number system.

The Country Vocabulary

The most obvious difference between country and most other styles is in the number of notes needed to get the job done. I had to hear this advice a couple of times before it finally sank in: "Think of the simplest thing you can play, and then play half of that." It's not as

Ex. 1

much of an exaggeration as you might think. One way to start reducing your note count is to avoid unnecessary fills and movement that conflict with the vocal line.

The country bass vocabulary has been fairly well laid out over the years, although many other influences have crept in as the music evolved and a new generation of studio players made their marks. Still, the main ingredients remain the same. The root and 5th are the primary notes in 2/4 (half-note) playing, and the 3rd, 6th, octave, and occasionally the dominant 7th enter the picture in basic 4/4 arpeggio-based patterns. Scalar movement comes into play in the classic walkups into verses and between certain chord changes, particularly from the I to the IV and the V to the I. Ex. 1 shows a two-beat feel with root-five motion; Ex. 2 is a quarter-note shuffle that uses arpeggios and scalar motion.

Obviously, more complex chord progressions open up the door to creating more adventurous bass lines that allow passing tones. Ballads also provide us a little more interpretation leeway. A key decision in these more "open" tunes is choosing your entrance point. Many times the bass can support a piano or guitar/vocal first verse, or even play a fill or two (gasp!) around the vocal. Coming in halfway through the first verse or entering at the "channel" (pre-chorus) can give the song a lift before the whole band comes crashing in at the chorus.

As in many other kinds of music, one of your primary functions is to tie the drummer's foot to the rest of the band (or vice versa in some cases). Depending on the song's require-

Ex. 2

ments, you can stay in unison with the kick or create additional light and shade by playing fewer notes, adding grace notes, or playing *around* the kick drum pattern. These techniques can make very subtle but effective differences in a track's dynamics. You're also giving the kick drum the illusion of pitch, so your register choice is important. Breaking up repeated roots with octaves is one way to keep a simple part from becoming monotonous.

Even in such a structured musical environment, we bassists still wield quite a bit of power as the band's harmonic and rhythmic cornerstone. Small note-placement shifts against the drum track can make a huge difference in a song's attitude. Another thing to listen for is the pianist's left hand. There's nothing quite like locking in with a really good piano player on a 4/4 shuffle—but the two parts can create a mudfest if both players aren't listening to each other. You can also reinforce the guitars' low end without necessarily doubling their lines. Think of this in terms of reinforcing key notes or phrases in the licks above your lines. Overall it's a matter of ensemble, and you have the power to emphasize what you feel are an arrangement's strongest elements. There are also times you need to go against the track's grain to keep it country; the most obvious example is a Chuck Berry-style rock & roll feel with a root-five bass part.

Focus On The Song

All things considered, never forget that the backbone of country music is the songs. There may be no other form of music so dependent on the power of words to move the listener. The importance of listening to the lyrics and connecting with the meaning of the song can't be overstated. Let's look at how a typical new song gets worked up in a Nashville recording session.

Much like a story that's been handed down until it barely resembles the original, a song and its component parts may have gone through many changes on its way to the studio. Sometimes the writer/artist/producer has lived with a home demo so long that every note has become firmly etched in his mind, and he "just can't hear it any other way." Still, it's up to you to keep the best ideas and do what you must to make the rest work.

Think of the simplest thing you can play, and then play half of that.

The Nashville Number System

The number system, the lingua franca of Nashville recording sessions, is as easy as 1-2-3—or, most often, 1-4-5. The system allows players with or without traditional reading skills to read and write charts, and it makes transposition easy. It falters on tunes with complex modulations or chord structures, but these seldom are a factor in country music.

In a typical Nashville session the producer plays a demo of the song to be recorded, and the players are either given a number chart or sketch their own by ear. This must be done quickly during expensive studio time, so top session players are adept at producing an accurate chart with one or two hearings. Since charts are transcribed as they're heard, no repeat signs are used, and for convenience most charts are only one page. Players write four bars a line down the left side of a page; they then go to the top right if more space is needed.

A typical number chart is shown here. The system simply assigns a numeral (Arabic, not Roman) to each chord by its scale degree. A number by itself represents a major triad; in the key of C, 1 is a C-major triad, 2 a D-major triad, and so on. Other rules:

- Key and time signature are written and circled in the upper left corner of the chart.
- A superscript minus sign (–) represents a minor chord; a superscript 7, a dominant 7 chord; Δ7 or maj7, a major 7 chord; o, a diminished chord; +, an augmented chord.
- In a "split bar" each chord lasts for two beats. The chords are separated by a slash, and the bar is underlined.
- A diamond (◊) around a number means the entire rhythm section plays a whole-note on that chord.
- A circled number is a 2/4 bar.
- MOD means modulation; NK, new key.
- Alternate upper structures are drawn like fractions: In the key of E, an E triad with a B in the bass would be $\frac{1}{5}$.
- A dot followed by a bar denotes an extra bar at the end of a phrase.
- Song form is noted by V1, V2 (verse one, verse two, etc.); CHO (chorus); and TA (turnaround).
- A sharp sign (#) after a number indicates a chromatic chord; in the key of C, 2# is a D# (or E♭) major triad.
- The classic country quarter-note bass walkup from 5th to root is notated by four small ascending slashes.
- Minor-key songs are usually written with the relative minor (the VIm) as the tonal center.
- Repeats, codas, and other devices from standard chord charts still apply, and important musical motifs are often written out above the numbers where needed.

Thanks to Tom McBryde for the number chart.

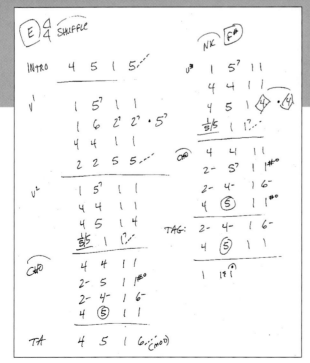

On the other hand you may be recording a song that was written right before the session, with a few lyrics still to be tweaked and with no musical arrangement other than a chord progression and melody. In this case the band can make or break a song.

In most Nashville sessions the arrangement is a collective effort, with players developing their parts while keeping up with the overall arrangement as it evolves. As a bassist you're generally expected to create, edit, and fine-tune your bass parts with little or no fanfare—in other words, get on with it and keep the verbiage to a minimum! Once the chart has been tweaked and everyone agrees on the tune's structure, the fun begins. Many times the "magic take" is the first one in which the majority of the band "found" their parts. Sometimes the more you record a song, the harder it is to sustain that freshness, especially on groove-oriented tunes. It's not a question of physical fatigue as much as avoiding the temptation to think too much and then lose the feel.

So how do you find the right part for a song? It never hurts to listen closely a time or two before picking up your bass; using your imagination instead of your fingers can lead you somewhere new. It's crucial to make adjustments as the other players work out their parts. It's a different kind of improvisation; rather than navigating complex chord changes or odd time signatures, think of yourself as part of a collective experiment in ensemble arranging and performance. Sounds important, doesn't it?

Rolling Tape

As you play the song, listen to everyone else. If the piano or electric guitar parts are busy, either simplify or tighten up your part to match what they're doing. Anytime you can leave out something that allows another part to come through, you're on the right track. Conversely, listen for holes in the upper-register parts that may allow you to make your own statement. Above all, follow the cardinal rule of country bass playing: Don't step on the vocal!

Of course, it's easy to over-analyze an arrangement and talk it to death. Run the song a few times before you tear it apart, and remember that listening closely to one playback is worth more than a thousand words. The better you are at getting your part together without talking, the more people will be amazed at how much you can accomplish quickly.

The bass/kick-drum relationship is the heartbeat of country music, so getting a quick read on the drummer's overall direction is a great starting point. The kick-drum pattern will have a lot to do with your rhythmic choices—but remember there's no law that says you have to mimic it exactly. Collaborating with the drummer to create longer phrases of one- or two-measure kick/bass patterns will help the dynamics and give the song a sense of motion. A less busy verse pattern will leave you somewhere to go in the chorus. Be prepared to go with the drummer's concept—but don't be afraid to offer a suggestion to improve the groove. A quick visit to the drum booth can be the fastest way to work out a problem without taking away valuable headphone time from the rest of the band.

Examples 3 through 6 show one-measure kick patterns commonly found in contemporary country. Ex. 3 is the backbone of the root-five 2/4 feel. The often-heard Ex. 4 is the most flexible for allowing the rest of the band to either push or not push the middle of the bar. Ex. 5 anticipates the back half of the bar, while Ex. 6 is a funkier groove in the style of The Band's Levon Helm or Kenny Buttrey from *Harvest*-era Neil Young. Program these patterns

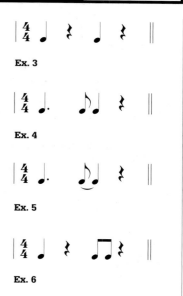

Ex. 3

Ex. 4

Ex. 5

Ex. 6

Common Nashville Session Terms

Push: An eighth-note that anticipates a downbeat or middle of the bar, usually played by the whole band. The push is noted on a typical number chart with a slash or an eighth-note tied to the subsequent bar or middle of the bar.

Right-hand push: When the upper-register instruments play the push but the bottom instruments play the rhythm straight. It can be written as "r.h." over the push mark or written in only by the players who will execute it.

Diamond: A whole- or half-note, often at the end of a verse or chorus, played by the whole band.

Stop: A quarter- or eighth-note, played by the whole band, that cuts off rather than rings out as a diamond would. A stop is written as a quarter- or eighth-note or occasionally as an inverted triangle (half a diamond).

into a drum machine and experiment with different ways of playing against them.

Assembling these kinds of rhythmic building blocks into longer phrases makes an arrangement more interesting. For example, a typical four-bar phrase might employ three bars of Ex. 3 and one of Ex. 4. When combining patterns, the kick can fill in some of the rests to create two-bar phrases. The bass has the freedom to play between these rhythms using grace notes, ghost notes, hammer-ons, walk-ups, slides, and fills. Just be sure what you add enhances the big picture—the singer and the song.

Another crucial element is the acoustic guitar part. It's safe to say the majority of country songs are written on guitar, and in the studio the acoustic part is often the skeleton the whole arrangement hangs on. A great acoustic player can bring a session to life, so it's very important to complement his or her rhythmic and harmonic approach. A great song can hold up in its simplest form, so don't be afraid to give the acoustic guitar some space.

There are a thousand ways to make a new song memorable: Leave space in a verse to let the track breathe. Try a rhythmic accent that shadows the vocal hook's phrasing. Use tasteful register jumps to emphasize the contrast between sections. Explore how right-hand muting changes the drums' perceived sound. (For instance, you can make the snare jump out of the track by cutting off your sustain on the backbeat.) Vary your lines by breaking up straight eighths in different ways. Every note is a universe in itself; don't underestimate the value of making each one count.

In the end it's all about making the song and the artist become one—and being comfortable with a support role that may make you feel invisible at times. You can bet they'll miss you if you're not there, and if you make everyone else sound good, you've done your job well. That's still the essence of great bass playing, no matter the style.

The late country session great Roy Huskey Jr.

Carlos Del Puerto of the
pioneering Cuban band
Irakere

Understanding Afro–Cuban Grooves: A Latin Primer

By Chris Jisi

Today's Latin music, which has both European and African roots, is built around two key rhythmical elements: *clave* (CLAH-vay) and *tumbao*. "The clave is an interchangeable two-bar rhythm to which all other rhythms must relate," explains Lincoln Goines, who has played bass for Dave Valentin, Dizzy Gillespie, Paquito D'Rivera, and Gato Barbieri and who co-wrote the Latin rhythm-section instructional book *Funkifying the Clave* with drummer Robby Ameen. "Depending on which bar the music starts on, it is referred to as 2:3 or 3:2 clave. The tumbao is the ostinato figure played on the conga drum

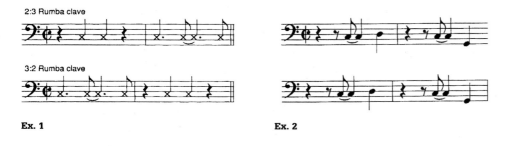

Ex. 1   **Ex. 2**

or bass that locks into the clave and creates the groove." Ex. 1 shows the two types of rumba claves; Ex. 2 shows a corresponding tumbao.

Goines suggests non-Latin bassists begin with the *songo* form. "It's the most exciting rhythmic form for bass, and it's also the most useful and easily adaptable style, because it's free and open. Songo introduced the drumset into the standard Latin percussion lineup; the style originated in Cuba in the '70s, when bands heard rock and funk on American radio stations but for political reasons had to disguise those influences within the traditional Cuban rhythms. Adding to its musical-melting-pot effect are Caribbean-based influences such as calypso and samba." Ex. 3 is in the songo form; Goines begins with a traditional rhythm and then adds a contemporary sound. "The piece is in 2:3 clave and, like most Afro-Cuban grooves, is felt in two or cut-time," explains Lincoln. "The traditional tumbao appears in bars 1–4; the slap technique beginning in bar 5 is in the style of Sal Cuevas, bassist for Rubén Blades and the Fania All-Stars. Attack each note sharply, but allow the lower tumbao notes to ring over into each other in legato fashion. The emphasis of the groove is in the tumbao, not the high-note syncopations." The tumbao roots of the tenths that first appear in bars 9 and 10 are played on the *E* string, with the *C* and *D* fingered at the 8th and 10th frets; the high *E* and *F#* are played on the *G* string at the 9th and 11th frets. Note the hammer-ons and pull-offs, especially in bars 14–20.

Ex. 3

Guaguanco is a more traditional, somewhat less flexible form than songo. "The great Cuban bassist Israel 'Cachao' Lopez was a master of riffing around within guaguanco," Goines continues. "It also has a correlation to the 'Bo Diddley beat' and New Orleans second-line feels." Ex. 4 shows the rhythmic backbone of guaguanco.

Ex. 4

The cha-cha bass tumbao is similar to the tumbao in Ex. 2, but it's played at a slower tempo—usually in the 88–132 BPM range. "Cha-cha is more rock- and funk-oriented, because it lends itself to the *two*-and-*four* backbeat with the bass on the downbeat. A good example would be the cha-cha feel of Santana's 'Oyé Como Va.'" Similar to cha-cha is mozambique, shown in Ex. 5 in the 2:3 clave. After the traditional mozambique line in the first four bars, Goines adds funk variations.

Ex. 5

Latin bassists (L to R) Jorge Reyes, Joseíto Beltrán, Orlando "Cachaíto" López, and Silvio Vergara

Introduction To Jazz: Navigating A Chord Chart

By Ed Friedland

Reading music is an important aspect of total musicianship. Most people think music-reading proficiency means being able to rip through pages of dense, syncopated 16th-notes. Certainly that skill will serve you well at some point in your career—but most of the time, particularly when you're playing jazz, you'll be given either a *chord chart* (chord symbols with slashes indicating the number of beats per measure, perhaps with some rhythmic kicks) or a *lead sheet* (the melody of a song with chord symbols written above each measure). You'll be expected to create something appropriate with this information. That might seem pretty easy—but those little chord symbols contain a lot of information. Let's take a close look at those letters, numbers, and squiggles.

Chord Construction

A prerequisite to understanding chord symbols is knowing how the different types of chords are constructed. If you aren't familiar with this information, look at the column called CONSTRUCTION in the listings of chord symbols that follow; it tells you how the chords are built. Practice playing the chords as arpeggios, from the root to the top note and back down. Also play each chord starting on different roots until you've played every chord type in every key. The ability to outline these arpeggios with walking bass lines (see page 92) is a fundamental part of playing jazz.

To get started, we need to know what a chord symbol tells us directly. The root is the most obvious piece of information. The symbol also tells us if the chord is major or minor; what type of 7th it has (if any); whether the 5th is perfect, flatted, or raised; and if there are any additional tones to be considered, such as a suspended 4th or upper extensions (the 9th, 11th, and 13th).

As shown in Fig. 1, a chord symbol is divided into two parts: the *prefix*, which is the first part, and the *suffix*, which is the last. The prefix is all that's used for triads; the suffix gets used in four-part (and larger) chords. Fig. 2 shows the five basic prefixes used for all chord symbols; the ALSO SEEN AS column lists other ways (both correct and incorrect) the chord is often written.

Now let's look at the suffixes. It's important to be able to visually separate the suffix from the prefix; when you see the symbol *C–7*, for example, the minor symbol (–) pertains to the *triad*, not the 7th. When you see a plain *7* in a chord symbol, that indicates the 7th is a ♭7. (The ♭7 is sometimes called a minor 7th, but don't confuse that with a *minor 7* chord.) When you see *Cmaj7*, the *C* is the prefix, meaning it is a *C* major triad; the major symbol (*maj*) is part of the suffix and pertains to the 7th. It indicates that the 7th is a *major 7th*, like the 7th note in the major scale (conveniently found a half-step below the octave). This may be a little confusing at first, but you'll be amazed how simple it is to read chord symbols once you've spent some time practicing.

Fig. 3 is a table listing *C* chords with various common suffixes.

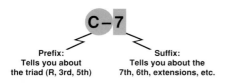

C–7

Prefix:
Tells you about
the triad (R, 3rd, 5th)

Suffix:
Tells you about the
7th, 6th, extensions, etc.

Fig. 1

SYMBOL	NAME	CONSTRUCTION	ALSO SEEN AS
C	C major triad	R–3–5–(8)	CM
	Note: A chord is always major unless you see a minor (m or –), diminished (dim or °), augmented (aug or +), or sus symbol.		
C–	C minor triad	R–♭3–5–(8)	Cm, Cmin
C°	C diminished triad	R–♭3–♭5–(8)	Cdim
C+	C augmented triad	R–3–#5–(8)	Caug, C+5
Csus	C suspended 4	R–4–5–(8)	Csus4
	The suspended triad uses no 3rd		

Fig. 2

SYMBOL	NAME	CONSTRUCTION	ALSO SEEN AS
Cmaj7	C major 7	R–3–5–7	CM7, C△7
	C major triad, with the 7th scale degree from the major scale		
C7	C7 or "dominant 7"	R–3–5–♭7	
	C major triad, with a minor or flatted 7th		
C–7	C minor 7	R–♭3–5–♭7	Cm7, Cmin7
	C minor triad, with a minor or flatted 7th		
C–7(♭5)	C minor 7♭5	R–♭3–♭5–♭7	Cm7♭5, Cø, Cø7
	C diminished triad, with a minor or flatted 7th (also called a "half-diminished" chord)		
C–(maj7)	C minor major 7	R–♭3–5–7	Cmmaj7, C–△7
	C minor triad, with the 7th scale degree from the major scale		
C°7	C diminished 7	R–♭3–♭5–♭♭7	Cdim7
	C diminished triad, with a diminished or "double-flatted" 7th (the double-flatted 7th is actually the 6th scale degree)		
C+7	C augmented 7	R–3–#5–♭7	Caug7, C7#5, C7+5
	C augmented triad, with a minor or flatted 7th		
C+maj7	C aug. major 7	R–3–#5–7	Caugmaj7, Cmaj7#5, Cmaj7+5
	C augmented triad, with the 7th scale degree from the major scale		
Csus7	C7 suspended 4	R–4–5–♭7	C7sus
	C suspended triad, with a minor or flatted 7th		
C6	C6	R–3–5–6	C13
	C major triad, with the 6th scale degree from the major scale		
C6/9	C6/9	R–3–6–9	C9 13
	C major triad, usually with the 6th scale degree substituting for the 5th, with extension 9 on top		
C–6	C minor 6	R–♭3–5–6	Cm6, Cmin6
	C minor triad, with the 6th scale degree from the major scale		

Fig. 3

You will also encounter chord symbols with bass notes that are different from the root notes; in these symbols the chord and bass note are separated by a slash. These alternate bass notes may be chord tones or perhaps notes that do not belong in the chords at all. For example, *C7/G*, which indicates a C7 chord with a *G* in the bass, can be considered an inversion of a C7 chord because the 5th is on the bottom. However, the *F♯* in a *C7/F♯* chord would be considered a truly alternate bass note. *F♯* is not part of the original chord; instead it's used to create a particular harmonic effect. In either case, you should approach this type of chord by playing the specified bass note. (If you're improvising a solo, play as if only the chord on top were on the chart—but incorporate the specified bass note as an additional tone in your line.)

A Typical Chord Chart

Now that you have an understanding of basic chord anatomy, look at the chord chart on page 91; it's typical of one you might encounter on a gig. In addition to the chords, this chart contains rhythmic notation as well as some common "road map" features, such as first and second endings, repeat signs, and rehearsal letters.

In the upper-left corner is the style marking. In this case it says SWING, which means you should walk through the tune. The chart gives you just the raw information about the song; the exact feel is up to the rhythm section. The large letters **A** and **B** inside rectangles are called rehearsal marks; they indicate the form of the tune. In this case, the song has an **A** section and a **B** section (bridge), and it has one of the most common forms around, **AABA**.

The repeat signs tell you more about the form. In this case, start at the top (bar 1) and play through the first ending; then take the repeat back to the top. Play until you reach the point where the first-ending sign starts, skip those two bars, and go directly to the second ending. Then play through the second ending and go on to the bridge (**B** section). The last **A** section goes straight through to the double bar line; this is the end of the form. (Each time through the form is called a *chorus*.) To continue the song, go back to the top.

The rhythmic notation in bars 1 and 3 of the **A** sections is to be played for the head (melody) only; when the solos start, you should walk through these bars in quarter-notes, using the chord changes written above in parentheses. In other words, for the solos play *Cmaj7* for bars 1 and 2 and *A7* for bars 3 and 4 of the **A** sections.

The tune's last bar has *D–7* and *G7* in parentheses; this means they comprise the turn-around, which takes you back to the top. When you end the song they are to be left out and replaced with an ending. As is the case with most charts, there is no specific ending indicated here; it's up to the band to come up with an ending that begins in the second-to-last bar. There are several choices, but Ex. 1 shows the #1 favorite, super-duper, can't miss, greatest ending of all time. The dotted semicircle over the last note is called a *fermata*, which means you hold the last note until a cutoff is signaled by the bandleader. This is usually done with a nod of the head, called a "head cue."

Ex. 1

Extensions

Some chord symbols list possible upper extensions: ♭9, ♯9, ♯11, ♭13, etc. In addition, each chord symbol implies one or more scales that would be appropriate for a given chord.

Chartin' A Course

Depending on the progression and the key, one or all of those possible scales may change.

You may encounter a poorly written "fake book" with horribly wrong and/or illegible chord changes, and you'll have to figure out what's right to play. Sometimes fake books have improper root motion; if so, the pianist might decide to play what he thinks is right and not tell anyone else. (For you, this is called on-the-job training.)

In time, as you gain experience with these situations, you'll be able to figure out what's happening. In the meantime, practice all of your arpeggios in all keys until they're second nature to you. Study the tables and become familiar with all the symbols and the various ways they can be written. Open up a fake book or some sheet music and practice reading the changes. Although sometimes you may need to play only the root, knowing about the rest of the chord will help you create walking lines, fills, and solos that make sense.

Walking Bass Techniques

By Mike Richmond

"**W**alking bass" refers to a type of line most commonly used in jazz. In its simplest form, a walking bass line consists of a string of quarter-notes derived from various scales, arpeggios, chromatic alterations, and modes (Ex. 1). Fundamentally, a walking line should establish both a harmonic foundation and a steady rhythm for the ensemble. If done well, it creates a pulse like a heartbeat, pumping renewed life into the music. It allows the other musicians to float along on the rhythmic undercurrent it creates.

In order to make the traditional quarter-note walking line more rhythmically interesting, it often helps to introduce various rhythmic elements—skips, slurs, triplets, ties, and syncopated rhythms—that punctuate the line and enhance the groove. It should be noted that while these figures can have percussive effects, the line's overall feel should be smooth and even. Also, they must be used at the proper tempo; if played out of context they can disturb the rhythmic flow and upset the line's forward motion.

As you apply rhythmic embellishments to a walking line, keep in mind that swing feel must be maintained. Rhythms such as ♪♪ must be felt and played as ♪♪♪, which is in keeping with the triplet swing feel. To execute the rhythmic embellishments you'll need to alternate your right-hand index and middle fingers.

The *skip* (Ex. 2) is the 16th-note of a dotted-eighth-and-16th figure and has the feel of a person skipping from one step to the next. It should be played clearly and perfectly in

Ex. 1

Ex. 2

meter, with a slight accent. When playing skips, remember they should *add* to the groove and give momentum to the line; the skip should never be rushed, as this would result in rushing the tempo.

The *ghost skip* (Ex. 3) is used rhythmically like the skip but doesn't have a definite pitch; ideally it has the crisp, percussive sound of a snap or click. When playing the ghost skip on the same string or on the string above the note that follows, don't press the string completely to the fingerboard; instead, mute the string by applying only slight pressure. Then play the next note with the same finger. When playing the ghost skip on the string *below* the next note, mute with your right hand, cutting off the tone as it plucks the string above.

A *pull-off skip* (Ex. 4) is a note plucked with the left hand only. One way to execute a pull-off is by plucking an open-string 16th-note after fingering the dotted eighth-note on the

These musical examples were adapted from Mike Richmond's Modern Walking Bass Technique *[Ped Xing Music, Box 628, Englewood, NJ 07631] and reprinted with permission from the publisher.*

Opposite: Karl Sevareid of the Robert Cray Band

Ex. 3

same string. After the pull-off, the next note (the same open string) can be plucked with the right hand. (⅜ indicates the left-hand 1st finger plucking the open G string.) In Ex. 4 the left-hand 1st finger plays the A♭ on the G string as the right index finger plucks the note; the left-hand 1st finger then plucks the G string as the right hand lifts off it; the pull-off is completed with the right index finger plucking the open G. (Again, this should be performed in one fluid motion.) The pull-off is most commonly used on the top string, but it's also possible on the D and A strings. Pull-offs are not often used on the lower strings, because their heaviness makes it difficult to get a clear tone.

Ex. 4 **Ex. 5** **Ex. 6**

Pull-off skips can also be executed from the D string to the open G above (Ex. 5). The left-hand 4th finger plays the F♯ on the D string as the right index finger plucks the note; then the left-hand 4th finger plucks the G string as it slides across, with the right-hand finger lifting off the D string in the same motion. This pull-off is completed with the right index finger plucking the open G following the skip; as it's plucking the G string it presses against the open D to deaden it.

A *slurred skip* (Ex. 6) is a skip that's slurred to the following note. It's played by plucking the 16th-note with the left hand and then sliding to the following note without plucking it.

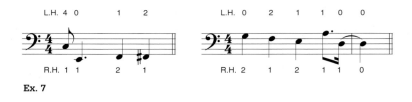

Ex. 7

The figures ♪ ♩. and ♪ ♩♪ are common rhythmic alterations that briefly suspend time. These syncopated rhythms create tension and give a feeling of anticipation, which is resolved when the walking line is continued (Ex. 7). Also, triplets (♪♪♪) can be used to briefly break up the rhythm and increase the excitement level. Slurs and pull-offs work well with triplets.

Ex. 8 is a walking line that uses all of these techniques—use it as the starting point for a long walk of your own.

Ex. 8

Thumbstyle Technique (Slap Bass)

By Alexis Sklarevski

Thumbstyle playing, or slap bass, was invented in the late '60s by Larry Graham (see page 178) and developed and refined by numerous players, most notably Louis Johnson, Stanley Clarke (see page 182), and Marcus Miller.

Thumbstyle technique can be broken into two building blocks: the *slap*, done with the thumb, and the *pop* (sometimes called the pluck), usually done with the index finger. Don't worry about your left hand for now—just concentrate on right-hand positioning. Place your right arm so your forearm is more parallel to the strings than it is when you're playing fingerstyle (see Fig. 1); this may mean you have to bring your elbow down closer to the bridge. If you're standing up and your bass is hanging too low for you to reach this position, adjust your strap accordingly.

While muting the A, D, and G strings with your left hand, strike the E string with your right thumb about where the neck meets the body, or over the last fret. If you make good contact, the string will hit some of the frets, producing that bright, metallic "zing" we want to hear. Don't press down on the string with your thumb; let it bounce off. Also, don't just brush the string—you have to actually hit it. Try playing each of the strings a few times to get a feel for this motion (Ex. 1). You'll notice it's harder to be accurate on the thinner strings, so play slowly and watch your hand.

Now for the pop. Using about the last half-inch of your index finger, pull the G string

Fig. 1

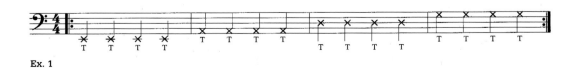

Ex. 1

Ex. 2

away from the bass, and then release it. Don't yank the string—just let its natural tension pull the string off your fingertip so it snaps down onto the neck. If you've kept the same hand position you had earlier, you'll see that your index finger is pretty much in line with where the neck and body meet. Pluck the *D* and *G* strings a few times to get a feel for this motion. Once you've done that, practice muting the string with your left hand immediately after popping it; this produces the staccato sound usually associated with popping.

The fundamental exercise for the thumb/pluck motion involves playing octaves on string pairs: *E* and *D*, and *A* and *G* (Ex. 2). Listen carefully to the sound, and try to strike a balance between the volumes of the slap and the pop; neither should be louder than the other. If your hand starts to hurt, take it easy. Build up slowly to the point where Ex. 2 is comfortable to play. Then try the different rhythms in Examples 3 through 5.

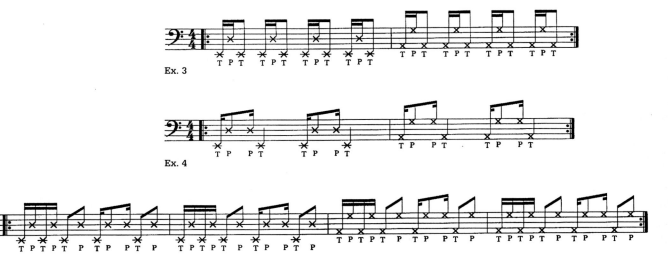

Ex. 3

Ex. 4

Ex. 5

Examples 6 through 17 are one-bar slap lines in the key of *E*. When you can play several of these examples, try combining them to produce two- and four-bar lines. As you're practicing, loop each example and play it several times, along with a metronome, until it really feels comfortable. Your goal shouldn't be to play these lines fast—instead, strive to be as *accurate* as possible.

Ex. 6 is a very standard slap line. Begin with open *E* and then play the *C♯* and *D* on the *A* string. Note the dot over the *D*; it's a *staccato mark*, meaning you should play the note short. Counting *one and two and three and four and*, play the two 16th-notes on the *and* of beat *four* as a hammer-on: Fret the second note sharply with your left pinkie without slapping the string again. (The hammer-ons are all indicated with a slur and the letter H.) Ex. 7 is a variation with four 16th-notes in beat *four*. For Ex. 8 play muted *D*'s for the first two 16ths of beat *four* by laying your left fingers across the strings as you slap and pop; muting while slapping creates a percussive sound rather than an actual note. Ex. 9 uses a two-16ths/eighth combination, and Ex. 10 is similar but has muted notes in beats *two* and *four*.

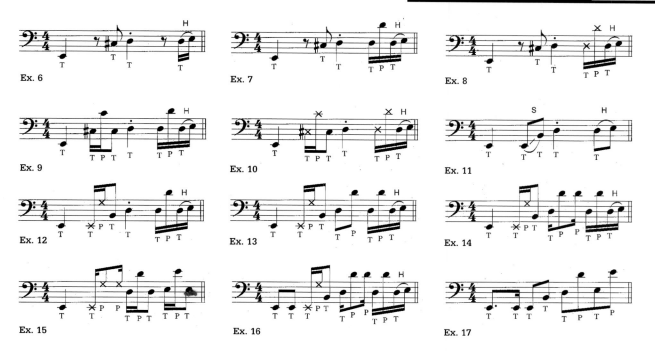

Ex. 6   Ex. 7   Ex. 8

Ex. 9   Ex. 10   Ex. 11

Ex. 12   Ex. 13   Ex. 14

Ex. 15   Ex. 16   Ex. 17

Play Ex. 11 with the thumb only; slide up the open *E* string to the *B* at the 7th fret and play the *D* on the *A* string without shifting. Ex. 12 through Ex. 17 are all variations on Ex. 11. In each case slide up to the 7th fret and continue the line in that position, as it's the easiest place to play the phrase smoothly. Be sure to articulate every note; don't gloss over any of them. You want to hear pitched notes and muted notes with the same intensity and attack.

So far all of our slap bass lines have been in the key of *E*. The great thing about playing in *E* is you don't have to worry about unintentionally hitting the string below it with your thumb. (On a 4-string, anyway.) Unfortunately—or fortunately, depending on how you look at it—not all tunes are written in *E*, so you'll sometimes find yourself having to play in keys where the lowest note is not an open string.

Ex. 18 is a two-bar phrase in *G* that can be played without any position shifts. Start with *G* on the *E* string; the hammer-ons are indicated by slur markings. The first two 16th-notes

Ex. 18

Ex. 19

in beat *four* of bar 2 can be played as a slap/pop on the muted *G* string, or you can mute the *D* string, thumb the first ghost note there, and then pluck the second one on the *G* string. Ex. 19 is a variation; be sure to place the *F* on the last 16th of beat *one*.

Ex. 20 is a four-bar bass line incorporating the eighth-note octave pattern from Ex. 2; try playing the octaves in bar 4 using tenuto (long) and staccato (short) notes, as written. Start

Ex. 20

Ex. 21

the last bar on *F* on the *A* string, and play the octaves on the *G* string. Be sure to keep the sound of the thumbed and plucked notes balanced.

In bar 1 of Ex. 21 play beat *four* using the muted *D* string for the ghost notes. Play the B♭ on the *G* string; this can be a little tricky, so be sure you hear both the ghost notes and the pitches. In bar 4 play the octave patterns with both tenuto and staccato articulations. Here again we're using the standard two-16th/eighth rhythmic pattern. Notice how bar 4 is a close variation of bar 4 in Ex. 20; this kind of rhythmic interpretation can help a bass line evolve without adding more notes.

These are just the bare fundamentals of slap technique. There are several books and videos devoted just to this area of bass playing, and I encourage you to pursue the technique with a qualified teacher as well. Most of all, though, listen to recordings of the slap-bass greats and try to emulate their lines and their sound.

Bass Harmonics

By Michael Manring

Harmonics are chiming, bell-like tones produced on a stringed instrument through a special technique. Harmonics are popular with bassists for several reasons. First, they just sound cool, and bass harmonics are generally loud and clear. This is partly because our ears are less sensitive to low pitches than to higher ones, so we tend to perceive high pitches as being louder than low pitches of the same amplitude. (That's why you need a more powerful amp than your guitarist to match his volume.) Second, harmonics are low-maintenance notes—once you play them, they ring until they're muted, leaving you free to play other things. Finally, harmonics are intonation-stable, giving fretless and upright players a reference for closed tones. (They don't always coincide with our system of "equal temperament," however—but that's a whole other story.) Knowing how harmonics work will improve your understanding of just about every aspect of music.

Also known as overtones, partials, *flageolet* tones, *flautando*, and a host of other names, harmonics occur in all vibrating bodies: bass strings, columns of air, drum heads, rocks, whatever. A vibrating string's motion is complex; it not only vibrates as a whole but in lots of subdivisions. The string vibrates in one part along its entire length, in two halves, three thirds, four quarters, and so on—all at the same time. To see this in action, in a darkened room, turn on the TV (no kidding) and hold your bass sideways so you can see the strings in front of the screen. Now pluck a string. The string will look like it's vibrating in an unusual way. The TV screen acts as a strobe, "freezing" the string's motion at a certain frequency. Different notes show different vibration patterns, depending on how the string's harmonic frequencies interact with the TV's—endless hours of fun!

Since open strings vibrate in even subdivisions of their length, when you play a harmonic you isolate one of those divisions. That's why harmonic points, or nodes, appear at even fractions of the string's length—at the halfway point (the 12th fret), the one-third point (the 7th fret), and so on. Here's how you play a harmonic: Lightly touch the string at one of these points with a left-hand finger (don't press the string to the fingerboard), and then pluck the string. You'll notice the string vibrates on both sides of your finger but not at the point directly under your finger. Your finger is simply stopping the vibrations of the fractions larger than the one you hear.

Most harmonics produce a pitch different from the closed tone at the same position. In some cases it's the same note in a higher octave, but often it's a different note entirely. This is helpful in that harmonics increase the number of notes available in one position. Harmonics also have a different timbre than closed tones, so they can lend variety to your sound.

It's a good idea to identify all of the harmonics. Even if you're using a tuning other than standard *EADG*, the harmonic ratios always remain constant (See Fig. 1).

There are harmonics beyond these at the 1/8th and 1/9th positions, and so on—but as they get higher in pitch they become increasingly harder to hear and to play.

Fraction of String Length	Interval Above Open String
1/2	1 octave
1/3	1 octave + fifth
1/4	2 octaves
1/5	2 octaves + maj. third
1/6	2 octaves + fifth
1/7	2 octaves + ♭ seventh

Fig. 1

Ex. 1

Ex. 2

With this information we can identify all of the most convenient harmonics available in standard tuning. Ex. 1 shows the first seven harmonics on the *E*, *A*, *D*, and *G* strings (including the open strings). We can also put all of these harmonics together on one grand staff (Ex. 2). Out of our original 28 harmonics (seven per string) we have 23 different pitches, since some of the tones can be played on more than one string. I've indicated which string or strings each harmonic can be played on.

Notice that the notes in the upper portion of the set are spaced closer together than those in the lower register; that's because the intervals between the higher partials on each string are smaller, so the information becomes more dense where each string's sets intersect. As a result, the most scalar harmonic patterns are found in the upper register.

Now let's consider the options for playing these harmonics. Since four of the notes in our set can be played on more than one string, we always have to make some choices with those—but there is yet another variable. Dividing a string into three parts, for example, means there are *two* places where you can play the 3rd harmonic—at the 1/3 point (over the 7th fret) and at the 2/3 point (over the 19th fret). As you get into the higher-numbered harmonics, there are more and more places on the string where they appear, giving you many more fingering options.

To find all of the places to play harmonics, you might want to make yourself a guide. Cut a thin strip of white cloth to the scale length of your bass, from bridge saddle to nut. By folding the cloth into halves, thirds, etc., and comparing the lengths of the segments, you can make marks on the fabric at the appropriate fractional divisions. Do this for each fraction up to sevenths, marking each set of divisions with a different colored pen. You'll end up with a color-coded guide you can hold alongside your bass to indicate where the harmonic sets appear. Remember that you always have one less position for a harmonic than its number: There are two positions for the 3rd harmonic, three for the 4th, etc.

There's a catch: 2/4, 3/6, and 1/2 are mathematically identical, so these three marks are all in the same place, at the midpoint of your guide. The same is true for 2/6 and 1/3, and 4/6 and 2/3. Therefore, when you touch the string at the "2/4" point, the string vibrates in halves, not quarters—giving you the 2nd harmonic instead of the 4th. The string always vibrates in the largest fractional length it can, limiting the number of positions for some of the harmonics; we end up with only two places to play the 4th harmonic and only two places for the 6th.

Now let's get back to our master set of harmonics. First we'll make a list of all the notes, regardless of the octave in which they appear. In the set of the first seven harmonics of the *E* string we have three *E*'s, two *B*'s, one *G♯*, and one *D*. (Notice that all of these notes are within an *E7* chord.) Using this procedure on all of the strings, we get the notes in Fig. 2. We can then combine the notes from each string, giving us Fig. 3.

Putting these in order of relative pitch gives us a kind of scale: *C, C♯/D♭, D, E, F, F♯/G♭, G, G♯/A♭, A,* and *B*. There are a total of ten different pitches—except for *D♯/E♭* and *A♯/B♭*, all of the chromatic pitches are represented at least once. This means all of the notes for the major keys of *C, D, G,* and *A* are available. (The other keys have either a *D♯/E♭* or an *A♯/B♭*, or both.) So in terms of harmonics, standard tuning is most convenient for the major keys of *C, D, G,* and *A* and their related modes. Other tunings, meanwhile, are better for other keys.

The possibilities for harmonics in standard tuning are virtually endless—and when you combine harmonics with alternate tunings, you open up another universe of possibilities. Good luck exploring—and have fun.

Number of Occurrences

String	3	2	1	1
E:	E	B	G#	D
A:	A	E	C#	G
D:	D	A	F#	C
G:	G	D	B	F

Fig. 2

Note	Number of Occurrences
D	6
E	5
A	5
G	4
B	3
G#	1
C#	1
C	1
F#	1
F	1
	= 28

Fig. 3

Freelancing 101:
Nine Steps To Nailing The Gig

By Ed Friedland

We bass players enjoy a unique position in the musical food chain: Every band needs a bassist, and there are never enough of us to go around. This gives us many opportunities to play a wide variety of musical styles, all in the same week. As a freelance bassist you can gig with a band, save the day, receive lots of strokes for doing a great job, get paid, and leave—all without having to load up the PA! Of course there's no one there to help you carry your SVT up the stairs when you get home, and you may never wind up on MTV. But you can make a good living, establish a reputation, and have many satisfying musical experiences.

1. Keep Time

There are several conflicting opinions on how to develop good time—but the bottom line is you *must* have it. It's at the core of everything we do as bassists, and if you can't keep time, don't wait for the phone to ring. So how do you develop good time? My answer is to use a metronome. I'm willing to believe there are other ways to get your time together, but this is the way I do it.

Here's one thing you can do right away to get started: Turn down your metronome to 40 BPM—the slowest setting on most metronomes—and play a major scale in half-notes. (That means you're playing 20 notes per minute.) Tape yourself. How was it? A little rushed, perhaps? It takes *focus* and patience to play that slowly and really nail it. Do this exercise at slow, medium, and fast tempos; record it, and be honest about how it sounds. Don't kid yourself into thinking your time is good enough—there's no such thing. If the exercise gets too easy, play only on beats *one* and *three*, then *two* and *four*, and finally only on *one*, only on *two*, then *three*, and *four*. It can always be made more challenging.

Often you'll play as a substitute with an existing band. You will find they have developed a group sense of where the time and groove are. It's your job to fit in with these people, not to force them to undergo major changes for a one-nighter. *The goal in freelancing is to make the people who hire you happy.* If you come in and find a way to groove with them, they'll be happy—even if they have time problems. When your time is strong, you can help smooth out any trouble spots. And if the band is solid already, they'll really like you.

2. Know Your Music

A good musical-knowledge base is very important if you want to take any call that comes in. You *must* be able to read music. Not every gig will require it, but you never know when someone is going to pull out a chart and expect you to read it. Reading means dealing with specific written notation as well as chord charts; for more information see Grooving On The Grid (page 50) and Navigating A Chord Chart (page 88). If you live in Nashville, you'll need to know the Nashville number system; see page 80. There are also many excellent books available to help you toward musical literacy.

You will need to know all the basic chord types and scales, as well as how to use them. You must have a complete knowledge of the fingerboard. A good fingerboard-familiarity

> **Don't kid yourself into thinking your time is good enough—there's no such thing.**

exercise: Start on low *E* and play every *E* up and down the neck. Then go to *F* and repeat. Do this with each note, and repeat the exercise daily—eventually you'll know the entire fingerboard. You also have to know the names of the notes in each key; if someone tells you to play I–VI–II–V in *G*, you have to know what the corresponding roots are. You might be able to get away with learning only fingerboard patterns, but gaps in your understanding will come back to haunt you.

Learn your key signatures, too. You need to know how many sharps or flats each key has, because it's common for a bandleader to indicate the key just by saying "two flats" or "three sharps." It's also common to signal the key with fingers. In most places fingers held up means sharp keys, while fingers down means flats—but make sure you know the local convention. In Boston, for instance, fingers up means flat keys—so three fingers up would mean the song is in *E♭*. In Providence, only 45 miles away, fingers up means sharp keys—so three fingers up would mean the key of *A*.

3. Know Different Kinds Of Music

Being a freelancer requires you to be familiar with many different musical styles. Even if you're into only one style, with a little common sense and an open mind you can play just about anything. When something different comes on the radio, don't change the station; check out the bass line. Do you hear roots, 5ths, and octaves? Let's face it—from one style to another, bass lines are made up of similar elements: outlining the root motion, hooking up with the drum part, and creating fills that enhance the feel. Of course, there are also specialized techniques you'll need to know even if you don't become an expert. Bassists are usually expected to be able to slap, for example, so you should be at least passable at the technique. And if you're a slap player, you need to know when *not* to slap! Few things are more obnoxious than someone turning every song into a funk tune.

Playing bass chords isn't usually called for—but if the keyboard breaks down or the guitarist doesn't know the tune, playing chords can save the day. Another handy approach is palm-muting, which involves plucking the strings with your thumb while lightly dampening them with your palm; this results in something approximating an old-style acoustic bass sound. Use it the next time you have to play "Fly Me to the Moon," and watch the old timers smile. (That means more gigs!) Palm-muting can also get you a deeper sound for reggae, blues, and other styles.

One of the biggest stumbling blocks bass players face is repertoire. Many times I've needed a sub and had to pass over a great player because he didn't know tunes. Many situations (especially the "pickup band") require you to come to the gig ready to play anything—'40s standards, '50s rock & roll, '60s R&B, '70s disco, '80s new wave, and '90s alternative. There may be no charts involved, and you have to make quick segues from tune to tune to keep the dance floor moving. How do you do that? Listen to all styles of music and absorb what you hear. Also, *play* different styles, and notice things that recur. Learn to recognize common root motions, such as I–IV–V, I–VI–II–V, II–V–I, IV–IVm–III–VI–II–V–I, I–♭VII, I–♭III–IV–V, and others. Of course, if your ears are together, you'll be able to "fake" through the tune the first time and have it nailed by the repeat.

Most often you'll be called upon to play good, old-fashioned, solid bass. Be prepared for that and you'll have few problems. If you are unfamiliar with a style or a tune, use common sense: Less is more. Listen to the melody, listen to the changes, and listen to the drums. Which brings us to the next requirement: ears.

4. Listen

BASS PLAYER columnist John Goldsby said it all when he wrote, "You don't get hired to play fast—you get hired to *hear* fast." Quick ears enable you to hear something and immediately play the right thing. To get working on your ears, start learning to hear diatonic and chromatic intervals. Find melodies that remind you of the various intervals (for example, "Twinkle Twinkle Little Star" for a perfect fifth), and make a list. Get a pitch pipe, a tuning fork, or even a harmonica, and start training yourself to recall pitches. When you listen to the radio, figure out the key for every tune you hear. While you're at it, learn to sing the bass line. You never know when you'll have to play it!

5. Get Equipped

Even if you have your chops together, your ears are in shape, and you know the tunes, there's more. You should have reliable and versatile equipment. This could mean several choices of instruments, or just one all-purpose axe. A fretless is good to have for special circumstances. If you have multiple basses, make sure the right one is in your gig bag before you leave. You should have at least two good working amps, including a head with at least 200 watts, and a choice of cabinets. I also recommend a good combo amp that will enable you to be heard and to get in and out of the gig quickly. Some places are "load-ins from hell"—and you'll be happy to walk through the front door discreetly with your 15" combo while the keyboard player waits for the security guard to open the loading-dock door. Make sure you have extra strings, a tuner, a strap, a good instrument cable, an extension cord (a 10' household cord will save you), a spare battery if you have an active bass, and an all-purpose tool for emergency adjustments. If you want to be a real Boy Scout, carry a power strip, a music stand, a portable soldering iron, extra cables, a spare power cord for your amp, and—the thing that keeps America running—duct tape.

It's also important to have a reliable car. You can mooch rides, but do you really want to wait for the drummer to break down his hardware, help him carry it, and then have to listen to his Buddy Rich tapes all the way home? Be punctual; leave yourself enough time to run into traffic, get lost, and set up your gear. It doesn't matter how good you are—if you consistently show up late, you won't get called back.

6. Get Organized

Time management is important, too. Get a datebook, and write things down. Don't take a gig unless you can check the book and be *sure* you're free. Double-booking yourself occasionally happens—but it's better to know far in advance. (Ever spend a Saturday afternoon trying to find someone who can cover your gig that night?) If you go for a "double"—two gigs in one day—make sure you have enough time to make the transition from one to the next. You may have to drive long distances, switch over your gear, change clothes, and eat. This is where having two rigs can come in handy; if necessary, you can have one amp set up and waiting for you at your second gig.

Once you get busy, choose your gigs wisely. If you take care of business, at some point you'll have your pick of many opportunities. Don't take a gig if you're sure something better will show up. If you commit four months in advance to a $50 Saturday night and later get a call for a $200 gig the same night, you'll kick yourself. In that case, don't call the leader of the first gig the day before to tell him you can't make it. You're better off losing the extra money than getting a reputation for being unreliable. If you need to get out of a gig for some reason, find your own sub, and make sure the sub is approved by the leader. If your sub can't cut the gig it's a reflection on you—and you will hear about it the next time you work with that band (if there *is* a next time).

7. Think Green

When someone calls about a gig, don't be shy about asking how much you'll get paid; after all, it's business, and you don't want to be surprised at the end of the night. (Of course, when you work for the same clients all the time you develop a certain amount of trust about money.) Before you say you're available, ask for details while you're "looking for your book." Ask what you need to wear, as well as who, what, when, where, etc. With this knowledge you can decide if you want to take it. If it meets your criteria, you can "find" your book and check the date. But don't be snooty about money; if the "bread is short," just say no. If you feel compelled to mention that the money isn't enough, do it tactfully and with respect—you might trigger a better offer.

8. Know Your Place

When you show up for the gig (on time), ask the leader where you should set up. If there's a "book" for the gig, stand next to the keyboardist or guitarist if possible; they can guide you through tough spots. Set up your amp close to the drummer. If he has to strain to hear you from behind the guitar rig, he may have a hard time nailing the groove with you. If it's your first time playing with the band, say hello, be polite and friendly, and avoid copping an attitude. In general, develop a relaxed professional demeanor—even if it kills you. Even if the band is not very talented, it may still be a source of income. If you can't stand playing with them, there's no need to alienate anyone; the next time they call, just politely say you're booked. Don't be a jerk—keep your gig karma clean! Remember: Even the lamest gig can lead to a referral for a great one.

9. Look The Part

Make sure you're properly dressed. If you're going to play freelance for a living, you men should purchase your own tux; you can buy them used in good shape for around $200. Keep your tux relatively clean; I always get mine cleaned once a year. Have a few shirts and a spare bow tie. Get comfortable black shoes (not black sneakers—only drummers can get away with those) and black socks. You'll need something to wear for "suit" and "jacket-and-tie" gigs; a black suit is all-purpose. The standard country-club outfit is a navy-blue blazer, white shirt, and gray pants. It's good to have some "real" pants (not blue jeans) and "cool" shirts for "dressy casual" gigs. The same rules apply for women; light blouses and dark slacks are always appropriate. Another fashion tip: Black jeans are very versatile.

It may seem silly to devote so much attention to your wardrobe—but people are looking at you as well as listening to you. And most likely they understand what they're seeing better than what they're hearing!

When it comes to making it as a freelancer, remember that at a certain level, tons of people have the chops to do the gig. The calls will come in for you because of your reputation for taking care of business, whatever the gig.

Requirements Of The Working Bassist

By Alexis Sklarevski

Students at every level often ask me, "What things should I know to become a well-rounded, *working* bassist?"

Let's assume you've decided to get serious about becoming a working musician, or perhaps you're already a working player and want to expand your knowledge so you can handle a wider variety of gigs. Fortunately, many general musical concepts are used universally, and if you've worked on them in one area you can transfer them to another. For example, if you've been playing in a country band all your life, you're probably quite used to locking in with the kick drum—which just also happens to be a widely used rhythm-section concept in funk and rock.

Developing a good sound is a major step toward being able to work. Clean, precise picking is very important; in general, I advise players to adopt an alternating two-finger picking technique, because your chances of being able to play a wide variety of bass lines are pretty slim if you're using just one finger. ("Yeah, that's obvious," you may say—although many of you don't do it, even if you *think* you do.) Aspiring players have a hard time with technical demands, including playing smooth glisses, cross-string picking, ghost-notes, muting, different articulations, and so on. These are all areas that need to be worked on until they become part of your playing—no matter what the style of music.

If you can read well (and I don't mean Zappa stuff), there will always be opportunities to use that skill. There's nothing wrong with working on your reading, and I seriously doubt it will diminish your feel and turn you into a mindless, no-soul robot. Once your reading is fairly proficient, there are all kinds of gigs you can (and probably will) be called for, as bassists are not generally known for their reading abilities.

You should have a working knowledge of different styles of music—rock, funk, swing, Latin, country, etc.—and you should know these styles' essentials and demands. Learn several tunes in each style; focus not so much on copying the bass line exactly (although that can be great practice) but on the style's essence and the things you notice happening repeatedly. Fortunately there are dozens of music books that cover just about every topic you could want.

Know your changes. The idea of hammering out the root note of every chord can get pretty boring if you do it on *every* tune. I'd never suggest that you overplay, but you might be amazed at the kinds of lines you can come up with using just triads and experimenting with them in creative ways. If you want to play jazz, you need to know your changes especially well, and you need to spend a lot of time experimenting with different ways to negotiate progressions, many of which are quite complex.

Your time and feel need to be as good as they can be, which may require spending so much time with your metronome or drum machine you'll wish you had never bought it at all. Eventually you should be able to clearly define a feel with nothing more than a click track. Your knowledge of feels and feel interpretations should be expanding constantly; no matter what the style or groove of a tune, you need to be able to come up with ideas that work right from square one.

> You need to be able to come up with ideas that work right from square one.

Personal interpretation is extremely important; what you can bring to the music in terms of your own personality and musical taste may get you more work than anything else. There will always be specialists in every field, but you should still bring a little of yourself into the music and come up with ideas that are all your own. Most writers and singers I've worked for have been open to lots of suggestions, and they seem to welcome the input of the people working with them.

You must attain a certain level of musical proficiency in order to get work, but you must also be able to get along with people in the most idiotic of circumstances. Without a doubt there will be times when you stand there in total disbelief at what's going on around you. Maybe my most useful piece of advice about working is: *Keep your sense of humor.* Believe me—you'll need it.

Fusion veteran Victor Bailey

PART

TWO

EQUIPMENT

How To Buy An Electric Bass

By Tom Mulhern

Think of all the hours you put in, slaving over a hot metronome: practice, practice, practice, tick, tock, tick. After all that work, would you entrust your hard-earned chops to a less-than-perfect instrument? Whether you're looking for your first bass, preparing to trade up, or expanding your arsenal, there's more to it than just reading a label or a price tag. "Shopper's know-how" can save you cash at the outset and help you avoid trouble later on, so don't take the task lightly.

Where do you start? Consulting your bank account is a good choice. No matter what anyone tells you, the real bottom line is what you can realistically afford. Don't go into the hole, especially on your first bass. It just might turn out to be your worst nightmare—and nothing disrupts a practice session like an irate bill collector pounding on the door.

The next step—closely related to your financial situation—is determining how badly you need a new bass. If you're shopping for your first one, okay, now's the time. However, if you've already got a bass, time is on your side—at least as much as you want it to be. You might not love your current model, but at least it's *yours*. If it weren't at least passable, you wouldn't (or maybe couldn't) be using it. Keep using it until you can afford that new dream bass, and while you're saving up, further educate yourself on the comparative merits of prospective purchases before taking the big plunge.

Now that you've determined whether you need a bass, assess your physique, your style, and the sonic personality you want to project. Let's start with your physique. How big are you? Do you have big or small hands? Long arms? Short arms? Basses are available in a range of sizes. Some have wide necks (extra-wide, too, if you're looking at 5- and 6-strings), and bodies can be large or small, thick or thin, conventional or oddly shaped. And while some basses seem to weigh a ton, others are marvels of lightweight comfort. Now, here's where you have to be brutally realistic: Do you plan to play bass as a career, as a hobby, or just as a "double" to another instrument? If you're going to make a career of it, make comfort a priority on a par with great sound. A heavy bass hanging from a strap for a few hours every day can cause plenty of physical problems, including a sore back and arm numbness. A long bass neck and short arms can also add up to trouble. And don't forget about how well a bass sits on your lap, unless you absolutely never play while sitting down.

Now let's go shopping. You've probably seen your favorite musician wailing on that one cool bass, and you love that sound—but before you plop down a wad of cash for the same instrument, remember that your favorite bassist also has a distinctive, personal style which contributes to his sound. Also, your hero's tone—however awesome—might not fit your style or your band's sound.

How do you get your best shot at selecting the right instrument? Do your homework. Research some of the available basses before you go shopping. Ask other players about their instruments, and read all you can. When you go to the music store, avoid the busy hours. Don't go on a Saturday afternoon, or after school hours on a weekday. Drop by in the mid-morning or mid-afternoon, when the salespeople may be cooling their heels and may spend more time showing you the ins and outs of the basses you try.

Don't be a jerk. Don't start talking prices, discounts, trade-ins, or other "what ifs" at this point. You aren't ready to buy, and the salesperson doesn't want to negotiate if you aren't sure what you want. And don't bring a gaggle of friends on your initial shopping forays. They'll just distract you, and because they're not there to buy, they'll make the salespeople edgy and perhaps even anxious to hustle you out. If you want your friends' or bandmates' opinions, bring them along once you've narrowed your selection to one or two basses. At that point, their input can be invaluable.

If possible, try basses through an amp similar to your own (if you have one). If no amp in the store is even comparable, ask the salesperson if you can bring your own. If the strings aren't up to par, find another of the same model with good ones, or ask if a new set can be put on. Use a good cord, and make sure you try the bass at a realistic volume level. Too quiet and you won't be able to hear its subtleties; too loud and you may find yourself laying back to keep from being blown out of the showroom.

Bring a small notebook and a pen, along with a checklist of features you want or need, and take notes. In addition, try basses you might not have had on your "hit list." Don't rule anything out. Also, for now ignore the finish; a purple bass with lime-green Brady Bunch caricatures sounds the same as a white one. Once you narrow your choices, ask the salesperson about available options. If he can't help you, contact the manufacturer directly. Few makers sell directly to consumers, but most can provide the information you need.

Sometimes you can't find exactly what you want, especially if you're left-handed. In such cases, don't overlook custom instruments. They almost invariably cost more than production models, but the extra scrimping and saving might well be worth it, especially if you get *exactly* what you want.

After you've selected a bass, *then* talk price with your salesperson. If it's available at more than one store, compare prices. But remember that price alone shouldn't be the final factor. Check out the store's after-purchase service. Your musician friends can help you here; if they've had bad dealings with a store, you might end up in the same hole. And, of course, the place with the higher price may be the one with better service. Some stores have a service department that can tweak your bass just the way you want it, do speedy repairs, and otherwise respond to your needs after you sign on the dotted line. Others will let you languish. Don't let a few bucks send you to a place that couldn't care less what happens to you or your bass after they get your money.

Here are some construction specifics to scrutinize on any basses you try:

Neck

We all know what we like to feel under our fingers, so the feel of your bass neck may be one of the most important factors. If you zero in on one model, try several "identical" ones, if possible. You may find some variation in the necks, and you may be pleasantly surprised to find one that feels even better than your (former) pick of the litter.

The method of joining the neck and body has long been disputed by builders. Some argue that neck-through-body construction yields the best sustain, tone, and stability, while others point to the success of Fender's Precision and Jazz Basses, both bolt-ons, as proof to the contrary. A third faction prefers a set-in neck—one glued in place by means of a dovetail joint. But perhaps the feel of the neck-body joint is more important. A through-body neck can provide such a smooth transition that it's virtually impossible to tell where the neck ends and the body begins. With properly designed cutaways, this can provide the best high-fret access. But new techniques in joining the neck and body have made very accessible the upper reaches on non-neck-through styles. Whether this matters depends on your style—if you rarely venture above, say, the 12th fret, the neck-to-body transition won't matter.

Like bodies, necks come in many different materials and can have either single-piece or multi-laminated construction. Again, though, you may have little choice in material or design. Manufacturers characteristically produce one "flavor" of neck for their basses. In general, woods such as maple, mahogany, and alder are used—often in two or three pieces, since laminating can help prevent warping or twisting. Weight is another factor in comfort and playability; if a neck is too heavy, the instrument can be unbalanced, unless the body is similarly heavy and acts as a counterbalance. Then you trade overall balance for extra overall weight. (Your poor, aching shoulder!) Always keep comfort in mind.

Because wood reacts to atmospheric changes, most wood necks contain a steel truss rod, with a nut at one end that lets you vary the tension and bowing in the neck. If strings buzz excessively, or if notes bottom out, have the store's repairman check to see if the rod needs adjustment. (For more on bass setup, see page 121.) Check for neck twist, too: Sight down the neck from the nut, and if the neck under either the low or high string seems to drop away, you're looking at one bad twist. Walk away from anything that bad—little can be done to fix it. Check the neck for excessive flexibility. Hit an open string and pull back gently on the headstock. If the strings bottom out, the neck may be too rubbery, possibly causing tuning problems and decreased sustain. Another testing technique checks the stability of the neck-body joint. Holding the instrument's upper horn with one hand, gently push the neck toward the floor while you pull up slightly on the horn. If the joint makes a cracking sound and the strings shift, you're looking at a bass with a not-too-stable joint. In that case, try tightening the joint's bolts and see if that improves the instrument's stability.

Such builders as Modulus Guitars, Moses, and Zon use a carbon-fiber composite (sometimes called simply graphite) for bass necks. It's an incredibly strong wood alternative that's immune to variations in humidity and temperature. Such necks are harder to produce, so they tend to cost more than wood. Also, some people prefer the sound of wood necks—but today many luthiers are incorporating graphite reinforcement into more traditional wood necks, combining the advantages of both materials.

Scale Length

Some basses have scale lengths as short as 30", while others cover a whopping 36". (Scale length refers to the distance between the bridge and nut—see Fig. 2 on page 13.) Most basses are of the 34" variety. If you choose a shorter length, you'll be accepting a compromise: Shorter strings usually mean a more rubbery feel, possible intonation problems, and a duller sound. For 5- and 6-string basses with a *B* string, a long scale is practically a must; otherwise the low string may have blurry tone and a floppy feel. You may not have a choice of scale lengths on a particular model, so if it's an insurmountable obstacle, consider a different bass.

Fingerboard

The fingerboard affects both the feel and the sound of the bass. Very hard materials such as ebony, maple, or phenolic (a synthetic) contribute brightness as well as sustain. Also important is durability: Rosewood is somewhat softer than ebony, but it can lend a more woody texture to the tone. Practically any fingerboard can stand up to years of sweaty hands, but strings are a real grind. Most modern strings are roundwounds made of very hard alloys, and if they can erode metal frets, just think what they can do to wood. This wear and tear is greatly magnified on a fretless, so you might want to opt for ebony or maple instead of rosewood. (Some manufacturers coat their fretless boards with a synthetic for extra resistance to string wear, and Jaco Pastorius coated his fingerboard with epoxy.) Some fretless basses are available with lines that act as handy position markers.

Number Of Frets

Get as many frets as you need. While 24-fret configurations (which offer two octaves' range per string) are common, the extended fingerboard means their pickups are often placed differently, which affects tone. Some players—particularly thumb thumpers—prefer the sound of a 21- or 22-fretter. Check this for yourself! Make sure you play in your usual style when trying a bass; this is no time to experiment.

The Body

Body shape is often a matter of visual style—but shape, contouring, and weight all affect comfort, too. Regarding body materials, don't expect a wide variety on production basses.

Most have traditional woods such as alder, ash, mahogany, or maple, although you might see more exotic woods, such as padauk, koa, and bubinga. (Environmentalists take note: Many exotic woods come from tropical rainforests.) While exotic woods are often exceedingly strong, tight-grained, and durable, they tend to be very heavy.

Body density and mass affect tone, and the tone differences between light and heavy woods can be significant—but when comparing similar woods, one body often sounds pretty much like another. For some people, the material's look is more important than the sonic qualities—particularly if you're going for a natural finish.

A related consideration: A body may be made of a number of pieces of wood glued together. Opaque finish? Who cares if the body is made of six pieces? But stripes of contrasting woods sandwiched together look great on a natural-finish bass. Regardless of the material or number of body laminates, take a good look at the body under a bright light from various angles. On a properly built instrument you shouldn't see or feel lines in the finish where the pieces are joined. An exception is an ultra-cheap bass; a few bumps on an otherwise perfectly playable instrument (especially a beginner's bass) won't hurt. On more expensive models, particularly those with natural finishes, improper lamination is unacceptable.

Finishes

Many new basses have extremely durable finishes of polyurethane or similar materials, which tend to be impervious to most scratching and dinging. A traditional finish material, lacquer, is often more beautiful, but it is also more easily cracked and chipped. What's better? If you're going strictly by durability, choose a synthetic; otherwise, both types are just fine.

Pickups & Electronics

In the '70s, electronics were quite an issue: active filters, phase switches, and multiple pick-ups were big selling points as bells and whistles were thrust upon the poor, bewildered bassist. Things have settled down somewhat, and today many players look for one great basic sound rather than a broad spectrum of tones. So if you're inundated with a lot of technical information about the electronic guts, skip down to the bottom line: How does the bass sound? Now how does it sound when you *aren't* playing it? Does it hum and buzz? If it has two pick-ups, does it hum and buzz more at one setting than another? Active circuitry, which adds a bit of preamplification and tone shaping, should also be checked for noise. When you aren't playing, do you hear a lot of hiss? Even if your amp is hissy, you can check pretty quickly: Turn the instrument's volume full up and then all the way down. If there's a big difference in noise, consider passive electronics. (Old batteries can contribute to hiss; ask your salesperson if they're fresh.)

If a bass has active circuitry, a bypass switch is desirable; if your batteries go dead during a gig, it's faster to flip a switch than to open your instrument and replace the dead power source. Regardless of whether a bass has active or passive circuitry, check how well the tone controls work. Passive controls merely cut signal (they remove either highs or volume), while active circuitry can boost and cut volume and tone.

Do you play primarily in clubs? Hum may be a loathsome problem, especially if the bandstand is near neon or fluorescent lighting. If you have a choice of humbucking pickups or single-coils, consider humbuckers. Historically, single-coils have had the edge when it comes to brightness, but with modern active circuitry and better pickup design, humbuckers don't necessarily mean a muddy tone. And even if you were to sacrifice a minute amount of brightness, it's far preferable to the sound of bumblebees emanating from your amp.

What knobs and switches do you really need? If you have two pickups, a blend knob is preferable to a switch. Separate tone and volume controls for each pickup are good features, too—however, since most bassists play at full volume, a single master volume will do the job. Placement of the controls, while not a big deal, can be a stumbling block. If you're a habitual knob-twiddler and they're hard to reach, you might be looking at trouble.

Hardware

The key word here is function. Most tuning machines and bridges are rugged enough, but they must be responsive to your needs. Tuners shouldn't have "slop"; when you turn them one way, they should have an immediate effect. If there's a click, or if you can turn them a little without the tuning changing, they're trouble from the get-go. Check that the tuners don't move when you bend or snap a string. You can always install new tuners if you need to, although it's not appealing to buy a new instrument that needs immediate upgrades.

The bridge saddles should allow individual height and intonation adjustment for each string. Height adjustment is necessary for when you want to tweak your setup—or when you switch to different string gauges. Intonation adjustment makes it possible to keep the string in tune throughout its length. Whenever you change string gauges, you should fine-tune the intonation as well as the saddle height; see Setup Essentials, page 121.

When buying a bass, the bottom line is simple: Steer clear of any instrument that falls short in its feel, sound, or look. Buy the best you can afford, and don't be bamboozled by hard-sell tactics. Careful scrutiny of an instrument can save you years of headaches. Remember the Trojan Horse? Pandora's box? Learn from history: Check it out thoroughly before you take it home.

Buying An Acoustic Bass

By Steve Rodby

I've always thought shopping for an acoustic bass is a lot like shopping for a used car: Yeah, maybe it's a little beat up, but it's better than what I've got now. (I sure hope it runs when I get it home.) Maybe it just needs a tune-up . . . .

Where to look. If you are fortunate enough to live near a big city, the best place to start looking for an acoustic is at one of the many fine bass shops around the country, such as David Gage and Kolstein & Son in New York, The Bass Viol Shop in Cincinnati, Guarneri House in Grand Rapids, Robertson in Albuquerque, Tom Metzler and Ye Old Rosin Shop in L.A., and Hammond Ashley in Seattle. These places have lots of instruments to try at a variety of prices, and experts to consult. Since many are also repair shops, their instruments are usually in excellent condition. Two publications have ads listing these shops as well as individuals selling instruments: *Bass World: The Journal of the International Society of Bassists* [4020 McEwen, Suite 105, Dallas, TX 75244], and *The International Musician*, the monthly paper of the American Federation of Musicians [1501 Broadway, New York, NY 10036]. However, many things in music come through word of mouth, and instruments are no exception—I came upon both of my basses through recommendations from teachers.

What to look for. It's essential to buy a healthy instrument—or else it will spend more time in the shop than your Jaguar. Though there are some excellent makers producing new instruments, good basses are frequently old and, for a variety of reasons (the trip across the Atlantic, the size and tremendous tension on the top, weather changes), often have more cracks than a Marx Brothers movie. Don't be fooled by cosmetic beauty, or lack of "newlook," but do check how well any cracks have been patched. Lightly tap cracks and edge seams with your index-finger knuckle; you'll hear a clicking if they're open. Listen carefully for dreaded buzzes—they'll drive you crazy, and they won't just go away when the weather changes. (Besides, weather always comes back.) Look for a sturdy, well-maintained bass with expert repairs.

An instrument's sound and feel is a matter of personal taste, but here are some things that should concern you nevertheless. I think of the sound's specific character as being separate from its ultimate quality. First, describe the sound: Is it dark or bright, loud or soft, open or "covered," nasal, vocal, punchy, delicate, deep, or tenor? Then ask yourself, is it beautiful? I've heard good and bad combinations of all these characteristics. So, what many bassists think of as one question is actually two: Is it the sound I'm looking for, and is it a good version of that sound?

Look carefully at the strings' tension—what I call the compression. Is the bass too stiff or too flabby? Does it speak quickly or slowly? Is it the right size? Smaller is better than too big, as your goal is to get around the bass easily. Check for evenness: Does one string, or one note, boom out too much? Is the string length (measure it) approximately what you're used to? If not, you'll play even more out of tune than you usually do. Or has it been tuned at the factory? Just kidding.

Try before you buy. Once you've got your eye on an instrument, the most important—and most difficult—thing to do is to play it as much as possible, in a way that tells you what you need to know. Definitely try the bass with your favorite strings. Where will you be using the bass? If you plan to amplify it, you *must* put on a pickup and try it amplified to check for feedback, resonances, character, and tone quality. If you do studio work, hear how it records. Classical players often take a prospective instrument to a concert hall to see how it works in an orchestral, solo, or audition setting. Play the bass. Play it for colleagues and for your teacher; get a second opinion; get several. Basses sound quite different out in front (to the people we are playing for and with) than they do where our ears are. Have someone whose playing you know play the instrument, and listen carefully. You may be able to alter the sound somewhat with soundpost adjustments and string changes, but as in love, you shouldn't expect to drastically change the bass you are about to cohabit with.

Some bass shops or individual sellers loan basses for trial, given an appropriate deposit, collateral, or a long-standing relationship. It can be tricky, but it's worth whatever it takes.

The bottom line. You used to be able to tell "classical" from "jazz" basses by the price tag. These days they all cost too much. Some work equally well for all kinds of playing, but these are rare. You'll generally see different strings and string heights on instruments set up for predominantly arco (bowed) and pizzicato (plucked) styles. I see the two as distinct projects with diverging requirements.

The bass market has gone completely crazy in the last 20 years. I know of instruments that have appreciated in value by 2,000% or more! These days most of us have to finance our basses. Banks, famous for their reluctance to loan money to musicians, will require you to put up something other than the bass itself as collateral. With interest, insurance, and maintenance costs, don't buy an instrument as an investment. Buy it to play it.

Are you experienced? The best advice of all is simply to play as many basses as you can. The most successful buyers I know are those who are always looking, asking around, trying instruments, and expressing interest. There is much to know about older European makers, the differences between countries, and shopping abroad, not to mention flat vs. round backs, how soundpost adjustments affect sound, plywood vs. hand-carved, etc.

Even if you're not in the market right now, you should act as if you are—that's the only way you'll recognize your bass when it comes along. So shop till you drop, and look for healthy basses that sound beautiful and feel right.

The <u>Right</u> Way To Install Strings

By Scott Malandrone & Jim Roberts

Ask ten bass players how to install strings, and you'll probably get ten different answers. Even the top pros can't agree—John Patitucci says he always cuts his strings to length, while Nathan East says he never cuts his. And East says problems can result if you twist a string around the post by hand before cranking the tuner. And so on.

The old rule about never cutting bass strings made sense in the days when a cut string's outer wraps could easily unravel. Today, thanks to advances in string technology, the outer wraps of most strings are effectively locked onto the core—so cutting the string is not likely to cause a problem. Even so, we recommend bending the string (as shown in these photos) before you cut it. And don't forget that if you cut the string so it's a little too long, you might get an extra wind on the post—but if you cut it too short you're out of luck.

Over the years BASS PLAYER has asked a number of bassists and techs how they install strings, and we've tried a number of different methods ourselves. Based on that research, we drew up some guidelines for the best results with minimum fuss. Here are those guidelines step by step, for both 4-in-line and 2+2 headstocks. If you're installing strings on a 5- or 6-string, the same procedures apply—you just have an extra string or two to handle. And please bear in mind there may be other string-installation methods that work just as well.

4-In-Line Headstocks

1. Unwind the old *E* string from the post. To make it easier to remove the string (and to protect the instrument's finish), cut it off as shown. Carefully pull the remaining length through the hole in the bridge.

2. Insert the new *E* string through the back of the bridge and run it over the saddle. Be careful not to scratch the finish.

3. Run the string past the tuning post and make a right-angle bend in the string 2" to 3" past the post. Cut the string just past the bend. (The bend prevents the wrap wire from slipping.)

4.   Insert the end of the string into the hole in the center of the post.

5.   Pull the string to the inside of the tuning post, and then wind the string onto the post by turning the key. The second wrap around the post (and subsequent wraps) should fall underneath the first wind; this pulls the string over the nut at a downward angle for better contact (and tone). Be sure to keep tension on the string during winding.

6.   With the string tuned about halfway to pitch, press down at the bridge to bend the string over the saddle and establish a good "witness point."

7.   Tune the *E* string to pitch and stretch it as shown. "Snapping" the string—by pulling it up slightly at the 12th fret and then releasing it—may help the string stay in tune.

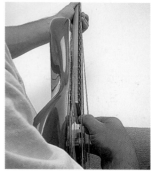

8.   Repeat steps 1–9 for the *A* string.
9.   Repeat steps 1–9 for the *D* and *G* strings, remembering to run the strings under the string tree on the peghead (if your bass has one).
10. Done! Notice how the windings hold the strings down against the peghead, creating a downward angle from the nut. If you cut the strings too short they will sit too high on the posts; this means there won't be enough tension across the nut, and string buzzes could result.

2+2 Headstocks

1.   Unwind the old *E* string from the post. To make it easier to remove the string (and to protect the instrument's finish), cut off the coiled part. Carefully pull the remaining length through the hole in the bridge.

2. Insert the new *E* string through the back of bridge and run it over the saddle. Be careful not to scratch the finish.

3. Run the string past the tuning post and make a right-angle bend in the string 2" to 3" past the post. Cut off the string just past the bend.

4. Insert the end of the string into the post.

5. Wind the string onto the post, making sure each wrap goes underneath the previous one.

6. Repeat steps 1–7 for the *A* string. The procedure for the *D* and *G* strings are in "mirror fashion" to that of the *E* and *A*.

7. Insert the end of the *D* string in the post.

8. Pull the string toward the center of the headstock.

9. Wind the *D* string onto the post. Repeat the same procedure for the *G*.

10. Done! Note the even windings on the posts.

After They're On

Once you've installed your new strings, take care of them. Wipe them down after playing, using a clean rag. Be sure to get *under* the strings—that's where crud tends to build up, especially in the area where you pluck.

Some players like to extend the life of their strings by boiling them (usually with a little vinegar) or zapping them in the kind of ultrasonic cleaners used for jewelry. This removes built-up oils and dirt and returns some "zing" to the sound. We've found that removing strings and reinstalling them changes their sound somewhat—but if cleaning works for you, go for it. Bear in mind, though, that a cleaned set won't sound as good (or last as long) as a brand-new set simply because strings wear out from the metal fatigue caused by thousands of plucks and snaps and strums. Strings are sort of like cars: Treat them right and they'll last longer, but sooner or later they'll wear out anyway.

Setup Essentials: Adjusting Your Bass For Top Performance

By Dan Erlewine

Electric basses have come a long way since Leo Fender introduced the Precision in 1951. Bass-playing technique has evolved along with the instruments, so today's bass has to sound and play great, from top to bottom.

Proper setup is the key to getting the most from your bass. Given your playing style and string-gauge choice, the nut, bridge, and neck must be adjusted to obtain the best possible action. (Action refers to the way the strings lie over the fingerboard.) With a little practice, you can make most of these adjustments yourself.

Here's the general order of these adjustments:
1. Install the strings. If the bass is new, play it awhile to get the feel of the action.

2. Sight the neck, looking for straightness or relief. (For more about relief, see Adjusting The Neck below.)
3. Make basic neck adjustments before adjusting the nut or bridge.
4. Adjust the nut and bridge together.
5. Check the neck adjustment again.
6. Adjust the pickup height.

Installing the strings. You should expect to go through several sets of strings until you find what's right for you. Begin with the manufacturer's string recommendation and go from there. (If your bass is new, check the warranty—it may be invalidated if you use certain types of strings.) Some guidelines:

· Roundwound strings are bright-sounding and easy to tune, but they suffer from finger noise (squeaking) and produce the most fret buzz.
· Flatwounds eliminate the squeaks but have a more mellow tone and are harder to get in tune.
· "Halfrounds" or "groundwounds" (roundwound strings with a surface that has been ground or compressed flat) offer low finger noise, decent brightness, and good intonation.
· "Exposed-core" or "taper-wound" strings are thinner at the bridge end. Some bassists prefer the sound and intonation of these strings.
· String tension is important. Equal tension from string to string gives a balance that feels right to both hands. For hard-to-adjust necks or those that tend toward upbow (resulting in a concave fingerboard) choose a light-gauge string, which requires lower tension to tune to pitch. Within a given gauge, flatwound strings require the highest tension, halfrounds the second highest, and roundwounds the least tension.
· If you're a 5-stringer looking for the optimum low *B*, go with a heavy string gauge, such as .145.

On Fenders and other instruments without an angled-back headstock, be sure you install the strings with enough wraps to create good down-pressure on the nut. [For info on proper string-installation technique, see page 118.] Basses with angled-back headstocks require fewer wraps to achieve good down-pressure.

Sighting the neck. All bass necks are either straight, back-bowed (with a convex fretboard), or up-bowed (with a concave fretboard). The straighter the neck, the lower you can set the action—but you must pluck close to the bridge, and with a light touch, to avoid buzz or fret rattle. If you play close to the neck and "dig in," you'll need some *relief* (controlled up-bow) to avoid buzzes.

A "perfect neck" is one that under string tension will: adjust straight for low action; adjust into a slight back-bow when desired (to counteract heavy strings); and loosen from straightness into controlled relief. A properly relieved neck (Fig. 1) has a gradual up-bow going from around the 9th fret toward the nut, remaining straight from the 9th to the last fret. The result is an overall curve in the fret tops between the 1st fret and the neck-body joint. This mimics the string's long arc as it vibrates, which eliminates a lot of buzz.

Sighting a neck is the simplest way to check whether a neck is straight, back-bowed, or up-bowed. Hold your bass on its side, with the highest string closest to the floor. Support the body, not the neck, and look from the nut down the neck toward the body. If you have trou-

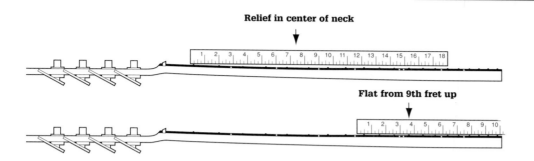

Relief in center of neck

Flat from 9th fret up

Fig. 1

ble looking along the fret tops, look along the glue-joint under the fingerboard. Other ways of checking a neck are: holding down a string at the 1st fret and last fret (a tight string is a good straightedge), or—for a truly accurate reading—laying a precision-ground 18" straightedge along the fret tops. Sighting the neck will determine if, and how, you'll adjust it.

Adjusting the neck. Most bass necks can be adjusted by tightening or loosening a truss-rod nut (Fig. 2). Tightening the truss rod (by turning clockwise) creates a backward tension that counteracts the strings' tendency to bow the neck; therefore tightening it will straighten an up-bow and remove neck relief. Loosening the truss rod by turning the nut counter-clockwise allows some back-bowed necks (necks that warp away from the strings) to pull straight or into relief. If you forget which way to turn the truss-rod nut, remember the old rule *lefty-loosey, righty-tighty*.

Keep the following in mind when making truss-rod adjustments:

1. The adjustment nut for many bolt-on necks is at the body end. It may be accessible only after loosening the strings and removing the neck, or there may be a plate on the instrument's face that covers the nut.

2. Always *loosen* the truss-rod nut first (Fig. 2), since it may already be as tight as it goes. In fact, remove it completely and brush or blow any dirt from the threads of both the rod and nut. Then put a bit of lubricant (Teflon Tri-Flow, Vaseline, Magic Guitar Lube, or household oil) on the threads inside the nut, being careful not to get any on the bare wood. Lubricating the threads makes for a smoother adjustment, especially on older instruments.

3. Re-install the nut until just snug, without putting tension on it. Then make a small pencil mark on both the nut and neck (Fig. 2). When the marks line up, that's your starting point—a handy reference when making adjustments.

4. One half-turn on a truss-rod nut is a lot. Once the nut is snug, tighten it one-eighth to one-quarter turn and then check your progress. If you had to remove the neck to adjust the truss rod, expect to remove and re-install it several times during this process.

5. The effect of the rod adjustment can take days or even weeks to be complete. You may adjust a neck perfectly one day, only to find later that the neck kept moving from the rod's tension and is now too straight or even back-bowed. If this happens, simply re-adjust it.

6. If the truss-rod nut is extremely tight on the rod, or recessed far into the hole, watch out! It was probably over-tightened by a previous owner. Some ill-informed people really crank those truss rods, which is a great way to break them (and to make your neck permanently non-adjustable). Over-tightening can also cause the wood to compress without straightening the up-bow. In this case, follow the removal, cleaning, and lubrication steps above, and

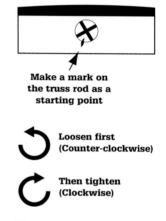

Make a mark on the truss rod as a starting point

Loosen first (Counter-clockwise)

Then tighten (Clockwise)

Fig. 2

Thin, flat washer between wood and barrel nut

Wood compresses here

Fig. 3

then add one or two thin washers (Fig. 3) before threading on the nut. This often gives the nut a new grip and allows further rod adjustments.

7. With a stubborn neck it may be best to loosen the rod completely, clamp the neck straight (or even into a back-bow; see Fig. 4), and then tighten the truss-rod nut. This method generally works when all else fails.

Adjusting the nut and bridge. String height at the nut is critical. If the string slots are too deep, or the nut itself is too low, heavy strings are sure to buzz against the 1st fret. After the neck adjustments have been made, check the nut height; with a little luck you'll still have a nut that's slightly tall, allowing you to lower the strings slightly if you choose. If the strings are too low at the nut, have a new nut made or shim up the original. Removing a nut without breaking it can be difficult, so leave this work to a professional.

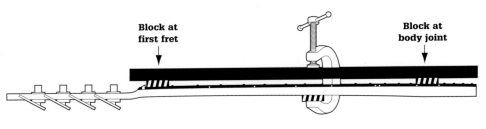

Block at first fret

Block at body joint

Fig. 4

Measure string height at the nut between the bottom of the strings and the 1st-fret top. A low-action measurement would read: *E* .035"; *A* .030"; *D* .025"; *G* .025". When I make a new nut I stop lowering the strings at .050" on the *E* and .030" for the *A*, *D*, and *G*. From that point I prefer to lower the strings gradually, with the particular customer's attack and playing style in mind.

Players with a strong attack—especially slappers—should use a fairly low-profile nut with string slots that aren't cut too deep. That way the edges won't break off (Fig. 5) as the string is strained in its slot. A good depth for the string slots is between one-half and two-thirds of the string's diameter. Bone is the usual nut material for many basses—but if you hit hard use a resilient plastic, graphite, or phenolic, which has less chance of breaking.

Nut often cracks here

Fig. 5

Bridge adjustments aren't hard to make—but don't rush. Expect to spend several hours getting things right. There's a delicate balance between neck, nut, and bridge, and their combined effect determines your action. Bridge setup controls the string height, matches the arch of the saddles to the curve of the fingerboard, and sets the intonation. Here are the basics:

• You'll usually raise or lower the string height at the saddle by adjusting small set-screws with an allen wrench or small screwdriver.

• Lengthwise saddle travel controls intonation. Pluck a 12th-fret open harmonic (see page 98) and compare it to the fretted octave note; if the fretted note is sharp, move the saddle back (away from the neck). If it's flat, move the saddle forward (toward the neck).

• Matching the arch of the saddles to that of the fingerboard makes the action comfortable to both hands and consistent across the strings. A radius gauge is handy for this task; radius gauges, and lots of other setup tools, are available from luthier's supply houses.

- For low action and minimum fret rattle, combine the following approaches: (1) Get the neck as straight as possible with very low action, and then eliminate any buzz by loosening the truss rod, thereby adding relief; (2) straighten the neck and then eliminate buzz by raising the bridge saddles.
- Remember that some buzz between metal strings and metal frets is normal.

The pros speak. String-height measurements vary from manufacturer to manufacturer. I discussed bass setup with five top luthiers: Michael Tobias, Ken Smith, Roger Sadowsky, Brett Carlson, and Bob Malone.

Tobias: "We never measure, because each bass is different. But our setups start out with 1/8" at the last fret all the way across, following the fingerboard radius. This gives a height of 1/16" to 3/32" at the 12th fret. When you press a string at the 3rd fret it should clear the 1st fret by .010" or .012". No bass will play without some relief. As a measure, hold down a string at the 1st and 15th frets—using the string as a straightedge—and adjust the neck until you can just slide a Fender thin pick in at the 8th fret between the string bottom and fret top. That's your relief."

Smith: "All basses must be set up individually. I use taper-wound strings in gauges of .044, .063, .084, and .106. You must have a little relief at the 9th fret, up to as much as 1/16". I don't actually measure string height at the nut, but I prefer an action where the player doesn't have to press too hard, with no buzzing on open strings. I consider a low height at the 12th fret to be 1/16" all the way across."

Sadowsky: "I shoot for a mostly straight neck with a little relief. I prefer string gauges of .045, .065, .080, .105. My standard setup has a 12th-fret string height on the fat side: 5/64" for the *G* and 3/32" for the *E*, measured from the bottom of the string to the top of the fret."

Carlson: "We use relief, except on fretless basses—with those we get the neck perfectly straight. Our relief, measured by holding down a string at the 1st and last frets, is set at .015". String height at the 1st fret is .025" under each string. At the 12th fret I shoot for 3/32" under the *G* and 5/32" under the *E*. Our standard strings are roundwounds, .045, .065, .080, .100."

Malone: "In any setup you can't go beyond what you have to work with. It all comes down to how straight you can get that neck. If you can get it straight to begin with, then your setup can go from there. I like a very slight relief, but I don't measure it—it's all by feel. For nut height, when a string is pressed at the 3rd fret it should just barely touch the 1st."

Adjusting the pickups. After re-checking your neck, finish by adjusting the pickup height to suit your taste—but don't raise the pickups so high the strings slap against them or get pulled into the upper frets by the magnets.

Amp Basics

By Jim Roberts

Whether you're looking for your first amp or getting ready to upgrade to a massive rack system, it's important to carefully assess your needs, consider your budget, and shop around. Don't be swayed by clever salespeople or your friends, no matter how convincing they may be. Your amp is a vital element of your sound—and if you rush into an unwise purchase, you'll be shopping again soon (and trying to unload a used amp). Here are a few things you should know before you spend your hard-earned dollars.

An amplification system has four main components: preamplifier, signal processor, power amp, and speaker cabinets. The *preamplifier* is where you plug in your instrument cable. The preamp's main job is to prepare the signal coming from your bass, primarily by boosting its amplitude (voltage). Most preamps have a *signal processor* section, which may be as simple as bass and treble tone-control knobs. In most modern amps, this section includes an equalizer (EQ), and it may also have built-in effects units, such as a compressor and/or chorus. (For definitions of these and other terms, see the Gear Glossary on page 148.)

After the signal has been adjusted by the preamp and modified by the signal processor, it's passed along to the power amp. This is where it's increased to the voltage level required to drive speakers. Because a low-frequency sound requires more energy to produce than a higher-pitched sound of the same perceived volume, bass amps must have lots of output power. Even small amps often produce 100 watts RMS or more, and large power amps rated at 600–800 watts RMS are becoming more common. The last link in the signal chain is the *speaker cabinet*, where electrical energy is converted into mechanical energy by the speakers. The electrical signal passes through a voice coil attached to a flexible cone; as this cone moves in and out, it produces sound waves in the air.

There are three types of bass amps. The simplest is a *combo amp*, which has all of the components in a single unit. Your first amp is likely to be a combo amp, and you'll probably have one throughout your career, for practicing and rehearsing. Combo amps typically have one or two speakers mounted in an enclosure that also includes the preamp, signal processor, and power amp. The most common configurations are 2x10 (two 10" speakers), 1x12 (one 12" speaker), and 1x15 (one 15" speaker), although many other combinations exist. Generally speaking, combo amps are the least expensive type, with list prices beginning around $300.

For most club gigs you'll use a *stack* or "piggyback system" consisting of a *head* (sometimes called a "brain") and one or more speaker cabinets. In this type of system the preamp, signal processor, and power amp are usually all contained in the head, which is often a two- or three-rackspace unit. A stack is quite flexible; speaker cabinets can be added or changed easily, and the head can be replaced by a different one. Typical two-piece systems for club gigs start at around $700, and prices range well into the thousands.

Today, many professional bassists rely on a *rack system*. This is a more sophisticated version of a stack, with separate preamp, signal-processing, and power-amp components mounted in a roadcase. Because a rack system is modular, it's easy to upgrade one component while keeping everything else the same, and various signal-processing units can be added over time. Many rack systems are either stereo (with separate power amps for left and right channels) or bi-amp (with separate power amps for high and low frequencies). While a rack is by far the most flexible type of rig, it's also the most expensive. If you want to put together even a fairly simple rack, the cost will probably begin around $1,000—and that's *before* you buy the speaker cabinets.

Here are five essential questions to ask yourself before you go amp shopping:

• *Where will I use this amp?*
If most of your gigs are in tiny clubs, don't buy a system that won't even fit onstage. And consider how you'll be transporting it—will it fit in your car?

• *How loud do I play?*
Generally, if you have to turn up your amp more than halfway to get sufficient volume, you

need more power. Clean bass requires lots of headroom, so make sure you've got enough power to handle the gigs you play.

• *Is it reliable?*
Most modern gear is built to stand up to years of on-the-road abuse, but it can't hurt to ask around. If there's a good electronics-repair shop in your town, check with the technician to see which bass amps are on his bench too often.

• *Can I try it out?*
A music store is not a real-world sonic environment. If the dealer won't let you test the amp *on a gig*, try another dealer. You may have to make a deposit or provide some other form of security, but that's a small price to pay when you're pondering a major purchase.

• *Can I afford it?*
There are two sides to this question. You obviously can't buy an amp if you don't have the money. (Beware of time-payment deals—they're usually a ripoff.) On the other hand, you shouldn't buy a "bargain" amp that's underpowered or unreliable; in the long run it will turn out to be *more* expensive. Balance the amp's cost against your real needs, and consider all the alternatives. Look at used amps, too; although they must be checked carefully, they often represent outstanding value.

A final point to consider is whether you prefer the sound of tube or solid-state circuits. For bass players this isn't *quite* as volatile an issue as it is with guitarists, many of whom would rather eat ground glass than plug into a solid-state amp. With regard to circuit design, modern bass amps are available in three "flavors": all-tube, all-solid-state, and hybrid. All-tube amps, which are available from Ampeg, MESA/Boogie, and other companies, have tubes in both the preamp and power amp. (Although even these amps usually have *some* solid-state circuitry in the signal-processing section.) Many bassists swear by this design, insisting that nothing sounds as warm as an all-tube amp; others are turned off by the heavy weight and maintenance requirements of tube amps, especially since good replacement tubes can be expensive and difficult to find. Not surprisingly, all-solid-state amps are far more common; they're offered by many manufacturers, including Carvin, Fender, Gallien-Krueger, and Peavey. Loud, reliable, and lightweight, these amps feature much more sophisticated circuitry than early "transistor amps," which were noted for their sterile sound and frequent meltdowns. Hybrid amps combine both types of circuits, using tube preamps and solid-state power amps. Made by Hartke, SWR, and others, these systems are growing rapidly in popularity. Which type is the best choice? That's up to you.

Effects Basics

By Karl Coryat

While there may seem to be hundreds of bass effects on the market, they're all really just variations on a dozen or so basic effects, which in turn fall into four categories: equalizers, dynamic processors, time-based effects, and synthesizing effects.

Equalizers. Audible sounds can be represented in terms of the frequency spectrum, a graph with the lowest frequencies on the left and the highest on the right. Since most sounds—the low *E* on your bass, for example—are actually a combination of many frequencies, a single note can stretch all the way across the spectrum. The proportions of these different frequencies determine a sound's *timbre* (tone color), which is why an instrument that puts out more high frequencies sounds brighter than one playing the same pitch with less highs.

Equalizers ("EQs") alter the balance of the different frequencies, which helps make instruments fit together in a musically pleasing way. For instance, if your amp is pumping out tons of lows but no mids, your bass will probably sound muddy and indistinct; in this case a little low-cut and mid-boost EQ will make your notes sound punchy, with better pitch definition.

There are several types of EQ. The simplest covers two frequency bands, with a bass control and a treble control. Add a midrange control and you've got a 3-band EQ; 4-band and

5-band EQs (and beyond) provide more sonic flexibility. Sometimes an EQ's controls are in the form of sliders; this is called a *graphic* EQ, because the physical positions of the sliders produce a graphic representation of the EQ's effect on the frequency spectrum. An even more flexible type is the *parametric* EQ; it may have several frequency bands with three knobs per band, allowing you to specify not only the boost or cut at that band but also the band's center frequency and the bandwidth or "Q," which determines how narrow or wide an area of the spectrum gets affected. The *semiparametric* EQ, commonly found on amps, is simply a parametric EQ without bandwidth controls.

Dynamic processors. These affect a signal's dynamics—loudness and softness. The simplest is the volume pedal, which is just a volume knob you control with your foot. More complex circuits do the dynamic changes for you. A *compressor* reduces the dynamic range of your signal by making the softest notes louder and the loudest notes softer. Compressors smooth out the signal and can make your bass more punchy and consistent-sounding from note to note. They also protect speakers from being dangerously overdriven—although this job is often left to a *limiter*, a type of compressor that limits your signal from getting any hotter past a certain point. The other type of dynamic processor is the *expander* or *noise gate*. By making the softest sounds even quieter, an expander can lower your signal's "noise floor" by reducing the levels when you aren't playing.

Even though compressors and expanders are technically opposites, they're often used simultaneously—with great results. The compressor evens out your notes, and the expander cleans up everything in between. Single-unit compressor/expanders are commonplace in recording studios and complex rack systems.

Time-based effects. These split your signal in half, electronically delay one of the lines, and then recombine them; the amount of delay determines the type of effect. Delays longer than about 80 milliseconds create discrete echoes, while delays from 20ms–80ms produce subtle "slap-back" echoes, popular for things like rockabilly vocals but not very useful on bass. Shorter delays (10–20ms) produce *chorusing*, making you sound like two or more bassists playing together. Delays shorter than 10ms create *flanging* and *phasing* effects, in which certain frequencies cancel out, changing the tone. Choruses, flangers, and phasers have a "modulation" function, which causes the delayed half of your signal to speed up and slow down; this imparts an animated quality and produces "whooshing" or "liquidy" effects, depending on how the modulation parameters (usually "rate" and "depth") are set. A delay unit with a broad range of delay times and modulation values can produce any of these effects—but for simplicity many bassists prefer boxes dedicated to specific functions, which is why you see chorus and flanger pedals for sale.

Synthesizing effects. The most common of these is the *octave divider*; it analyzes your signal and synthesizes a note one octave below. Most effective when you're playing high on the neck, octavers allow you to explore the upper range of your instrument without losing the low end. They sound especially good with fretless; an octave divider is a big part of fretless whiz Pino Palladino's sound.

Distortion units count as synthesizing effects because they give your signal high frequencies that weren't there before. A drop of distortion makes your sound ruder and rawer, although some distortion units work much better with bass than others. As with any type of equipment, try several units and choose the one that works best for you.

The key to smart signal processing is using effects judiciously. Your playing—not the effect itself—should be what the listener hears; the effect should act merely as a spice or accent. Even though an effect may sound cool, it can also sound gimmicky and distracting—and it may cause listeners to think you don't have much to say musically. Listen to the way the masters employ effects, and then do the same: Use them tastefully.

Setting Up An Amp & Speakers

By Steve Rabe

Before you leave for your next gig, make sure you've got the following: an AC-receptacle tester, spare fuses for your amp, and two 9-volt batteries. These items won't take up much space—in fact, they should all fit in your bass case. Here's why you'll need them:

After arriving at the club and getting your gear onstage, the first thing you'll do is locate the nearest AC outlet. But wait—before you plug in, grab that receptacle tester and check the socket. These little gizmos are available at most hardware and electronics stores for less than five bucks, but they're worth their weight in gold. The best type will not only check for correct wiring but will tell you the exact nature of any problem that exists. Armed with one, you will know *beforehand* why your amp won't go on, why it will blow a fuse, why it will hum like crazy—or why you will get shocked.

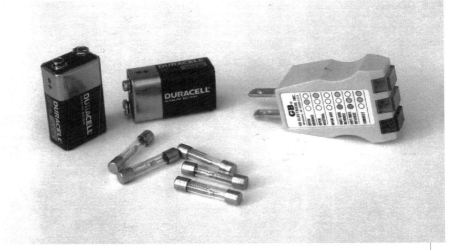

Essential tools: spare batteries, fuses, receptacle tester

Having found a good, well-grounded outlet, you're ready to set up. First, check your cables. Every cable you use for your bass or for patching in effects should be made with shielded audio cable. Make sure the cables you buy are specified for musical-instrument use, and avoid types with molded ends, because they're next to impossible to repair. To prevent signal loss, cables should be as short as possible.

When using an effect, it's generally best to use the *effects loop* found on most modern amps. Since most effects loops are located after the amp's initial preamp gain stages, this should reduce the hiss coming from your speakers, as noise generated by the effect will be amplified less overall. However, even today some effects units on the market have gain loss—that is, less signal comes out than goes in. With these units the volume with the effect bypassed is higher than when the effect is activated. This change in volume will be more prominent when the effects loop is used—so, if the effects loop does not have a level control to compensate for this, or if the level change is too drastic, you may have no other choice than to place the unit between your instrument and amp. Before purchasing an effects unit, try it in the effects loop of *your* amplifier.

When you're plugging in, never route instrument cables directly over or under your amplifier. Because of the high impedance (resistance) of most pickups and the high input impedance of your amp, hum can be injected into your cable from the amp's internal power supply. This is especially important in rack systems.

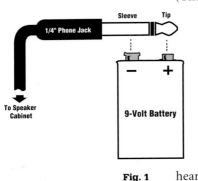

Fig. 1

A 9-volt battery can be used to test a cable.

On to your speaker cabinets. Speaker cable should be made of at least 18-gauge wire. (The thicker the wire the *lower* the gauge number, so 18-gauge is heavier than 20-gauge, and so on.) *Do not use instrument cables to hook up your speakers.* This can result in intermittent power loss, cause your power amp to oscillate and damage itself and/or your speakers, and render the cable useless for any purpose.

If you're having a problem with your speakers and suspect one (or more) of your cables, use a 9-volt battery as a cable tester. Plug one end of the questionable cable into your speaker cabinet, and then touch the phone plug on the other end to the battery's two terminals (+ and −), contacting the tip and sleeve as shown in Fig. 1. A good cable will pass the voltage to the speakers, creating an audible noise and causing the cones to move out. When you disconnect the battery the cones will move back in. If you don't hear anything and your speakers don't move, that means the cable is bad.

You can test for an intermittent cable by keeping the battery on the phone plug while swinging the wire like a jump rope. If the cable is good, the speaker will remain in one position and not make any noise. This test can be especially handy after making new cables or repairing old ones, and it can also be used to check speaker phasing—more on that soon. (A couple of notes: Holding a battery on the phone plug will drain the battery quickly, so don't overdo it. And this test will also tell you if you have a dead 9-volt; if you know the cable is good but the speakers don't move, toss the battery.)

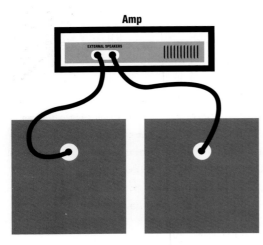

Speaker Cabinets

Fig. 2

When cabinets are connected to the speaker jacks on an amp head, they are hooked up in parallel.

Before you turn on your amp, check one last time that all of your cables are connected properly—especially your speaker cables. If a cable is loose while you're playing, your AC or speaker fuse can blow. For reasons like this, it's always wise to carry several spare fuses.

Now you're plugged in and switched on, but during soundcheck you find out you're not quite loud enough to carry the room. A member of another band generously offers to let you use his speaker cabinet. That's great—but ask yourself three questions before you hook it up: (1) What's the impedance of *your* cabinet, and what's the impedance of his? (2) What will the total combined impedance be? (3) Is that a safe load for your amp?

When an additional speaker is added to a system, it's generally hooked up in *parallel* to the other speaker(s); see Fig. 2. This is the case when you use your amp's extension speaker jack or the in/out jacks (if provided) on your cabinet's input panel. As you add speakers in parallel, the total impedance the amplifier "sees" becomes *less*. Also, in a parallel-wired system no other wiring is necessary; you just plug in an additional speaker in an existing jack. In a *series* arrangement, on the other hand, the existing circuit must be broken and the new speaker inserted; in this case the total impedance becomes *greater*. Let's look at parallel impedance, since it's more common.

To figure out the total impedance of two or more cabinets of equal value hooked up in parallel, divide the impedance of *one* cabinet by the number of cabinets:

$$\frac{\text{one cabinet's impedance}}{\text{number of cabinets}} = \text{total impedance}$$

Let's say your enclosure has an 8Ω impedance and the cabinet you borrowed is 8Ω. The formula is $8 \div 2 = 4$, so the total impedance will be 4Ω. Likewise if you had four 8Ω enclosures, the total impedance would be 2Ω ($8 \div 4 = 2$). Now, it may be just your luck that the second cabinet is 4Ω and yours is 8Ω. No problem—just think of the 4Ω cabinet as *two* 8Ω cabinets (we know this is true from the first example), so you now have, in effect, three 8Ω enclosures. The formula is $8 \div 3 = 2.67$.

Your amp's owner's manual should state the lowest (or minimum) impedance your amp is designed to drive. This may also be indicated next to the speaker-output jacks. If the total impedance of the cabinets you want to use is 4Ω, your amp must have a minimum load rating of 4Ω or *less*. This being the case, you turn off your amplifier, hook up the second cabinet, and then turn your amp back on. To your disbelief the sound is not louder—in fact, it's tinny with no body, and turning up the gain makes it sound even worse.

Most likely, the two cabinets are *out of phase*. This means that while the speaker cones of one cabinet are moving out, the cones of the second cabinet are moving in. The net result is little or no sound at all. To check for this situation, get out that 9-volt battery again. Turn off the amp and unplug the speaker cable, leaving the other end still connected to the cabinet. As shown in Fig. 1, touch the battery's + side to the plug's tip and the – side to the sleeve. When you do this, the cabinet's cones should move *out*. Now repeat the procedure with the second cabinet; if the cabinets are wired out of phase (see Fig. 3), the cones will move in the opposite direction—in.

The guy who loaned you the cabinet is really upset, because it's brand new. He even made a new speaker cable for it himself. Hmmm. Take your battery and recheck the phasing of both speakers, using your speaker cable instead. If they check okay, you know the homemade speaker cable is miswired—that is, + and – have been reversed. Give the cable back to its owner and suggest that he rewire the connectors (or buy a properly wired commercial cord). Whenever you replace a speaker or have one replaced, use this test to make sure it has been properly installed in the cabinet. You should also check all new or repaired cables the same way.

Thanks to all your trouble-shooting, the night turns out to be a complete success. And, as an added bonus, you get an offer from the club to be its house stage tech!

The next day you set out to find a second speaker cabinet. Before going, list all the items pertinent to your additional enclosure, including: impedance, power-handling capacity, function, and price range. In your amp's owner's manual it says the minimum load is 4Ω. Since your existing cabinet is 8Ω, you know you can add one more 8Ω speaker safely ($8 \div 2 = 4$). You could also add one, or even two, 16Ω cabinets: two 16Ω cabinets in parallel have the same total impedance as one 8Ω speaker.

To get the most efficiency out of your system with the fewest cabinets, your best choice is one 8Ω enclosure. Since the two cabinets are of equal impedance, each will receive half the power your amp can deliver. If your amp puts out 200 watts RMS at 4Ω, each cabinet will receive 100 watts maximum before clipping. (Clipping is the point where the power amplifier runs out of headroom and begins to distort.) If you had four 16Ω enclosures, each would receive a maximum of 50 watts RMS before clipping. It should be noted that continuous clipping is very harmful to speakers, especially in a bass system: the lower the note, the longer the duration of DC (direct current) content in the clipped signal. To understand what happens under this condition, remember what your speakers did when you applied the 9-volt battery to them. Now imagine what 20 or even 50 volts would do at the rate of 40 times a second! The results can be overheating, voice-coil disfigurement, overall fatigue, and—eventually—complete failure.

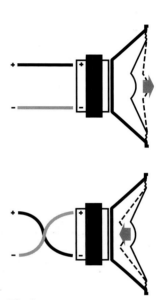

Fig. 3

When speakers are in phase, the cones move in the same direction. When they are out of phase, the cones move in opposite directions, canceling each other out.

After figuring out the power rating you need, look at the power specifications of cabinets carefully—they can be deceiving. Some companies rate their speakers in terms of "music power" or "continuous program power" or just plain "watts." The *only* specification you should be concerned with is "watts RMS." RMS is short for root mean square, and I won't bore you with the mathematical explanation; suffice it to say that a rating in watts RMS indicates true power. In musical terms this means that with a cabinet rated at 100 watts RMS input, you can play 16th-notes on your 100-watt amp at full volume (under clipping) constantly for extended periods. If a cabinet's literature does not have this spec, call the manufacturer and find out before you purchase it.

Last, ask yourself why you're buying this cabinet in the first place. What do you need: More volume to cut through in live situations? Lower lows for better articulation on your 5-string? Crisper highs for slapping? If the most critical need is for more apparent stage volume, consider a cabinet with good punch and midrange response, such as a 2x10 or 4x10. (The ear "hears" mids and upper mids better than low notes, which is why a solo on a 50-watt guitar amp blows away your 100-watt or even 200-watt bass amp.) In such a case a 1x15 or 1x18 may not be a good choice, especially if that's the configuration of the cabinet you currently own.

Now that most of the parameters have been defined, go to the music store and ask what they offer in an enclosure with good punch and midrange response, 8Ω impedance, and power-handling of at least 100 watts RMS. Try out everything in your price range that qualifies, preferably with your own amp and instrument. And while you're there, don't forget to pick up a good speaker cable along with a couple of spare 9-volt batteries. You'll need them.

Acoustic–Upright Amplification

By Scott Malandrone

E lectric bassists have it easy. Buy a good axe, plug it into a modern amp, and *boom*— instant tone. But it's a different story for upright players. Amplifying the acoustic's organic tone is a nasty job, one usually plagued with feedback and thin sound. What's the problem? Just slap a pickup on that bad boy and crank it up, right?

Wrong. That wooden body is designed to resonate. After all, that's what gives acoustic upright its big, blossoming sound and unique decay. But that air cavity makes amplification difficult, as other nearby instruments can excite resonant frequencies inside the chamber and send your amp into full-blown feedback. And just when you think you've got it tamed, the demon returns.

A good amplified acoustic tone captures the air and wood of the instrument's body, the string's nuances, and the note's attack and pitch. Player preferences determine the individual blend of these qualities, but the goal is mud-free, clean volume that accentuates the instrument's natural tone. So how do you achieve this golden sound?

There are three popular methods of electrifying the upright. The most common involves equipping the bridge with a special pickup system that uses piezoelectric crystals, usually installed directly underneath each string. Piezo pickups offer wide bandwidth and good feedback resistance, a good blend of qualities. The type of piezo material—which can be quartz, ceramic, or film—and the method in which the piezos are installed into the bridge

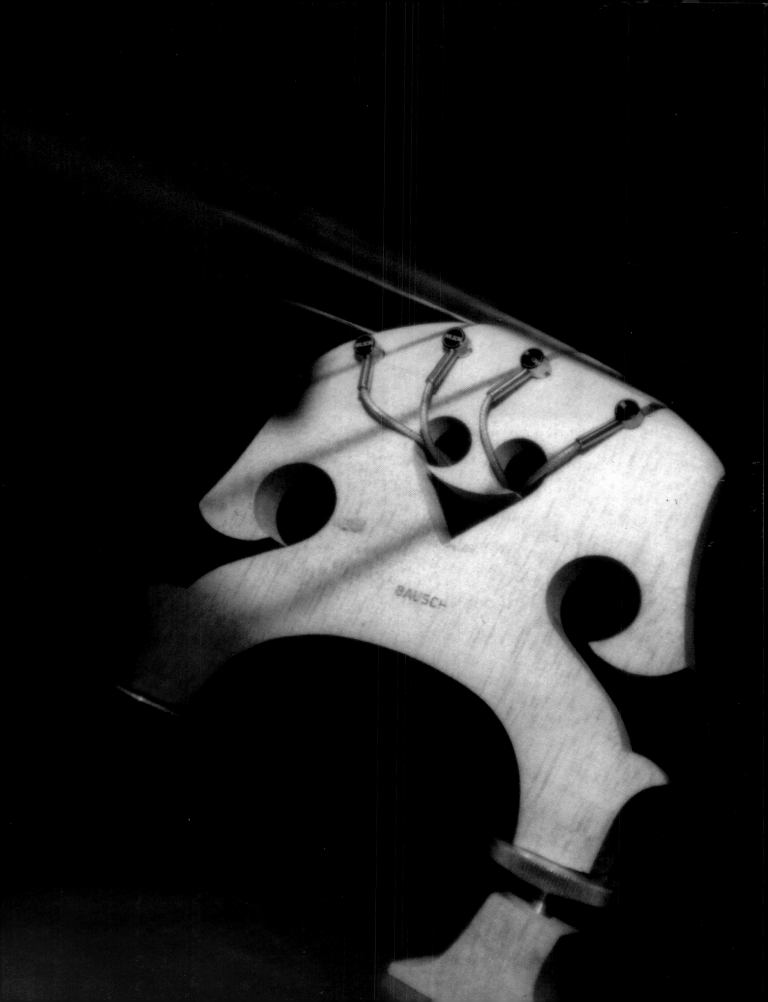

both affect tone. ("Piezo" is Greek for "pressure." When a piezo crystal is stressed or vibrated, for example from the downward pressure of a string, it develops a voltage between its surfaces which can then be amplified.) Popular piezo systems are made by Barbera, Barcus-Berry, Fishman, Underwood, and Wilson.

There are drawbacks to bridge-mounted piezo systems. Piezos don't capture the instrument's entire sound, as there's more to upright tone than what's present at the bridge and top. Piezos also exhibit very high impedances and require a high-quality buffer amp to properly operate. Simply plugging into an electric-bass amplifier, which has inputs designed for magnetic pickups with much lower impedances, will roll off the lows and make the highs thin and scratchy-sounding. The remedy? A buffer preamp between the bass and amp. Fishman, L.R. Baggs, and Schertler all make buffer preamps for piezos. Another popular preamp, although designed primarily for electrics, is the Sadowsky Bass Preamp.

Magnetic pickups that attach to the end of the fingerboard, such as those made by Pierre Josephs Violins and Biesele, are also available. Magnetics have a more electric-type sound and typically do not have the extended frequency response of piezos, although they are very feedback-resistant.

Another amplification method involves placing a small microphone into one of the instrument's *f*-holes or wrapping a mike in foam and stuffing it under the bridge. (There are also transducers that adhere to or clamp onto the bridge.) This captures more of the upright's air, warmth, and resonance than a piezo system can. Barcus-Berry, David Gage, Pan Electric, Polytone, and Schertler manufacture transducer systems. Small mikes by Audio-Technica, Crown, and Countryman are also effective. The problem, of course, is that mikes are very susceptible to feedback and handling noise—and they may not offer enough sonic detail to bring the upright out in the mix. Placing a larger mike (such as the popular Electro-Voice RE20) a few feet in front of the instrument eliminates handling noise, but bleed from other sources (cymbals, etc.) introduces a whole other variety of problems.

The best overall solution uses both piezos and a mike, which are mixed together via an external preamp/mixer box such as Fishman's Acoustic Bass Blender. This allows full control over the amount of body and bridge sounds. The blend may also be controlled at the mixing board if desired, although you'll be at your soundman's mercy. (If he's a guitar player, for example, you're probably in trouble.) Need more thud? Turn up the transducer. Want a bit more articulation? Bump up the piezos. It's a very flexible system, but it requires more cash and setup time.

If you play in a lot of different rooms, you'll benefit from a good EQ. (Some buffer preamps, such as the L.R. Baggs Line Box Pre-EQ, have this built in.) Parametric EQs, which allow you to zone in on the exact frequency area to cut or boost, are the best choice. Room size, wall and stage material, and even air temperature all affect the way sound travels, and a parametric will keep those EQ hot spots in check. If you're looking for an excellent parametric in a pedal format, look for the discontinued T.C. Electronic Dual Parametric Equalizer, a favorite of many electric and upright players.

What type of amp should you use? When it comes to uprights, smaller is usually better. (High-powered 4x10s are usually not required.) Standards include combo models by Gallien-Krueger, Polytone, and SWR. Many upright bassists swear by the tiny but powerful heads made by amp wizard Walter Woods. Whatever you choose, the amp should offer distortion-free volume and relatively flat frequency response. On the other hand, amps such as the Polytone Mini-Brute combo have a low-mid bump that's popular with upright

> **With an acoustic, keep it simple. Don't go overboard with the outboard.**

players. Tip: Plugging uprights into amps with tons of low-end accentuation usually equals feedback.

Although there are many options to boosting that acoustic, the best advice is to keep it simple. Don't go overboard with the outboard. Use good cable, buy quality components, and don't forget that buffer preamp. Spend the money right the first time and you'll save in the long run. That way you'll have more cash left to invest in that 16th-century Amati.

Recording Electric Bass: A Step-By-Step Guide

By Karl Coryat

IS bass the most difficult instrument to record? It would be hard to argue otherwise. Basses produce frequencies as low as 30Hz, and in this region of the audio spectrum, notes get mushy, blurry, and muddy *very* easily. But basses don't just go low: They also produce frequencies that stretch into our hearing range's highest regions, especially when played slap-style. If that doesn't make things difficult enough, the bass is a very dynamic instrument—and since low frequencies carry a lot of energy, it's easy to overload a stage of your signal chain (or an entire mix) even when you can barely hear the bass over the other instruments. So recording a bass sound that's clean, punchy, distinct, deep, and powerful is a *tough* job.

Onstage, things are easier. Dynamic range isn't much of a problem—it's limited pretty much only by the pain threshold of the audience or the local noise ordinances (or, hopefully, by your mercy and good taste!). But the recorded medium has some important limitations: The dynamic range of compact discs is only about 90dB, some 40dB less than the dynamic range of human hearing (cassettes have a range that's another 20dB or 30dB narrower); as a result, recorded music must be "squeezed" into this dynamic region. Furthermore, lows tend to distort stereo loudspeakers more easily than the speakers in your amp. And when music is played on boom boxes and cheap car stereos, the speakers are often too small and inefficient to reproduce the lows faithfully, sometimes causing the bass to get hopelessly lost.

Fortunately, there are techniques that make our lives a little easier when we enter the land of RECORD buttons and mixing boards. Some of the techniques in this article are aimed at the beginning home recordist, while others—especially those explained by the pros we spoke to—can be applied by advanced players, producers, and engineers. Whatever the situation, our goal is the same: to make our recorded bass lines more exciting, interesting, and "there."

What To Shoot For

It's often said that the one rule in recording is that there are no rules—but that's not 100% true. While it may be the case on a strictly artistic level, if you want your recordings to sound as professional as possible, you have to strive to achieve several of the qualities that distinguish good records.

First, a recording should be *quiet*. No professional recording sounds like it was recorded next to Niagara Falls. (No musical recording, anyway.) Second, a recording should be *clean*. Even if you're trying to get an overdriven sound, the signal you hear on playback should have no more distortion than the signal that went into your tape machine. (Unless, of course, you're using your tape deck's input as a source of distortion, a technique sometimes used by lovers of truly raunchy sounds.) Third, a recording should have *clarity*. If all the high end is wiped out somewhere in the recording process, the end result is a muffled sound—not good. Finally, a recording should have *competitive levels*, a highly overlooked factor. There's a psychoacoustic phenomenon that causes music to sound better when it's played louder.

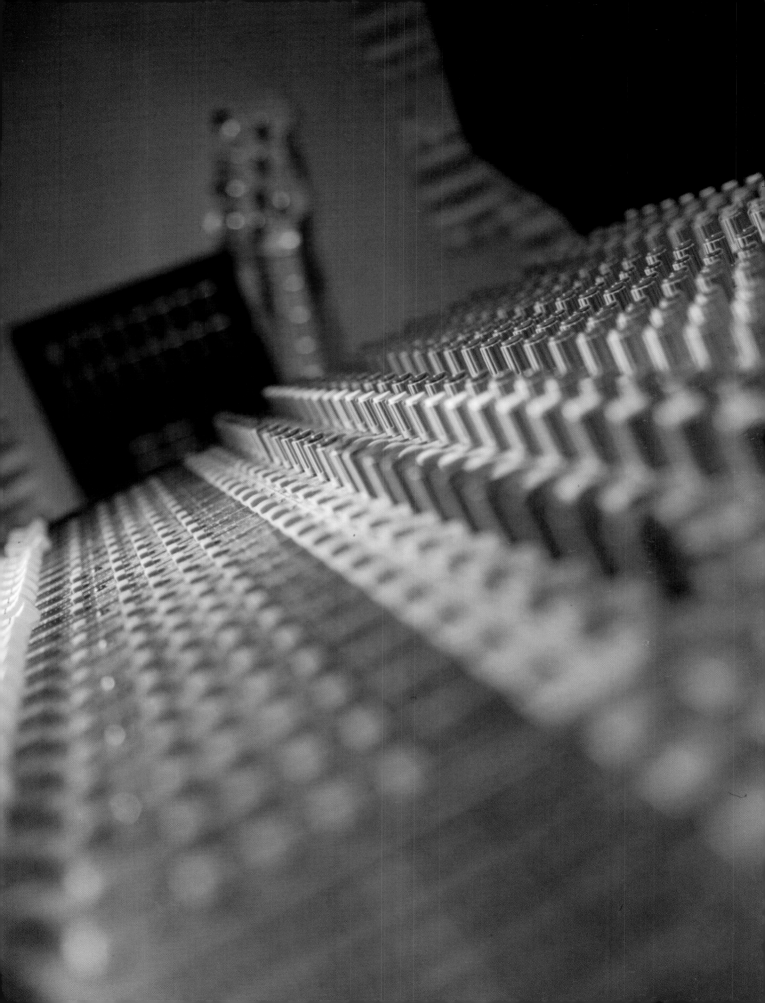

(You headbangers know what I'm talking about!) This occurs because the human ear is more sensitive to midrange frequencies than to highs and lows, so boosting the overall level makes the lows sound deeper and the highs more brilliant. The result is that if someone is listening to your tape along with others, the ones recorded at the highest possible levels (without reaching the distortion point, of course) tend to sound best and have the most impact. Sure, the listener could turn up the volume for the quieter tapes, but that would just increase the amount of background noise—and wouldn't you rather make a tape that sounds great right off the bat, without the listener having to do a lot of knob-tweaking?

The Signal Source

With any audio signal chain, the source is the most important link. In a stereo system, it's the CD player or turntable; if you're recording bass, it's the bass itself. Why? Because no matter how good your gear is, if the signal is screwed up to begin with, nothing in the world can fix it—at least not without side effects. So it makes sense to begin your recording setup with a good bass that has good pickups and electronics. If you use a less-than-stellar axe for live performance, when you're getting ready to record, borrow or rent the best bass you can find—one that sounds good and clear and whose electronics don't hum or buzz. (Most pro studios have a few instruments on hand for this purpose.) If you have to settle for a buzzing bass, try to reduce the noise by checking for nearby fluorescent lights or rheostats (light dimmers); these are notorious for contaminating electrical signals. You might also try changing the direction you're facing as you play—with some basses, especially those with insufficient shielding, your physical orientation can have a marked effect on the amount of noise the instrument picks up.

Don't add onboard EQ when you're recording. Just try to get a good, clean sound—you can worry about EQ later, when you have access to EQ circuits that are probably better than the ones in your bass. If your instrument is active, try switching to passive mode, if possible; sometimes that can yield a cleaner, quieter source sound.

Recording Direct

"Going direct" is the most common way to record the bass. Invented by engineers Geoff Emerick and Ken Townsend for the Beatles' *Sgt. Pepper's* sessions, direct recording is done by running the output of a bass (or guitar or keyboard) directly into the mixing board. This way, the signal doesn't need to be passed through an amplifier and microphone, as was done during the early years of rock & roll; your sound stays clean and true as a result.

But there's a problem: If you simply plug a cable from your bass into a 1" input jack on a mixing board or tape deck, you'll get a sound that's lifeless and dull. Why? The explanation is complicated, but it basically results from an impedance mismatch between your bass and the input stage of the board or deck. The result is a "rolling off" (attenuation) of high frequencies—the ones that give your bass sparkle, bite, and growl.

To keep those frequencies intact, you need to put a *direct box* or *DI* (direct input) between your bass and the board. These fairly inexpensive units contain transformers that match the impedances, allowing high frequencies to pass through unhindered. Most DIs have balanced XLR outputs, requiring hookup to your mixing board via a balanced-line mike cable. The good news is that since the direct box's output is balanced, you can run a long cable between the box and the mixing board without picking up a lot of noise. The bad news is you need a board with XLR inputs, or some other piece of gear that can adapt an XLR cable for your mixer's input jacks.

There are several kinds of direct boxes, ranging from simple stomp-box-like units to rackmountable ones; some are driven by tubes, and others have elaborate signal-shaping circuitry built in. It shouldn't be too surprising, then, that they also *sound* quite different; if you're buying one, try out several with your bass and decide which you like best. In any case, if you want a good direct sound, you *must* have a DI box; simply plugging straight into the board and cranking up the highs just won't do the trick.

Michael Manring, during the sessions for his *Drastic Measures* CD

Preamps

Most direct boxes don't really amplify your signal; they just match impedances. And since basses generate fairly low voltages, you need to bring up your signal's level to the line levels that operate in a mixing board or tape deck. That's why you normally plug the line from a direct box into the mike input of the board; the board then treats your bass signal like a mike signal and uses its own mike preamps to bring it up to line level.

The difference between a mike-level signal and a line-level signal can be up to 60dB—so when using top-quality mikes, many engineers opt for sophisticated mike preamps. But since basses produce a signal that's quite a bit stronger than that of most microphones, the preamp you use isn't as critical. Most modern consumer mixing boards have mike preamps that are more than adequate for bringing a bass up to line level. It should be noted, though, that some cassette 4-tracks with built-in "mixers" have terrible-sounding mike preamps—so it's wise to avoid them for all but the most low-tech projects. If you record with a cassette 4-track, compare the sound of its mike preamps (using either a microphone or bass) with those of a "real" mixing board; if you notice a significant difference, it may be time for an equipment upgrade.

In professional contexts, some engineers like to use high-end dedicated mike preamps on the bass. One such engineer is Tom Size, who built the most elaborate signal chain ever to appear in BASS PLAYER: Billy Sheehan's studio rig. For Mr. Big's *Bump Ahead* Tom recorded five tracks of bass—two of them direct lines, one from each pickup on Billy's Yamaha Attitude Limited bass. The signals from the DiMarzio Model One neck pickup and Model P bridge pickup each went through separate James Demeter tube direct boxes, and then through Demeter tube mike preamps, bypassing the mixing board completely. Tom also likes the top-notch sound of equipment by George Massenburg and John Hardy.

Another favorite preamp of pro engineers is the venerable Neve 1073. The vintage Neve circuit is renowned for its distinctive, highly musical EQ section—one reason why so many engineers like to record on Neve boards. One big Neve fan is Paul Northfield, a veteran who has recorded many classic prog-rock records, including discs by Rush, Yes, and Gentle Giant. "Neves produce extraordinary low end," Northfield comments. "But what's interesting is the lows remain very *tight*. With an old Neve, you can get quite obscene with the low end, producing a very powerful sound. Other consoles tend to produce a sound that's rather cardboardy when you turn up the bass." Be on the lookout for Neve modules when you're scouting prospective studios. And remember, you can still achieve excellent results with much less expensive gear.

Recording Media

Thanks to the technology explosion, these days there are numerous ways to record bass (or any other instrument). The traditional recording medium—good ol' analog tape—is still the favorite among most pro engineers, thanks to its characteristically warm frequency response and so-called "tape compression," which tends to make a bass sound full, punchy, and even. Analog tape is cheap and readily available, it's reliable, and it comes in several standard formats that can be used in virtually any studio in the world.

One of the most popular analog tape formats for the home recordist is the cassette 4-track. For years, inexpensive units by Tascam, Fostex, and other companies have allowed musicians to layer instruments and vocals, greatly aiding the songwriting and arranging processes. The tradeoff, of course, is sound quality: While some cassette 4-tracks sound remarkably good, most are useful only as musical sketchpads, and none truly approaches CD sound quality. Better results can be achieved with 1" 4-tracks and 8-tracks, which use tape that's twice as wide moving four to eight times faster; the tradeoff is increased equipment cost, tape cost, and maintenance. Things start to get really good with 2" 8-tracks and 16-tracks, which offer excellent sound quality at reasonable prices. Finally, the pro-studio standard is the 2" 24-track. A good 24-track can cost tens of thousands of dollars, and a 25-minute reel of tape costs upwards of $150—but the sound, at least in the analog realm, is unbeatable.

Then there's the world of digital recording, gaining rapidly in popularity both in small home studios and in pro facilities. Digital machines record sound in terms of numbers rather than waves, resulting in recordings that can be copied generation after generation with no sonic loss. They're also extremely quiet and accurate, although many people complain that digital recordings sound cold and sterile compared to analog recordings. This is especially important to us bassists, since the low end tends to suffer the most from digital media. It's not that going digital hurts your tone—on the contrary. Digital is the most faithful way we know to capture and reproduce sound. Analog decks, however, tend to add pleasing colorations that have come to be associated with recorded music. If you want the crisp, clean sound of digital, though, you can get excellent results by combining old technology with the new—by running your signal through tube equipment before recording, for instance.

The least expensive and most widely available digital recorder is the DAT (Digital Audio Tape) machine. Although they record only two stereo channels, DAT machines are fairly inexpensive (prices start under $700) and use standard-format tape cartridges (a 90-minute tape costs about $10). DAT machines are ideal for recording solo bass, and they're excellent for recording other performances live to 2-track.

If you want digital multitrack, you can take either the tape route or the hard-disk route. The Alesis ADAT, which uses S-VHS video tapes, and the Tascam DA-88, which uses 8mm video tapes, are two machines that offer digital multitrack recording at breakthrough prices. And as computer equipment gets faster and less expensive, the fastest-rising method is hard-disk recording. Usually requiring peripheral hardware such as an internal card or rackmount interface, hard-disk recording and onscreen digital editing offer incredibly powerful, flexible convenience. There are even a bunch of 4- and 8-track "mini-studios" that use this technology for maximum flexibility in an audio-sketchpad context. Keep watching—things will only get better in this arena.

Compression

One of the most popular studio effects for bass is compression. (See page 129.) In general, compression is effective in the studio because it makes mixing easier; when the dynamics of any one instrument are varying uncontrollably, it's hard to get the instrument to "sit" in the mix and maintain a consistently balanced level relative to the others. Compression is especially good for bass—it can make a tone fatter, more punchy, and more present. "I like to use a lot of compression," says George Drakoulias, staff producer/bassist at American Recordings and the man behind the Black Crowes' breakthrough disc, *Shake Your Money Maker*. "I don't know if you can go too far with it; I don't think I ever have, except when I was going for a certain effect." Very fast attack times and somewhat slower release times (between 200ms and 400ms, depending on the context) generally work best for bass. The compression ratio determines how dramatic the effect sounds; it can range from 1.4:1 (for subtle compression) to 10:1 and beyond (which can yield "squashed" sounds).

It's common to compress an entire bass signal, but Paul Northfield has had success splitting the signal with a crossover and compressing the highs and lows separately. "One of the things I like in a bass sound is the sense of somebody's fingers on the strings digging in, as well as a sense of depth," he reports. "And sometimes EQ won't do that, because if you EQ a certain region too much the signal tends to get spiky. So I use a crossover, set at around 250Hz, to split the signal and send the two components to different compressors. I'll make sure the low end is packing the compressor nicely, and I'll do the same for the high end. Then I'll put the returns from the compressors on two faders and balance them until it just feels right. I've found this gives me an easy control over the sound, and I can get quite radical about the amount of brightness or bottom I bring in." Northfield adds that this technique is especially effective on slap bass, which tends to have a lot of transients (high-frequency spikes at the attack of each note); if the highs are treated separately, they can be compressed without thinning the lows. Northfield points out that although there are self-contained units that perform this function (such as Trace Elliot's SMX dual-compressor preamp circuit, also available in a footpedal), they aren't as flexible as a pieced-together system—which can be critical in the studio.

Another technique makes use of the compressor's "side chain" function. The side chain is a separate input that triggers the compression circuit but doesn't show up in the output. Since in most cases the only instrument directly competing with bass fundamental frequencies is the kick drum, some engineers like to send a kick-drum line to a compressor's side chain and then run the bass through that unit. By setting the compressor for a very fast attack and release, the bass momentarily "ducks" under the kick's attack—so the kick and bass never muddy each other up. And since the moments when the kick and bass coincide are usually when overall levels tend to peak, ducking the bass in this manner can yield a tighter, more even low end. It should be noted that since this technique reduces the attack on the bass (at least whenever a note coincides with the kick), it's not a good idea to use it when bass attack is an important element in the song—especially when the bass is slapped or played with a pick. If you use bass ducking, it's probably best to save it for fingerstyle playing.

Miking The Amp

Recording direct is great, but in many cases the resulting sound is just *too* clean. If your goal is to make a song sound like it's being performed live, a direct-recorded bass may sound artificial and out of place. For this reason it's very common to record the direct line on one track and also send a line to a bass amp—and then mike the amp and record that on another track. In most cases, producers like to use the direct line for the lows, while the miked-amp track provides the highs. This is especially effective for hard rock, where the sound of a bass amp being driven hard helps give the bass an aggressive, on-the-edge feel.

Not just any mike will do for these applications—it must be able to handle the low end well and also be able to take the high SPLs (sound-pressure levels) bass amps produce. This eliminates most condenser mikes, which aren't very tolerant of high SPLs. Tom Size prefers the Electro-Voice RE-20 and, especially, the AKG D112. "The D112 has proven to be very good for low end," Tom says. "Plus it has a little bump [frequency-response emphasis] around 4kHz, which helps bring out a bass tone's 'snap.' And it can take a lot of SPL—it's made to be inside a kick drum." In most cases the microphone is placed close to one of the cabinet's drivers; for a brighter sound, the mike is aimed at the center of the speaker. When you're close-miking this way, the room usually isn't a huge factor—but parallel studio walls can set up standing waves that cause certain notes to boom, which could harm your recording. (That's why pro studios usually have oddly shaped rooms.)

While some producers and engineers prefer to mike the player's stage rig, the standard rigs in studios are the Ampeg B-15 and the Ampeg SVT. Paul Northfield believes in striking a balance between the sound of vintage speakers and the power-handling capabilities of newer ones. "Some of the lower-wattage drivers sound great but tend to blow up," he says. "But if you use speakers designed to take high levels, their distortion tends to be rather clinical and clear. The art of getting a great bass sound is to get all of that fatness and depth, plus a growl that connects with it on top. And you can do that only by ear—by messing around with different systems."

Another miking technique is to use a guitar amp instead of a bass amp; this works well when you're looking for a very heavy, grungy tone. "Chris Squire used to run his Rickenbacker into a Marshall with a 4x12 cabinet," Northfield remembers. "Guitar amps can give interesting bass distortion, and you don't have to rely on pumping the cabinets that much." Since guitar amps don't reproduce bass frequencies well, they act as a kind of crossover—so if you use one, get your lows from a direct line.

Billy Sheehan (right) in the studio with Mr. Big

The Mixdown

This is the big payoff: You've gotten a great bass sound and made sure all the other instruments sit perfectly with the bass. Or maybe not—perhaps you've gotten only an *okay* sound and decided to "fix it in the mix." Either way, mixdown is your last chance to add EQ, effects, and anything else necessary to make your bass shine.

Most experienced engineers avoid adding EQ before going to tape, because you can never tell exactly what will be needed at mix time. "When I'm tracking I'd much rather not use any EQ than use one that harms the signal," says Tom Size. "If I don't have access to either a Massenburg or tube EQ, I'll put down the bass flat and deal with it in the mix."

When thinking of EQ for bass, it's helpful to consider four main frequency bands: lows, low mids, high mids, and highs. The lows range from 30Hz (roughly the fundamental of a 5-string's low *B*) to about 100Hz; boosting this region increases the amount of "woof" and "depth" in your tone, although adding too much can muddy a mix or make it overly boomy. The low mids range from 100Hz to about 600Hz; this is the "meaty" part of the bass spectrum, providing fatness and note definition—but if it's used clumsily, the bass can get boxy-sounding or cardboardy. The high mids, which range from 600Hz to about 3kHz, control growl and edge; too much boost here can make a bass sound harsh, and it can make finger and fret noise unpleasant. Finally, the highs extend above 3kHz to the limits of human hearing (as high as 20kHz); this region determines your sound's brilliance or transparency, especially if you're slapping. The tradeoff to boosting highs—and there's always a tradeoff—is it increases background noise.

The key to successful EQing is simply to try many different settings and decide which works best. If there's a frequency you want to cut, use the board's parametric EQ (or an outboard unit), add a ton of boost, and then turn the frequency knob until the sound is really bad; then cut that frequency to taste. And when EQing a bass track, EQ other instruments *around* the bass and the bass around the other instruments. For instance, if a guitar track is eating up the bass, try slightly cutting the guitar's frequencies in the region where you're boosting the bass. This technique, known as "frequency slotting," is a key to getting instruments to remain clear and distinct instead of turning into sonic mush.

Mixdown is also the best time to add effects. Even if you're *sure* you want that chorus sound on your bass, record a dry (unprocessed) track just in case you want to change the effect later. During mixdown you can also add some grit from a distortion box; keeping the direct line mixed in will keep the bottom from thinning out. Tom Size sometimes likes to get bass grunge from a Tech 21 SansAmp, and he also likes Zoom 9030 and 9050 signal processors for bass distortion and chorus.

Even if a miked-amp track has been recorded, sometimes the bass sound just doesn't cut it at mixdown. In that case, engineers often put up a different amp, feed it the direct line, mike the amp, and add *that* signal to the mix. As long as the direct line is clean and quiet enough to be re-amped, this technique can let you fine-tune the amp sound to fit precisely around the other instruments; distortion, amp EQ, mike placement—everything can be tweaked at the last minute.

There's one more thing to consider during mixdown: *signal phase*. If you're using one direct track and one miked-amp track, the signals can get out of phase with each other; in other words, on track one the bass waveform may be going in one direction while on track two it's going in the other direction. If this is the case, when you combine the two the bottom can drop out completely. To remedy this problem, some mixing boards have a PHASE button on each channel that phase-reverses the signal. If your board lacks this feature, you can make your own phase-reversing adapters in a few minutes with some solder and a few parts: Take a male-to-female extension cable, make two cuts one or two inches from each end, and solder the core wire of one end to the shield of the other and vice versa. (Do this only at line-level stages, where cable shielding isn't a big concern.) Ideally, though, you should check signal phase when you're tracking—by either moving the mike around or phase-reversing on the board—so the bass tracks sound great when combined.

As any seasoned engineer will tell you, it's important to make sure your mixes sound good on many different speaker systems; if you mix on the wrong system, the low end is often the first thing to suffer. For instance, your bass may sound fine on your big home stereo, but when you play the tape in the car or on a boom box, the bass may be inaudible. And if you mix only on small speakers that can't reproduce the lows, there could be hideous things going on down there that surface when you play your CD on a good stereo. Pro studios usually have three sets of speakers: one pair of expensive, built-into-the-wall monsters with near-perfect specs, a set of cheaper speakers like ones you might find in a typical home stereo (Yamaha NS-10s have been a standard for years), and a pair of one-driver bookshelf speakers. By switching among the three systems, the producer and engineer can quickly tell where the mix needs help. If you can't set up such a speaker array, make a cassette (or better yet, a test CD) and play your mixes on several systems, using commercial recordings as a reference. Listen as critically as you can, take notes, remix, and then re-monitor until you're sure the balance between the various instruments and frequencies is just right.

Mastering

This important step is often overlooked by unsigned bands on a budget. Some people think "mastering" just refers to putting the songs in proper order and adding the right amount of space between them—but it's an art form in itself. (Look in a commercial CD's liner notes and you'll probably see an acknowledgment to the mastering engineer.) Professional mastering, performed at a facility dedicated to this purpose, involves adjusting the level and EQ of the songs against each other, adding an overall EQ if necessary, and compressing and/or limiting the entire project. Since songs are mixed one at a time, they're rarely exactly equal in terms of level or EQ; mastering gives them a consistency so all the songs sound equally good. And remember "competitive levels"? Well, since nearly all pro-recorded CDs are compressed quite a bit in the final stage, your music won't be able to compete on the same playing field if it isn't compressed, too. That's because even if you have just one signal spike that's 3dB louder than everything else on your recording, when you try to fit your music into the dynamic-range limitations of a CD, that imperceptible, millisecond-long peak will have to be your disc's loudest moment—so you're effectively wasting 3dB at the top of the dynamic range for over 99.9% of your recording. As a result, your music will sound at least 3dB quieter than the latest Alanis Morissette or Cracker CD—not what you want. The last stage of mastering evens out the peaks and brings up the overall level so your music has maximum perceived loudness and impact. That's especially good news for bass, which is often responsible for these peaks; after a good mastering job the low end is usually much tighter, bigger, and stronger.

The End Result

There are no set rules about how the bass should sound in your finished product; the determining factors should be your taste, the sounds of the other instruments, and the arrangement. Most important, though, is the purpose of your recording. Are you trying to show off your playing, with the other instruments merely acting as a backdrop? In that case the bass should be up front and as clear-sounding as possible. If you're going for more of a groove, the bass should blend in. George Drakoulias puts it best: "In the context of a song, listeners shouldn't necessarily know they're listening to the bass—but they should know it's moving them. You don't necessarily want people to say, 'Wow, that's a great bass part'; instead, they should say, 'Wow, that feels great, but I don't know why. There's something on the bottom that's making me go crazy.'"

By far, the best way to learn how to make great recordings is to *practice*. Record songs in diverse styles, use many different recording techniques, and compare your work to contemporary (and not so contemporary) records you admire. Try to copy your favorite bass sounds and grooves, and listen again and again to the results. Record as much material as you can—after all, it's one of the best ways to get your music heard. And that's the point of it all, isn't it?

Gear Glossary

By Karl Coryat & Rick Turner

AC: Alternating current; a form of electric current that oscillates with a specific frequency. AC most commonly refers to the current that comes from electrical outlets—but a musical signal traveling through a cable is AC, analogous (in amplitude and frequency) to the sound waves we hear. Compare DC.

Action: The feel of the string height. Established by the height of the strings at the bridge and nut, the string gauges, the scale length, and the neck relief. On more subtle levels, action is affected by neck and body construction and materials.

Active electronics: Amplification circuitry built into an instrument, requiring a source of power (usually a 9-volt battery). Active pickups have circuitry built into the pickup housing itself.

Alnico: A combination of aluminum, nickel, and cobalt, commonly used to make pickup magnets.

Analog circuit: One that carries an AC signal whose waveform is analogous (in frequency and amplitude) to the sound wave it represents. Compare DIGITAL.

Auto-wah: See ENVELOPE FOLLOWER.

Balanced line: A 3-conductor signal-cable or output-jack configuration that reduces noise. Two of the conductors carry signals that are identical but 180° out of phase. At the end of the line the reverse-phase signal is brought back in phase and added to the other signal; this cancels out noise picked up along the line but doesn't affect information that was in the line at the beginning.

Bi-amping: An amplification method in which a signal is split into low-frequency and high-frequency components (divided at a CROSSOVER point), each signal going to a separate power amplifier. Bi-amping allows optimization of the different amplification requirements of low and high frequencies.

Bridge: A metal component near the butt end of a bass that anchors the ball ends of the strings. Also see SADDLE.

Capacitance: A property of many electrical components, including capacitors, pickup coils, and even cables. The capacitance of pickup coils affects their high-frequency limits, and the capacitance of cables can roll off highs by shunting them to the ground established by the cable shield. Capacitors are electronic components that block harmful DC signals while letting audio AC signals pass through at a frequency that depends on circuit impedance. Capacitors smooth power to a circuit and isolate audio signals from DC current.

Carbon fiber: See GRAPHITE.

Ceramic: A mixture of metal and a clay-based substance, commonly used to make pickup magnets.

Chorus: A delay-based effect that simulates two or more instruments playing in unison. See Effects Basics, page 129.

Combo amp: A preamp, power amp, and speaker cabinet combined in a single unit.

Compressor: An effect that reduces dynamic range. A compressor often makes a bass sound punchier by making the notes more consistent in volume. See Effects Basics, page 129.

Crossover: A circuit that divides the audio spectrum into two or more parts; these parts can be amplified separately and sent to separate amplifiers or speaker systems. See BI-AMPING.

dB: See DECIBEL.

DC: Direct current; a steady stream of electrons, such as the current produced by a battery. Compare AC.

Decibel: A unit that expresses amplitude, loudness, or intensity.

DI: See DIRECT BOX.

Digital circuit: One that converts a signal into a number-based signal, performs mathematical calculations on the digital signal (such as creating reverb effects), and converts the signal back into a waveform-based analog signal. Compare ANALOG CIRCUIT.

Direct box: A device that converts your bass signal's impedance and sends the low-impedance signal down a balanced line, which can then be sent to a recording console or PA.

Driver: Another word for speaker—the cone, voice coil, magnet, and frame as a unit. A more specific term than "speaker," which can include the cabinet or enclosure as well.

Dynamic range: The range of loudness, in decibels, that an instrument, amp, or other device can handle. It's the difference between the quietest possible signal (where the signal and the noise are at the same level) and the loudest (where significant distortion sets in).

Effects loop: A set of jacks that breaks an amplifier's circuit and lets you add a device (such as an effect box) inside the unit's signal chain. An effects loop normally consists of a SEND jack, which outputs a signal, and a RETURN jack, which receives the signal and thus completes the circuit.

Enclosure: See SPEAKER CABINET.

Envelope follower: An effect that adds an EQ peak whose center frequency varies with the signal level. The sound is similar to that of a wah-wah pedal, since EQ sweeps follow the decay of each note.

Equalizer (EQ): An effect, often built into amps, that lets you boost or cut certain bands of the frequency spectrum, thus changing the tone.

Exciter: A circuit designed to make a signal sound more clear, punchy, bright, or loud, without using ordinary EQ or gain.

Expander: A circuit that increases dynamic range by making the loudest notes louder and the softest notes softer. See Effects Basics, page 129.

Flanger: A delay-based effect that produces a "whooshing" sound. See Effects Basics, page 129.

Flatwound strings: Strings made of a core wrapped with a flat, ribbon-like winding. Compared to roundwounds, flatwounds produce less finger noise and are more mellow-sounding.

Folded horn: A speaker-cabinet design that reflects and then projects sound into a room. On their own, folded horns produce loud, deep bass, but not much highs—so they require additional high-end drivers (sometimes built into the cabinet).

Fundamental: A "pure" tone with no harmonics; the fundamental is the lowest-frequency component of an overtone series. The fundamental of *A*-440 is 440Hz; the fundamental of an open bass *E* string is 41.2Hz. See HARMONICS.

Graphite: A form of carbon used in modern instrument construction. Graphite fibers in a resin matrix can provide very high stiffness-to-weight ratios for improved bass-neck performance.

Groundwound strings: Roundwound strings that have been ground or burnished to reduce finger noise and fret wear.

Half-rack: A format for mounting equipment. Two half-rack units mounted side by side take up one standard 19" rackspace.

Half-round strings: See GROUNDWOUND STRINGS.

Harmonics: Multiples of the fundamental tone present in a note's sound. Technically the 1st harmonic is the fundamental, the 2nd harmonic (or 1st overtone—just to confuse things!) is an octave higher, and the 3rd harmonic (2nd overtone) is an octave plus a fifth higher. Subsequent harmonics proceed in ever-decreasing intervals.

Head: A preamp and power amp in a single unit. Sometimes called a top or brain.

Headstock: The enlarged area at the end of a bass neck where the tuners are located.

Heel: The area on the back of a bass where the neck meets the body.

Hertz: A unit that expresses frequency; 60Hz is equivalent to 60 waveform cycles per second.

Highpass filter: A circuit component that lets through high frequencies but cuts low frequencies.

Humbucking pickup: One that cancels electromagnetic noise (hum) by using two coils wired out of phase and two magnets oriented with opposite polarities.

Hz: See HERTZ.

Impedance: The AC equivalent of DC resistance; impedance can be thought of as a load on a signal. It's important to consider impedances when connecting any two electronic devices, such as amp and speaker or pickup and amp. (See Amp Setup Basics, page 131.) Also important in pickup design: Although a low-impedance pickup usually has a low output level, active electronics can boost that level while maintaining the low noise level of the low-impedance pickup.

Intonation: The degree of "in-tuneness" of a string as you play it up and down the neck. Due to strings' stiffness, the scale length must be adjusted in order to play in tune. Generally, the thicker and stiffer a string is, the more compensation is required. See Setup Essentials, page 121.

J pickup: A bright-sounding bar-shaped pickup associated with the Fender Jazz Bass. J pickups traditionally have a single coil, but many modern J's are double-coil humbuckers.

Limiter: An effect that sets a maximum output level. If a signal is limited, once the limiter's threshold level is reached, increased input won't result in increased output.

Load: A circuit's character that works against the current of an incoming signal. Also see IMPEDANCE.

Lowpass filter: A circuit component that lets through low frequencies but cuts high frequencies.

MIDI: Musical Instrument Digital Interface—the digital language that MIDI-equipped devices use to communicate with one another. Bassists can use MIDI to automate effect-program changes or to drive synth modules with a MIDI bass controller.

MIDI controller: Any musical instrument that produces MIDI signals.

Multi-tap delay: A delay that produces multiple independent echoes rather than one echo.

Neck-through-body design: An instrument-building method in which the neck passes all the way through the body. The body is actually two "wings" glued onto the side of the neck block.

Noise gate: A circuit that reduces the output level when no signal is coming through, thereby reducing noise and increasing the signal-to-noise ratio.

Nut: The piece of plastic, bone, phenolic, etc., that forms the end of the strings' playing length where the headstock meets the neck.

Onboard: Built into an instrument.

Overdrive: A circuit that boosts signal and/or adds distortion.

Overtone series: The fundamental and harmonics, the proportions of which determine a sound's tone. Also see HARMONICS.

P pickup: A warm-sounding pickup (split into two staggered halves) associated with the Fender Precision Bass.

Pad: A device that cuts or reduces ("pads down") an audio signal's level.

Parametric EQ: An equalizer that allows you to change the frequency bands it is affecting. See Effects Basics, page 129.

Passive electronics: A circuit that requires no external power source. Compare ACTIVE ELECTRONICS.

Peak EQ: A type of EQ band with a frequency center that can be cut or boosted, with reduced effect on surrounding frequencies. Compare SHELVING EQ.

Phantom power: A feature of an amplifier, mixer, etc., that sends DC current to power the active electronics of an instrument, microphone, or other device.

Phaser: A delay-based effect that produces a liquidy or shimmering sound.

Phenolic: A synthetic resin commonly used for fingerboards and nuts. Also called ebonol.

Pickup: A device that turns string-vibration mechanical energy into AC electrical energy.

Piezoelectric pickup: A non-magnetic pickup, commonly used in upright basses and acoustic bass guitars and occasionally in electrics. The mineral-crystal substance in a piezo generates a voltage potential when vibrated or stressed. Piezoelectrics, which have high impedances, need to be buffered by an appropriate preamp in order to produce a good sound. See Acoustic-Upright Amplification, page 134.

PJ configuration: A pickup arrangement in which a P pickup is near the neck and a J pickup is near the bridge.

Pot: Short for potentiometer; a variable resistor used in tone and volume controls.

Preamp: An amplifier circuit that alters an instrument signal's impedance and/or amplitude, thereby preparing the signal for a power amp. Preamps may also include EQ sections, compressors, effects loops, etc.

Pre-post switch: A feature, sometimes found on preamps, that lets you bypass the EQ section, giving you a "pre-EQ" output signal.

Programmable: Capable of storing user-customized data, such as EQ settings or effect configurations.

Rackmountable: Capable of being installed in a standard 19"-wide equipment rack.

Relief: The slight up-bow a neck needs to avoid fret buzz. See Setup Essentials, page 121.

Reverb: An effect that simulates the sound of playing in a room or hall.

RMS: Root mean square. "Watts RMS" is a unit that expresses average power along a waveform, rather than at its peaks and troughs. RMS values represent true amplifier power output; figures that use terms such as "peak power" can be deceptively large.

Roundwound strings: Strings made of a core wrapped with a round winding. Roundwound strings are bright but squeaky, and they tend to wear down frets and fretless fingerboards.

Saddle: A portion of the bridge over which a string passes. Forms one end of the strings' playing length, the nut being the other end.

Scale length: The playing length of a string measured from the nut to the theoretical bridge position; also, twice the length from the nut to the 12th fret.

Sealed cabinet: A speaker cabinet without a vent (an opening or hole); compare VENTED

CABINET. Sealed cabinets can handle large amounts of power and have excellent "damping" (controlled cone movement), but they aren't very efficient. Sometimes called infinite baffle.

Shelving EQ: A type of EQ band (usually the lowest or highest one) that cuts or boosts all frequencies past a central frequency, with reduced effect on frequencies toward the mid bands. Compare PEAK EQ.

Shielding: The use of a grounded conductor surrounding an instrument's circuitry, the wires inside a cable, or anything else that carries an electrical signal. Pickups, instrument control cavities, and audio cables should all be shielded to reduce electrostatic noise.

Soapbar pickup: Generic term for any rectangular humbucking pickup.

Solid-state circuitry: Electronics using transistors instead of vacuum tubes to amplify signals. Compare TUBE.

Speaker cabinet: A unit that contains one or more drivers; speaker cabinets are often built to control and optimize the sound of the driver(s). Also called an ENCLOSURE or speaker system.

Speaker-cabinet configuration: A figure that describes the size and number of drivers in a cabinet. A 1x15 cabinet contains a single 15" driver, a 4x10 contains four 10s, etc.

Subwoofer: A cabinet designed to handle very low frequencies.

Transducer: Any device that transforms electrical energy into mechanical or acoustical energy, or vice versa. Pickups, microphones, and loudspeakers are all transducers.

True diversity: A wireless-system design in which two receivers add their signals to reduce drop-outs and other undesirable effects.

Truss rod: A rod inside an instrument neck that, when properly adjusted, counteracts the tendency for string tension to bow the neck. See Setup Essentials, page 121.

Tube: An amplifier component with signal-boosting electronics encased in glass under a vacuum. Also called a vacuum tube or valve. Many players prefer the "tube sound" over the sound of solid-state amps, though tube amps tend to be larger, heavier, and more fragile than solid-state amps.

Tuner: Either the tuning machines that bring a string up to pitch, or an electronic device that aids the tuning of an instrument.

Tweeter: A small driver designed to handle high frequencies.

Two-way (or three-way) system: A loudspeaker system in which different portions of the audio spectrum are assigned to different sizes and/or types of drivers, each optimized for a particular frequency range.

Vented cabinet: A speaker cabinet with a "port" (hole) in one of its walls. Vented cabinets are more efficient than sealed cabinets, but the speakers blow more easily. Also called ported cabinet. Compare SEALED CABINET.

Wah-wah pedal: An effect that adds a narrow boost sweepable across the frequency spectrum, often producing a "talking" or "quacking" sound.

Woofer: A large driver designed to handle low frequencies.

XLR jack: A 3-pronged jack commonly used with microphones and other balanced lines. See BALANCED LINE.

Zero fret: A fret used in front of the nut. Most often found on headless basses.

Donald "Duck" Dunn and Al Jackson Jr.

with Booker T. & the MGs

The Great Basses

By John J. Slog

1951 Fender Precision

Lionel Hampton, one of the top cats in the jazz scene in '51, saw Monk Montgomery pouring out his soul on a Czech upright at a small jazz club in Indianapolis. Hamp offered Monk a steady gig with his big band, and then he handed him a strange new instrument: a Fender Precision Bass. Montgomery gave this new challenge his all—and his trail-blazing work helped pave the way for the rest of us. (Other early Fender Bass pioneers included Roy Johnson, Monk's predecessor in the Hampton band; Shifte Henri of Louis Jordan & His Tympany Five; and several country & western bassists.) Many scoffed at first, but it soon became evident that the Precision Bass—with its clear tone and easy-playing 34" scale—was indeed history in the making.

Born from the ideas of Leo Fender and George Fullerton, the slab-bodied ash-wood '51 was the first electric bass guitar mass-produced and marketed to the public (for a whopping $195.50). The look of the butterscotch-blond body, bolt-on maple neck, black Bakelite pickguard, and chrome-plated covers was easy to recognize onstage. And that Fender Bass sound was unmistakable—even without looking!

1959 Fender Precision

This bass is an absolute milestone. For musicians it's as much an American icon as the Ford Thunderbird with the "porthole" hardtop. This P-Bass version debuted in 1957—and it left a mark on the bass world that endures to this day. It is simply the most copied 4-string design *ever*.

During the mid '50s, Leo Fender's Telecaster-style Precision evolved through efforts to contour the body and make other small improvements. In '57 Leo decided to give the instrument a complete redesign. More important than the larger headstock and gold-anodized aluminum pickguard were the high-output split pickup and fully adjustable four-saddle bridge, which made it possible to intonate the bass more precisely. The combination of the gold pickguard and maple neck lasted only through mid '59—but it's astounding how many great bassists have used a Precision from this era. Duck Dunn played one for years with Booker T. & the MG's; Nokie Edwards was pictured with one in Ventures photos from the early '60s; Chuck Rainey did much of his best studio work with a '57; Bruce Hall put one through studio and stadium abuse with R.E.O. Speedwagon; and Mark Egan has done a lot of work with a modified '58—to name just a few. Countless other bassists have sworn by the gold-guard P-Bass for its unmistakable look and unique growl. If you're lucky enough to try out one of these beauties, you'll be playing an instrument whose sound and feel inspired scores of hit songs in every imaginable style of popular music.

1960 Fender Jazz Bass

Many consider the "stack-knob" Fender Jazz the ultimate collectible vintage bass. Leo Fender began work on the design in 1959; the concept was to add sonic flexibility with a dual-pickup design and improved playability via a narrower neck: 1 7/16" at the nut. (The narrow neck was originally touted as a feature that would allow guitarists to play the bass with ease.) The Jazz also had an "offset-contour" body that provided a more comfortable, balanced feel. As early Fender photos show, the Jazz prototypes had wide, five-pole pickups and a three-knob configuration: a volume control for each pickup plus a master tone.

In 1960 the production Jazz Bass was introduced; it featured a pair of the now-familiar narrow pickups and a different electronics package with separate volume and tone controls for each pickup, thanks to its concentric or "stacked" knobs. (Sometime in mid-to-late '61, Fender reverted to the three-knob design found on the prototypes.) Brazilian rosewood was used for the fingerboard. The slab board introduced in 1960 lasted until '62, and the "clay" position markers made their way through mid '64.

Although it was made for only about 18 months, the stack-knob Jazz attracted a good number of pros, including studio legend Joe Osborn. Not many were made, though, and the later three-knob version is the vintage Jazz best associated with many top players. John Paul Jones, Noel Redding, and Sting (who owns a stripped '63) have all been lured by the magic of early Jazz Basses. Even Bob Dylan was pictured with one in an old Fender catalog. Patrick Dahlheimer of Live has been bitten by the playability and tone of early Fenders, taking no fewer than six with him onstage. And, of course, Jaco—having pulled out the frets and epoxy-coated the fingerboards—coaxed more musical colors out of early-'60s J-Basses than anyone we know!

Truly a legend, the original Jazz Bass is still producing some of the sweetest tones in the history of modern bass.

1964 Hofner 500/1

Produced since the mid '50s in various forms, the Hofner 500/1 was the first choice of working-class English bassists in the early '60s—mainly for financial reasons. While Fenders sold for about £100, a Hofner could be had for only about £30. Another attractive feature of this hollowbody bass was its symmetrical violin shape, which looked fine whether played right- or left-handed. One such southpaw was Paul McCartney, who bought a Hofner at a small Hamburg music shop in 1961 and subsequently used it on all of the Beatles early live performances and recordings. After being stolen in 1963, that bass was replaced with another 500/1 similar to the '64 pictured here.

The "staple" pickups with small surrounds, a narrow control plate, the thin "violin burst" finish, and the arched top are a few of the distinctive features of the four-pound Hofner. Considering it was in McCartney's hands when he dreamed up the melodic bass lines on dozens of great songs like "Can't Buy Me Love" and "Eight Days a Week," it's no wonder the 500/1 is now known the world over as the "Beatle Bass."

1967 Rickenbacker 4001S

This unassuming 4-string may look similar to other Rick models made at the same time (and to later versions of the 4000 series)—but it's the most sought-after bass ever produced by Rickenbacker. Why is this plain Jane so desirable? For one thing, because of its famous users. Over the years we have seen Chris Squire with his '65 4001S on many Yes tours and heard its famous twang on many Yes albums. Squire's choice of a bright, wiry tone—especially evident on "Roundabout" [*Fragile*, Atlantic]—gave the impression the 4001S was a brash, in-your-face kind of instrument. (Squire's use of Roto-sound roundwound strings, a pick, and Sunn tube amps with 10" and 12" guitar speakers also contributed.) Another notable 4001S user—Paul McCartney—played a '64 model lefty and sought a somewhat deeper tone on his recordings. The body of Paul's beautiful Fireglo Ricky was reversed but had a right-handed neck, so the truss-rod cover and RICKENBACKER badge pointed the opposite way. Some years later Paul stripped the paint from that bass for a more natural look and feel.

The other reason for this model's appeal is its rarity. In the '60s Rickenbacker's U.K. distributor had requested instruments with a more traditional look for the British market. The export hollowbodies got *f* holes instead of the usual "slash cuts," and the export basses had dot markers on the neck rather than large triangles. When a Model 4001S bass reached England, it became known as a Model 1999. Under either name, it's a classic.

The First Alembic Bass

This fine example of custom craftsmanship was built in 1971 by the Master Guru of Extravagance, the King of Creative Inventiveness, and the Sultan of Defined Sound. This description is not worn by an individual but by an entity called Alembic. The idea for this revolutionary organization was spawned in the late '60s by the Grateful Dead, who felt that the era's commercial musical products were insufficient for their sonic needs. No three-piece suits, three-martini lunches, or stuffy accountants were needed—just some long-haired creative types devoted to the creation of pure sound through advanced technological design and craftsmanship.

Alembic was conceived by "Bear" Owsley, started by Ron Wickersham, and enhanced by the contributions of Bob Matthews and Rick Turner. Alembic brought about the first major revolution in bass guitar history since the Precision's introduction in 1951—and that revolution began with this instrument. It was built for Jack Casady of the Jefferson Airplane, and it can rightly be considered the very first high-tech bass.

Although Rickenbacker had been building neck-through-body basses since the late '50s, this instrument represented something completely new. For one thing, it was *active*: Wickersham had been installing electronics in guitars and basses since 1969, but Alembic #71-001 was the first instrument designed to be active from the ground up, with low-impedance pickups and an onboard preamp and tone-filter system. Turner was responsible for the unique woodwork and hardware—and when Casady couldn't decide what he wanted, Rick came up with the idea for interchangeable sliding pickups. He also carved zebrawood to create the body wings that flanked a multi-laminate neck with stringers of purpleheart and maple. Tiny red LEDs served as neck-position markers. The face originally sported plates of bird's-eye maple, but when the electronics were modified these were replaced by the purpleheart seen here. The scale length (as specified by Casady) was 32", and the ebony fingerboard had an elaborate abalone, sterling silver, and mother-of-pearl inlay designed and installed by Turner.

Many high-end bass companies have sprung up since Alembic first hit the scene, but we should all remember it the next time we plug in a beautifully crafted multi-laminate instrument with active electronics. This bass changed everything.

1979 Music Man StingRay

Leo Fender refused to rest on his laurels after selling Fender Musical Instruments to CBS in 1965, and he went to work on the Music Man StingRay shortly after his CBS consulting contract ran out. The new bass was designed to do everything the original Fender bass did—only better.

This ash- or alder-body instrument with a bolt-on maple neck was first marketed in 1976, and the early models had strings that passed through the body—a feature found on P-Basses made between 1951 and '57. (The string-through design was abandoned when the Ernie Ball company took over Music Man production in the early '80s.) The StingRay's 3+1 peghead took some getting used to, but the ballsy sound produced by its massive single pickup and active circuitry quickly became popular.

Although the StingRay was criticized by some for having only one tone, it was very good at doing what it did. In his funky fretwork with the Brothers Johnson, Louis Johnson proved the StingRay was a powerful vehicle for thumbstyle bass. Queen's John Deacon took a more melodic approach to his Music Man, and Pino Palladino's superb work on a fretless StingRay has shown another side of the instrument's up-front tone. "Up-front" doesn't begin to describe what Flea of the Red Hot Chili Peppers did for years with his StingRay—or *to* it! His in-your-face concept of physical playing helped inspire a whole new generation of StingRay-wielding bassists.

Opposite: The Funk Brothers — James Jamerson and drummer Benny Benjamin with the Motown band

PART THREE

INNOVATORS

James Jamerson: Interview With A Ghost

By Dr. Licks, with James Jamerson Jr.

Ghosts are people who died with unfinished business, or so they say. Trapped in the ethereal mists, they are forced to haunt the land of mortals until their business is concluded. For several years before his tragic death in 1983, James Jamerson tried in vain to interest the media in his story. Unfortunately there were only a few takers, and the full story of Jamerson's accomplishments was never told.

The great Motown bassist died with this on his mind. By 1987 he was nearly a forgotten man—even to most bass players. That same year I began breaking ground for the book/cassette documentary *Standing in the Shadows of Motown: The Life and Music of Legendary Bassist James Jamerson*. After some detective work which led me to Jamerson's widow, Annie, I took off for Detroit. Little did I know someone was looking over my shoulder.

What was supposed to be a one-hour meeting turned into three days, as tale after tale poured out from Jamerson's family, friends, and fellow musicians. As they fondly recalled his impact on their lives and music, it became increasingly apparent a book of transcriptions wouldn't be enough. The story was much bigger than just a collection of bass lines. It would grow even larger when I had my first visit from the ghost.

I had been up until 3 AM talking to Annie Jamerson, and she suggested I nap on her couch before my 6:30 flight back to Philadelphia. Lying there in the dark, I was in awe as the realization swept over me that this was the house where James Jamerson lived while helping to create pop masterpieces such as "I Was Made to Love Her," "Get Ready," "Ain't Nothing Like the Real Thing," "You Keep Me Hanging On," and dozens more by Smokey Robinson & the Miracles, the Supremes, the Four Tops, the Temptations, Stevie Wonder, Marvin Gaye, and many other Motown artists.

As I recalled the events and conversations of the last three days, something directed my attention to the wall behind the stairway. I was suddenly transfixed by a large photo of James. As we stared at each other, it was almost as if he were saying, "Help me get my story out."

While I never got the chance to speak with James about his music, I interviewed the Funk Brothers—the great Motown rhythm section led by keyboardist Earl Van Dyke—and many other musicians who played with him during Motown's "glory years" (1963–68). And, most important, I spent many hours talking to his son, James Jr. Drawing on that background, I constructed this interview with the ghost of James Jamerson.

* * *

Your Motown career entailed massive output and great variety and creativity. Was the hit-factory mentality stressful?

No, not in the beginning—but toward the end of the '60s it started to get on my nerves. We were recording around the clock, sometimes six or seven days a week, and it got to the point where we started hiding out at local bars and clubs just to get the hell away from the studio and the producers. It was also hard to play the same stuff over and over. Motown began

Opposite page: Jamerson with Motown drummer Uriel Jones

recutting songs that had hit earlier with other groups—like recording "I Heard It Through the Grapevine" with Marvin Gaye a year after Gladys Knight & the Pips hit with the same song. It was tough taking something you had recorded previously and redoing it in a totally different style with all new ideas, because you always heard the original in your head. Then you'd get angry at yourself and play it a different way just to get out of the studio.

During Motown's glory years, were your working conditions very different from the early '60s, when you were with Jackie Wilson and then the Miracles?

Well, we weren't cutting as much in the early days. And besides, in 1960 and '61 I had been playing electric bass for only about a year or so, and I was basically just digging into my jazz thing from playing upright, because that's all I knew. Jackie's music wasn't very sophisticated harmonically, and neither was the early Miracles stuff. A lot of that music was easy 12/8-feel ballads or shuffles I could play standard walking-bass things on. But even then my style was different from the rest of the guys on the scene. It was more syncopated and chromatic; I'd probably have to credit that to my jazz background also. If you check out a '62 Marvelettes tune called "Strange I Know," you can hear how I was taking a standard '50s type of line and giving it a new twist.

Were your approaches to the upright and electric much different?

That depends on what period of my life you're talking about. In the early '60s I was trying to play the Fender bass more like an upright, because that was my background. By around '64 I started to find my identity on the electric and started moving away from the walking-type things I had been doing. But don't get me wrong, I still walked on electric. One of my favorite Fender walking parts was "The Hunter Gets Captured by the Game" by the Marvelettes. I was nasty on that. Paul Chambers would have been proud of me.

When did arrangers start writing specific parts for you, as opposed to just giving you chord sheets?

Around '67 or '68, particularly when [songwriters] Ashford and Simpson came in. They started to put reins on me a little, but I'd still stick stuff in that was all me. Nobody could really write for me because I'd always come up with a better part than was on the paper. A lot of times these guys were just writin' out old lines of mine anyway and using them in new tunes. On Marvin Gaye's "What's Going On?" Dave Van dePitte had studied my style and wrote out a whole bunch of my old lines that worked in that tune.

All your parts were distinctive, but you really seemed to shine more with certain stars than others. Why?

Two reasons. Take the Supremes or the Contours—their music didn't need real busy lines. The simple stuff worked better for them. You got to play what works best for the artist, not yourself. Now on Stevie Wonder, or Marvin Gaye, or the Four Tops stuff, I'd really lay into it. Also, if I liked the person a lot I'd put out a lot more. Like Shorty Long. Most people just remember him for that "Here Comes the Judge" stuff, but he was one of the funkiest guys at Motown. I loved that guy, and my bass playing on his records showed it. The *Here Comes the Judge* album is some of my best work.

Did you miss the road after Berry Gordy pulled you off in 1964?

Once in a while—but for the most part I was happy to be home with my family. I loved to cook and eat, and I couldn't do that on the road. Even in the late '70s, when I did road-work it was lousy. I remember I used to make everybody sick on the Joan Baez tour I was doin' at the time, because I'd be backstage before a show eating sardines out of a tin can. That ain't no way to live.

How did your live playing differ from your studio approach?

Not at all. Your approach should change from song to song and artist to artist, but *where* you're playing shouldn't make a difference. Let the sound crew worry about that. I know guys who play simpler in a big boomy hall. That's wrong, see? You got to play what you feel, 'cause if you hold back you're not giving the audience your best, which is what they paid for. You could say I tried to make my live performances like a record date: I wanted them to be perfect.

You could make the Fender sound like an upright and vice versa. How did you do that?

I think the two sounded similar because I treated the Fender the same way as the upright in many ways, like using a lot of open strings and fingering the Fender like an upright. My hands were unusually strong from being an upright player. I think most guys who went right to electric don't have the hand strength, so it's hard to get that upright sound. Probably the most important reason, though, was that I always picked with just my index finger, and that gave my sound an evenness and consistency. It didn't matter what kind of instrument I was playing—it always sounded like me.

Your son said you never used any other right-hand fingers, no matter how complex the passage was. It's hard to believe you could pull off a very technical part like "Bernadette" so cleanly with just one finger.

That's why they called that finger "the Hook." This first finger of mine would be dancin' around pretty good on my bass when I was in the mood. If Wes Montgomery was playing all that fast stuff with just his thumb, why couldn't I do the same thing with just my index finger? But see, I didn't do it for show. I did it for the sound—always the sound.

Your open-string concept created many interesting dissonances in straightahead pop harmonies.

The open-string thing wasn't as planned out as you make it sound. On the upright it's a standard technique to play an open string almost like a ghost note to help you shift positions or cross over strings. The dissonance sounds for only a very short time. It's actually a lazy trick to cover up the position shifts. But sometimes, I did kind of lay on a dissonant note because I liked the tension it created—especially in the flat keys where the open strings aren't diatonic. Like in "Home Cookin'" by Junior Walker: The tune is in A♭, but I'm playing all these open D's. Your ear tells you something is a little strange there, but it works. I could have played E♭ instead of the open D's, but it wouldn't have sounded as good and it would have played and felt more stiff. The big thing about the open-string technique is that it won't work as well with the modern roundwound strings. They're too alive, so the dissonances become overbearing.

Your bass, and the way it was set up, was critical in your approach, wasn't it?

My thing was heavy bottom. That's why I played a Fender Precision, and that's why I used flatwounds. That was the only combination that gave me the sound I wanted. You can't get that with a lot of the modern basses and them rubber-band strings everyone is playing now. I wanted my bass to sound like a *bass*—big, fat, and round. You also never hear fret buzzing on any of my performances, because of the flatwounds. My action was very high, which also helped a lot. Most bassists couldn't play my bass, but it felt easy to me because I was used to the upright. And the mute and the bell most bassists take off—hell, that's half the sound. They ain't just for looks. [*For many years stock Precisions had a metal bridge cover with a foam-rubber string mute and a metal "bell" over the pickup.*] And I hardly ever changed strings—not unless they broke or started to unravel. I used to say, "The dirt keeps the funk."

The key is I wanted to lay down the bottom for the whole recording. I didn't want to solo, and I didn't want to draw too much attention to myself. I just wanted to make the rhythm section kick ass so people would get up and dance. There was one time I did solo for Motown, on a Junior Walker cut called "Mutiny." I really took it out, but that was rare for me.

There's amazing variation in your touch. You push certain notes and lay back on others, and not just on obvious accents.

Stevie Wonder's "Uptight" is a great example. If I felt I had to be strong on a certain note, I'd play it that way. Or if I needed to lay back somewhere, I'd do that. It's all in the attitude. And not just pushing the notes but pushing and pulling the beat around also. Sometimes I'd stretch the key and the beat so far, the band couldn't find where the beat was at. At times it would get so funky there was too much music for the singers to handle, and we'd have to recut the whole damn song. I was just trying to make things interesting. If you constantly have a solid *one* and *two* and *three* and *four* you get Lawrence Welk. You have to create tension rhythmically as well as harmonically. You don't always have a strong downbeat in every measure; you can tie some notes over on beat *one*, or use a rest and come in on the upbeat.

But that's all very technical. I really didn't think about those things. I just did them and felt them. Dig this—when you walk down the street, is every footstep exactly the same? Of course not. Music's the same way—it has to breathe. My best ideas didn't come from textbooks or computers or synthesizers; they came from life. Just look at a flower, or a wave in the ocean, or the way someone walks, and if you really look close you'll see music. Visual images are very important to a musician's creativity.

Your performance on the Isley Brothers' "This Old Heart of Mine" was a sign of things to come in rock, particularly when you pedaled those eighth-note roots.

Yeah, a lot of rock & roll bands in the '70s were getting into that—but I did it in '65. On that tune I needed something driving, and it just felt right. My style was to have no style at all. You couldn't predict what I would do. The Marvelettes' "Too Many Fish in the Sea" was so simple and easy it could be played by a little kid. But then on songs like the Temptations' "For Once in My Life" and the Four Tops' "Reach Out," I was all over the place.

Again, you have to go with what the song needs and how you feel. On songs like "Precious Love" by Marvin Gaye and Tammi Terrell or the Temptations' "Get Ready," I had to play those lines exactly the same every time because I was being doubled by the guitar. On "Too Many Fish" nobody was doubling me, but still I kept it the same every time. You can't make rules and get too analytical. Go with your heart, and it will always be right.

Motown producer/songwriter Frank Wilson said that when you played, it was "a song within a song." What do you think he meant?

I didn't want to play standard bass patterns my whole career. I mean, I had some stock things I would dip into from time to time, but I usually tried to hear something in my head and communicate it to my fingers. Even when I played a root-5th figure I always tried to make it melodic. Bass players are allowed to play melody, you know. Like on "Bernadette": That's built off a root-5th thing, but you can sing it like a song. Probably my best melodic performance was on the Marvin Gaye/Tammi Terrell version of "Ain't No Mountain High Enough." I should have written a pop tune off that melody. I could have retired to Jamaica. A lot of bass players play patterns because they fit nicely under their hands—but when you just play what you hear and feel, it takes you into places on the neck where it might be harder to play, but you have to get over that. Otherwise you're just a machine.

Goofing around at Motown's Studio A was a big part of the scene with you and the rest of the Funk Brothers.

Well, probably me more than anyone else. See, now I don't have any problems—no pressure, no heartaches, just total peace. But it amazes me when I think how crazy I was sometimes with all the fightin' and drinkin'. In that situation you had to do some crazy things just to keep from losing it. You know what it's like to cut a track over and over—25, 30 times in a row? I'd play it differently each time, and they'd all be good, but they kept making me do it over. On one Smokey session we were doing a song called "Flower Girl," and I got so sick of repeating it I stormed out of the studio. My son was sitting there, and when I walked out he wound up cutting the tune. But usually I'd just start messin' around to lighten things up before I walked. Otherwise, I might have hit somebody.

How important were the Funk Brothers to your music and your emotional stability?

My eventual failure in Los Angeles should tell you that. [*Motown moved from Detroit to Los Angeles in 1972. Although Jamerson and other musicians followed, the Funk Brothers never worked together again.*] That was the baddest rhythm section ever. I loved those guys; it was such a creative experience. I understood them, and they knew where I was coming from. Going out to the West Coast, where no one knew who I was and what I could do, was frustrating. A lot of the time they just made me read—no creativity at all. The Funk Brothers were like my family, and I guess I needed to be surrounded by that to be at my best musically.

There was so much magic in your Precision Bass. The Funk Brothers looked at it with a kind of reverence. Its theft in 1983 must have hit you hard.

That almost killed me more than the booze. We'd been together day and night for 20 years. Maybe the person will come forward and turn it in. I'd love to see it in the Rock & Roll Hall of Fame.

Any parting words for our readers?

I'd like to thank all the bassists who participated in the *Standing in the Shadows* book. I never dreamed everyone would come out for me like that. It's nice to know I wasn't forgotten.

Paul McCartney: Meet The Beatle

By Tony Bacon

Deep in the Sussex countryside, a few hours' drive out of London, is the secluded drive that leads to Paul McCartney's studio, a converted mill with a warm, friendly atmosphere. You can't help noticing the clear ambiance of the studio's owner and his impressive history at every step: here an aging map of Liverpool on the wall, there a yellow sticky with a note to ring George Martin, over in the corner a big acoustic bass propped against the wall.

Paul arrives. He ignores my inane grin, shakes my hand, grins himself so I don't feel alone, and steers me to a seat. Within seconds he has picked up the upright and announces that his wife, Linda, bought it as a present, and that it used to belong to Elvis Presley's original bassman, Bill Black. "I went into a guitar shop in America a few years ago," he offers, putting down the big bass, "and some guy asked, 'What kind of bass strings do you use, Paul?' I said, 'Long shiny ones.' I don't know the model names of basses, I don't know about amps, I don't know about serial numbers. With us it was always just Vox, Hofner—I never really got into the analytical end of it." I'm not about to press the great man too much on his self-analysis. But you started out as a guitarist, Paul, didn't you?

"I would have been about 15 or something, and me Dad bought me a trumpet, because it was kind of a heroic instrument at that time. Me dad had been a trumpet player, so he showed me a bit. But I realized I couldn't sing with the trumpet, and I wanted to sing as well, so I asked him if he wouldn't mind if I traded it in for a guitar."

So the young McCartney picked up a Zenith acoustic and started to learn to play. But he soon realized something was wrong. The guitar was right-handed; Paul wasn't. "I didn't know what you did about that. Nobody talked about being left-handed. Then I saw a picture of [singer/guitarist] Slim Whitman in one of the music papers, and I noticed—hang on, he's got the guitar on the wrong way 'round. I thought, That's good, you *can* have it the other way 'round. Then I changed the strings around.

"I met John and George about the same time. George used to get on the same bus; we got to chatting because he had an interest in guitars and music like I did, and we kind of hung out and became friends. Meanwhile I'd met John through another friend of mine, and he'd asked me to join the Quarrymen, which was my very first group. I went in as lead guitarist, really, because I wasn't bad on guitar. When I wasn't onstage I was even better—but when I got up onstage my fingers all went very stiff and found themselves underneath the strings instead of on top of them. So I vowed that first night it was the end of my career as the lead guitar player.

"Then we went to play in Hamburg, Germany, and before we left I'd bought a Rosetti Solid Seven electric guitar. It was terrible—really just a good-looking piece of wood. It fell apart when I got to Hamburg, so with my guitar bust I turned to the piano.

"Stu Sutcliffe was a friend of John Lennon's—they were at art school together—and Stu had won a painting competition. The prize was 75 quid [about $150]. We said to him, 'That's exactly the price of a Hofner bass!' He said, 'It's supposed to be for painting materials,' but we managed to persuade him over a cappuccino."

> "Once I got over the fact that I was lumbered with bass, I did get quite proud to be a bass player."

Sutcliffe became the Beatles' bass player after his prize money had been handed over the counter at Hessy's music shop in Liverpool for a lovely new Hofner 500/5 bass, a full-size hollowbody model. "It kind of dwarfed him a bit," says Paul. "He was a smallish guy, but it looked kind of heroic. He stood a certain way, he had shades, he looked the part—but he wasn't that good a player. He hadn't played anything up to buying that bass. Any of our mates could look at the group and spot it and say: 'Lousy bass player, man.'"

Sometimes they'd even find themselves telling the hapless Stu to turn away if someone was taking photos, because they didn't want the more sharp-eyed to notice Sutcliffe might very well be playing in the wrong key. A bit paranoid? Well, Paul remembers that the first thing they'd do when they saw a photo of a band in action was to check out the fingering on the guitars. "We always used to look for that, and I still do," he laughs. "You know, to see if Elvis could play guitar, in [the movie] *The Girl Can't Help It* or whatever. That was one of the things we used to love about guys in the audience: The girls would look at *us*; and the guys would look at the *chords*. We'd nudge each other and say, 'Look, this guy down here'—and he'd be looking deadly serious at you. You could see him copping all the chords."

Ticket To Ride

"None of us wanted to be the bass player," admits Paul. "It wasn't the #1 job. In our minds it was the fat guy in the back of the group who nearly always played the bass. We wanted to be up front singing, looking good, to pull the birds."

The Beatles played a second grueling season of Hamburg gigs in mid 1961. "Stu said he was going to stay in Hamburg. He'd met a girl and was going to stay with her and paint. So it was like, Uh-oh, we haven't got a bass player. And everyone sort of turned 'round and looked at me—it was like, 'Well … it'd better be you, then.' I don't think you would have caught John doing it; he would have said, 'No, you're kidding—I've got a nice new Rickenbacker!' I was playing piano and didn't even have a guitar at the time, so I couldn't really say I wanted to be a guitarist."

You may have seen the Beatles' Hamburg period portrayed in the movie *Backbeat*. In one scene McCartney's character picks up Sutcliffe's right-handed bass and plays it left-handed and upside down. Did you really do that, Paul? "I did, yes. I had to—guys wouldn't let you change their strings around! When John wasn't there I'd pick up his guitar and play it upside down. John did that with mine as well; he got pretty good playing upside down because of me."

Paul had to find a bass guitar of his own, so one day in 1961 he went shopping in Hamburg. Eventually he found a little shop with a violin-shaped bass guitar in the window. This was the famous "violin bass," a Hofner 500/1, made in Germany and similar in shape to Gibson's early Electric Bass model. McCartney recalls buying his first violin bass for the equivalent of about $45, and he insists it was a right-handed model he turned upside down—although all photographic evidence of those early years shows him with a production left-hander. McCartney has had a number of different versions of the Hofner 500/1 over the years, but he stuck to the model as his sole Beatles live-performance bass as well as his principal studio bass until the late '60s.

Paul still owns a Hofner from the Beatles days, and he still uses it for touring. "Because the Hofner's so light you play it a bit like a guitar. All that high trilling stuff I used to do, I think, was because of the Hofner. When I play a heavier bass like a Fender, it sits me down a bit and I play *just bass*. But I noticed in the *Let It Be* film that I play the Hofner right up there. Really, it led you to be a bit freer."

Did he listen to other bass players much? "Funnily enough, I'd always liked bass," he says. "I remember me dad giving me little lessons—not actual sit-down lessons, but maybe there'd be something on the radio and he'd say, 'Hear that low stuff? That's the bass.' So when I came to the Beatles I had a little musical knowledge through him—very amateur.

"Then I started listening to other bass players, mainly Motown. James Jamerson became my hero, although I didn't actually know his name. Jamerson and later the Beach Boys' Brian Wilson were my two biggest influences: James because he was so good and melodic, and Brian because he went to very unusual places. With the Beach Boys, the band might be playing in *C* but the bass might stay on the *G* just to hold it all back. I started to realize the power the bass player had within the band. Even though the whole band is going along in *A*, you could stick in *E*," he says, singing an insistent, repeated bass note. "And they'd say, 'Let us off the hook!' You're actually in control then—an amazing thing. So I got particularly interested in playing the bass."

Eight Days A Week

"Interested" is something of an understatement. Gradually the Beatles' bass parts became more and more important to the songs' melodic and harmonic development, and McCartney's thoughtful and often unconventional approach began to liberate the bass from its traditional role of simply providing unexciting and unchallenging roots beneath the chord progression. Not only that, Paul's engaging bass lines began to move forward in the mixes, and the band's interest in recording matters became almost as revolutionary as their composing skills.

"In the studio," Paul remembers, "it was very much us and them in the beginning. You entered by the tradesmen's entrance, set up your stuff, did your session, and left by the tradesmen's entrance. We were hardly ever asked to come up to the control room. Maybe at the end of a session it would be, [*adopts plummy upper-class British accent*] 'Would you like to come up and hear it, boys?' 'Oh *could* we? Thank you, mister.'" Engineers had to wear shirts and ties, and all the maintenance men had white coats. We hardly ever worked in the evening; only later did we get into those evening sessions. We mainly worked the two day-sessions, so it was down to the pub in the evening to talk about our exploits. For us it was like a job."

This recording regime led the band during the same day's session to record tracks as diverse as the blasting rocker "I'm Down" and the soothing ballad "Yesterday." How did they cope with that? "We just had to," McCartney shrugs. "Sing the rocker, that's done; sing the ballad. We had to be there at 10, ready to go at 10:30. So you'd let yourselves in, test your amps, get yourselves in tune. It didn't take long." Overseeing the proceedings, of course, was producer George Martin. "George would ask, [*adopts another plummy voice*] 'Right, chaps—what are you going to do?' And John and I would just show everyone what the song was. In the early days we all knew, because it was from the stage act. *Please Please Me* [released in the U.S. as *Introducing the Beatles*] was actually done from 10 in the morning until 10:30 at night. We just stayed all day and did the whole album. By the end of 'Twist and Shout' John couldn't have done another song. You can hear it on the record; his voice was just ripped. But we liked that—as long as we had a day off after, no problem. It was very, very loose. It would have bored us to rehearse too much; we knew the songs, so we'd get quite a lot done at those sessions."

Listening back to the early Beatles albums now, there are only a few bass parts that stand out. The problem was often not so much Paul's playing but the ill-defined recorded bass sound. Even so, it's hard not to be impressed by the sheer energy of the bass playing on "I Saw Her Standing There," or by the growing awareness of light and shade within "Please Please Me" and "A Taste of Honey." By spring 1964 there is a new confidence evident in the bass on tracks like "I'm Happy Just to Dance with You," while "When I Get Home" sounds like someone beginning to revel in the sheer sound of his instrument.

Getting Better

"Unlike people now, we were very keen that every track sounded different," Paul remembers. "We thought in singles, see. John and I we were always writing singles, so our albums—right up to *Sgt. Pepper*—were albums of singles. We thought the Supremes were a bit boring; it always sounded like the same song, or very near. They were trying to keep that Motown/Supremes sound. Well, we *weren't* trying to keep the Beatles sound—we were always trying to move on. We tried to get a new sound on every single thing we did."

A Style Is Born

Live at the BBC, the two-CD release of early Beatles recordings for the British Broadcasting Corporation, provides us with a wonderful portrait of the group's evolution from 1963–65. This was a critical period in the Beatles' development—and in the development of the electric bass. As you listen to these quickly recorded live tunes, you can hear Paul move away from the simple bass patterns he learned from early R&B and country music and begin to develop the melodic, contrapuntal style that would soon become his trademark.

Unfortunately the tracks are not arranged chronologically, so it takes a bit of skipping around to trace the evolution of McCartney's style. On the earliest cuts, such as "Keep Your Hands Off My Baby" (recorded January 1963), the bass playing is rudimentary: Paul's sound is blurry, and he sticks to root-five alternation broken up by the simplest of fills. Even so, you can tell he has a good feel for bass playing, and the other instrumental parts, even at this point, seem to hinge on his lines. By July 1963, Paul's lines are beginning to progress, and he occasionally breaks up the root-five patterns with walking lines and pumping triadic figures. *Something* is going on.

McCartney's bass playing really began to blossom as the Beatles wrote more original material. The BBC version of "I Saw Her Standing There," recorded in October 1963, is a big step forward—Paul's playing is more imaginative and has terrific rhythmic drive. And, on a cover of "Johnny B. Goode" recorded in January 1964, we hear a bass line that develops continually throughout the song, becoming more and more complex without ever losing the groove—a characteristic of many of the lines played by Paul's hero, James Jamerson.

Everything comes together on the version of "All My Loving" recorded at London's Piccadilly Theatre on February 28, 1964. The walking line under the verses is surprisingly sophisticated (especially since Paul is singing the lead vocal), and the bass line just *drives* the band. It's essentially the same part McCartney had played on the song's studio version (recorded six months earlier), but on this live track he's much more confident and prominent in the mix. For my money, it's the first truly great Paul McCartney bass line—and a sure sign of what was to come.

—*Jim Roberts*

A lot of this invention was necessarily spontaneous. In the early sessions, when the band was trying to squeeze out a couple of songs (or more) in a day, there was no time for philosophizing. The ability to think on one's feet and apply discipline—and, of course, just a little talent—began to spill over into the Beatles' individual instrumental contributions. "As time went on I began to realize you didn't have to play just the root notes," McCartney remembers. "If it was *C, F, G,* then I normally played *C, F, G.* But I started to realize you could be pulling on the *G,* or just stay on *C* when it went into *F.* And then I took it beyond that—I thought, Well, if you can do that, what else could you do, how much further could you take it? You might even be able to play notes that aren't in the chord. I just started to experiment."

Those experiments gradually led McCartney to come up with lines that were independent from the arrangement. "Michelle," recorded in November 1965, is an early example of this trend. "That was actually thought up on the spot," Paul reveals. "I would never have played 'Michelle' on bass until I had to record the bass line. Bass isn't an instrument you sit around and sing to. I don't, anyway. But I remember that opening six-note phrase against the descending chords in 'Michelle'—that was like, oh, a great moment in my life. I think I had enough musical experience after years of playing, so it was just in me. It's quite a well-known trick—I'm sure jazz players have done that against a descending sequence—but wherever I got it from, something in the back of my brain said, 'Do that. It's a bit more clever for the arrangement, and it'll really sound good on those descending chords.'"

By this time McCartney had added a left-handed Rickenbacker 4001S to his trusty Hofner for studio sessions, but he stuck with the Hofner for live work. "I was known for the violin bass," he says. "It's like Charlie Chaplin, you know? The little walking cane, mustache, and bowler hat. If he comes on with a bandanna and he's shaved and he's on a bike, it's like, 'Who's that?' Also, it was very light and I'd always played it live, so I might have been playing safe a bit, just using the instrument I'd always used."

Paul had been given the new Rickenbacker bass on the Beatles' August 1965 U.S. tour, and he started using it in the studio during October and November to record songs for *Rubber Soul.* From that point on in the studio he would alternate between the Rickenbacker and the Hofner—although by the time he recorded the superb "lead bass" parts for *Sgt. Pepper* in late 1966 and early '67, he was using the Rickenbacker as his main studio instrument.

Does Paul remember receiving the Rickenbacker? "Well, once we got to America we were quite famous, and Mr. [F.C.] Rickenbacker met us and said, 'John, we'd like to give you a presentation Rickenbacker,' and, 'Paul, we have a bass.' Oh, great! Freebie. Thank you very much! But it's very difficult to remember a lot about the Beatle tours, because when we weren't playing we were off, and we were either being whisked around or having a party. Actually, remembering it the morning after was difficult—never mind 30 years after!"

Paul says the long-scale Rickenbacker felt different and stayed in tune better than the Hofner. "It sounded a little clearer, too, and it seemed a little heavier—not just literally heavier, but it played a little more solid than the Hofner." From *Rubber Soul* onwards "it could have easily swung either way" between his using the Hofner or the Rick.

I show Paul a picture from the *Rubber Soul* sessions where he's using a capo on the Rickenbacker. "I'd try anything once. I often use a capo when I'm writing a song—just so it's a different instrument than the one I normally play. Everything goes up a little and goes more tingly, and you get a song that reflects that. So it may have been that we'd written a song on guitar in a certain key and I only knew it in that key, or maybe it was to get a higher sound. I often tuned the strings down a tone, too, so the *E* would become a *D*. I would mess around with any experimental effects. I'd try anything!"

Day Tripper

By the time of *Revolver* (recorded April–June 1966) McCartney's bass playing had become wonderfully fluent, roaming pretty much wherever he wanted. "Rain," released on a single during that period, is an all-time highlight. And when *Sgt. Pepper* appeared in June 1967 rock bass playing moved up another notch. The Rickenbacker's directness and clarity aided Paul's new quest for distinctive bass lines. "I was thinking maybe I could even run a little tune through the chords that doesn't exist anywhere else," he remembers. "*Sgt. Pepper* ended up being my strongest thing on bass. On 'Lucy in the Sky with Diamonds', for example, you could easily have had root notes, whereas I was running an independent melody through it, and that became my thing. It's really only a way of getting from *C* to *F* or whatever, but you get there in an interesting way. So once I got over the fact that I was lumbered with bass, I did get quite proud to be a bass player. It was all very exciting. Once I realized the control I had over the band, *I* was in control. They can't go anywhere, man. Ha! Power!

"I then started to identify with other bass players and talk bass with the guys in the bands. In fact, when we met Elvis he was trying to learn bass, so I was like, 'You're trying to learn bass, son? Sit down and let me show you a few things.' As it went on and I got into that melodic thing, that was probably the peak of my interest."

McCartney was probably responsible for more people becoming aware of the power and potential of bass guitar in the mid-to-late '60s than anyone else. "I think Jamerson, him and me, I'd share the credit there. I was nicking a lot off him. That was the thing, though—it did become a lot more of a funky instrument. It was becoming almost like a drum, the rhythmic possibilities."

Around the time the group recorded *Magical Mystery Tour* (April–December 1967), Paul's Rickenbacker got a psychedelic paint job; you can see the hippie-dippy colors in the film. "Yep, I got out the old aerosols," Paul confirms. "We were all doing that: George did his guitar, and we did the cars. If you did the cars, you might as well do your guitars. It looked great. It was just 'cause we were tripping—that's what it was, man. Look at your guitar and you'd trip even more. I sort of grew out of that, like most people did. But you know, I'm a bit of a visual man. I paint a lot, and we were always involved in album covers and fashions. John went to art school, Stuart was a painter . . . ." And Ringo? "Ringo was a drummer," he laughs, "but he could paint a nice apartment—two coats, one afternoon."

Despite McCartney's own estimation that his bass playing reached a creative peak with *Sgt. Pepper*, the group's last three albums—*The Beatles* ("The White Album," recorded May–October 1968), *Let It Be* (January–May 1969) and *Abbey Road* (April–August 1969)— are not exactly undistinguished when it comes to bass. Highpoints include the insistent line underpinning "Dear Prudence" from *The Beatles*, the swooping, joyous part on "I Want You (She's So Heavy)" from *Abbey Road*, and of course the fantastic lick underpinning "Come Together" from the same album.

Hello, Goodbye

When the Beatles closed shop in 1970, McCartney felt a huge void in his life. "It was very difficult to suddenly not be in the Beatles, after my whole life except my childhood had been involved with being in this very successful group. Once it was clear we weren't doing the

Beatles anymore I got real withdrawals and had serious problems. I just thought, I'm not even getting up—don't even ring, don't set the alarm. I started drinking, not shaving; I just didn't care, as if I'd had a major tragedy in my life and was grieving. And I was."

Gradually Paul began to get out of that, greatly helped by his wife's support. "She'd say, 'Come on—this can't go on too long, you know. You're good. You're either going to stop doing music or you'd better get on with it.' So then we started to put little things together, and it sort of got me back into being interested in music. It got rid of a bit of the fear of, well, how do you follow the Beatles?"

The answer, of course, was Wings. Although McCartney could have assumed any role he wished in that band, he chose to be the bass player. Why? "Because I always approach a tour by thinking as if I'm not there: 'Well, this geezer McCartney's going on tour. What would I like to see him do? Well, I'd like to see him play bass. He's good on that old bass.' So I'd think: I must play bass. And the audience would probably want me to do 'Yesterday,' so we'll sling that in somewhere."

Paul looks back on his Wings bass playing as less pioneering than the Beatles work. "I think it was okay, but I never quite had the interest I had during that period around *Rubber Soul* and *Sgt. Pepper*. I think that was a 'prize period' when I was playing my best bass. I could concentrate everything on writing the song, singing harmony with John, and playing the bass—pretty much my role—or maybe playing a bit of piano or guitar or something. Other than that I really didn't have much to do, so I could put all my energy into that. After that I sidelined the bass role a bit, in favor of the frontman role. It was not really my favorite thing to do, but there was nothing else to do. With Wings I was the bandleader, the business manager, the this, the that. We didn't have Apple, we didn't have [Beatles' manager Brian] Epstein, we didn't have anything—it was me doing it all. That was the biggest headache. In the Beatles I'd been free of all of that; we had a manager, and we had three other great guys.

"With the Beatles we'd play onstage for about 25 minutes, if you were lucky—and I did only about ten minutes, because John would do ten, George would do a bit, Ringo'd do a song, and we'd be off. And we'd do it quicker if we were annoyed—we'd be off in 20 minutes. If you think about it, I was 20-odd then and I was doing maybe 15 minutes. It's incredible that I can even handle two hours these days. But life goes on—there it is. I'm still at it."

Larry Graham: One In A Million

By Tony Green

The '60s and '70s funk tradition produced more than its share of unsung virtuosos—players whose styles and sounds have become staples of the pop vocabulary, leaving indelible marks on our ears and minds. But if you want to hear the most influential, distinctive, innovative funk musician of all time, there's only one name you need to know: Larry Graham, a.k.a. Mr. Thunderlicks, the original—and still supreme—thumb-slapper.

Born on August 14, 1946, Graham can still rattle sternums and rearrange tectonic plates—and the mere mention of his name can cause even a bass Stagolee like Bootsy Collins to gush. "When I got with Funkadelic," remembers Bootsy, "Larry once invited me up to his room to jam. He handed me his bass, and I said, 'Don't even try it. *You* play the bass, and I'll watch.' I will never be able to do that technique as well as he does. He's the ultimate slap machine."

Nonetheless, Graham may be the most influential bassist nobody knows. Sure, he's a household name to the bass cognoscenti—but the world at large thinks of him only as the voice behind the 1980 hit ballad "One in a Million You." Most folks don't remember him for his groundbreaking work with Sly & the Family Stone, nor do they think of him as the man who defined an entire musical genre with his thumb. Even so, people know Graham's sound—even when they hear it done by someone else. Louis Johnson, Marcus Miller, Stanley Clarke, Me'Shell NdegéOcello, Les Claypool, Flea … anyone who has ever whomped a bass string or snapped it off the fingerboard is honoring the most honorable Mr. Graham.

Although slapping had been used by upright players for decades (Milt Hinton and Cuban legend Israel "Cachao" López are good examples), Graham's thunder-thumb approach—first with Sly and later with Graham Central Station—turned the electric bass world on its ear. "I was in high school when I first heard Larry," says Jamaaladeen Tacuma, who played with Ornette Coleman's Prime Time band and has several acclaimed solo albums under his belt. "I thought, Man, this is crazy—this makes no sense." Graham, however, still has an aw-shucks attitude about his status. "The thing is, I never saw myself as a revolutionary," he has said. "All I was doing was what sounded good to me. But it has become an accepted way of playing the bass, to the point where people take it for granted. Most of the young kids you see doing thump-and-pluck don't even know who I am. Even people who came to my shows back in the Sly & the Family Stone days didn't know I was the man behind the bass."

Oakland Roots

Though he's Texan by birth, most of Graham's musical and personal growth took place in Oakland, California. His family—which included a guitar-playing father and a jazz piano-playing mother—moved there when Larry was two. An early student of drums and tap dance, Graham later picked up the clarinet, guitar, and sax, listening to such musicians as Ray Charles, Nat King Cole, and Frankie Lymon & the Teenagers.

By the time he was 15, Larry was accompanying his mother at clubs around town. "We had a trio," he remembers. "Me, my mother, and a drummer. One club we played at had an

organ with bass footpedals, and I found a way to use the footpedals while playing the guitar." When the organ broke down, Graham switched to bass, hoping to fill in the low end until the organ was back in commission. As fate would have it, the organ never got fixed, leaving Larry on an instrument he never intended to play full-time. "So I went out and got an old St. George bass. I wasn't concerned with playing it in the traditional way, because I didn't see myself as a bass player. In my mind I was still a guitar player, so I didn't care that bass players might think I couldn't play or was doing it wrong." Then something even more crucial happened: The band lost its drummer, leaving Graham as the entire rhythm section.

"That's when I started thumping with my thumb. It was the only way I could get that rhythmic sound."

In the process, Graham tapped into not only a new sound but an extremely powerful musical legacy. The "every-instrument-a-rhythm-instrument" concept is a major part of West African music and has found its way into all African-derived styles, including Afro-Cuban, Afro-Brazilian, reggae, and rock. The layered rhythms of Bo Diddley, the famous New Orleans "second line" style, and the soul-funk of James Brown all have roots in the musical approaches of West Africa and Afro-Latin America. But Graham didn't just adopt a rhythmic attitude; he transferred actual drum figures to the bass. His thumb would play the kick-drum parts, and his plucking fingers would simulate snare rhythms. This simple-sounding concept turned the bass into a hybrid instrument, capable of interacting with a drummer or percussionist with the same force as a conga, timbale, or trap drum while still holding down a supportive, melodic role.

Like A Rolling Stone

Graham mastered his new approach while he and his mother gigged around San Francisco's Haight-Ashbury scene. After a few shows at a place called Relax With Yvonne in 1968, Larry caught the attention of a popular local deejay named Sylvester Stewart—also known as Sly Stone—who was looking to put together his own band. "One particular woman came in all the time and loved us," Larry remembers, "and she was also a fan of Sly. When she heard Sly was trying to put together a band, she told him to come check us out. And he did."

Stone was impressed. Graham—armed with either a Fender Precision or a Vox bass—soon was part of what was to become one of pop's greatest outfits. Sly's songwriting and arranging genius and the Family Stone's churning rhythms garnered the band fans from Haight-Ashbury to New York's 125th Street.

Drummer Greg Errico propelled that rhythm. Graham had felt his style might explode when set against a percussion instrument, but in Errico he found a near-perfect match: a drummer powerful enough to match Larry's aggressive playing yet sensitive enough to leave space. "Greg knew how to play *around* me instead of colliding with me," Graham says. "He wasn't busy to the point where there wasn't any room to do anything. He was a solid foundation man—and that's where all the good funk starts, at the bottom. It's just like building a house."

As Sly's music grew in popularity, so did Graham's bass style. It took a while for the thump-and-pluck technique to catch on—but once it did, it spread like mad. Sly's songs were hits, which meant that if you were playing his songs in a cover band, you had to play Graham-style bass. At the time, that was a daunting task for even the most talented players. "I first saw Larry around the time I was with James Brown," says Bootsy Collins. "I thought, How is this cat playing with his thumb? He was doing amazingly unheard-of things."

Despite the many high-profile players who followed in his wake, Graham's pick as the next-best thumb-slapper is Kenny Burke, who played with the R&B group the Five Stairsteps. "Kenny used to hang around a lot during the early Sly days," says Larry, "so he picked up that technique directly from me. At the time there wasn't a bunch of guys copying me yet, and there was no such thing as an instructional video—so a bass player had no way to find out what I was doing unless he saw me at a show. And even then he still might not know. But Kenny had a head start on everybody."

Soon Sly and Larry were riding high on a string of hits—but the group's fame and success magnified Stone's egocentric and often self-destructive tendencies. By the early '70s his behavior had become increasingly erratic, resulting in a slew of missed appointments and concert no-shows. Sly also alienated band members by overdubbing tracks himself, including several on the epochal *There's a Riot Goin' On*. Still, Graham was a strong presence, making a huge contribution on hits like "Smilin' (You Caught Me)" and "Runnin' Away," as well as the crushing slow-groover "Thank You for Talkin' to Me Africa," from *Riot*. But the internal and external pressures spelled doom for the Family Stone. "I wasn't the first one to leave," says Larry. "I left in '72, but it had started to deteriorate long before that. There's always a chance we'll get back together, as long as Sly is alive and working. But that's on him. It's his decision."

The Station Mutation

The disintegration of the original Family Stone left the door open for Graham to form his own group—something he hadn't thought about until the Stone situation became too much to take. Even then, he wasn't interested in performing. He had planned to write for and produce a group he had assembled called Hot Chocolate—but after a single jam with Graham, everyone knew Larry was going to be the bassist.

Renaming the band Graham Central Station, Larry went on to carve his own niche. While Sly's success lay in his ability to meld deadly beats with unforgettable pop hooks, Graham Central Station's sound ran the gamut from ballads to doo-wop and excelled at over-the-top, take-no-prisoners funk. It seemed nothing made them happier than setting a groove loose—giving it a good running start and then running it down like a pack of hunting dogs (as on the eight-minute workout "The Jam," issued as a single and available on *The Best of Larry Graham and Graham Central Station, Vol. 1*). And Graham's bass was usually leading the charge.

"When we wrote songs for Graham Central Station," Larry remembers, "we'd often start with the bass line. On 'Hair,' for example [*Graham Central Station*], the drums were built around the bass pattern. And when we did covers, like our version of Al Green's 'It Ain't No Fun to Me' [*Graham Central Station*], it would always sound like us, because I'd always play the bass line in my style."

Standing In The Shadows

Even as the Larry Graham sound spread throughout the music world, his name remained unrecognized by the general public. That got even worse as things got better. He scored the biggest hit of his career, "One in a Million You," in 1980 [*One in a Million You*]—only it was his voice, not his fingers, that brought him fame. The lush R&B ballad, which showcased Larry's full-grain baritone, earned him his highest visibility as the tune shot to #1 on the R&B charts and #9 on the pop charts. "One group of fans would come to shows all dressed up for ballads, and the other would be in jeans, wanting to hear the funky stuff. But when I went onstage, people found out the 'One in a Million' guy was the same person behind the funk."

Things are a little better now, says Graham. There's more education about the music, and more and more people are waking up to his playing. "When it comes to who the musicians are, people generally don't know any better," he says. "But the music speaks for itself. You play some of the old funk stuff for a kid today, and he'll go, 'Wow! What's that new jam?' It's not new—it just sounds good because it's always going to be good music."

Stanley Clarke: Stan Is Still The Man

By Karl Coryat

Stanley Clarke is among the most elite of bassists: His name is a household word. But unlike Sting and Paul McCartney, whose fame rose out of the popularity of their hit bands, Clarke got to where he is the hard way—with only his hands and his instrument. He made important contributions to the bass world with Return To Forever and in guest appearances with such artists as guitarists Al DiMeola and John McLaughlin, being the first jazzer to lean heavily on the slap-and-pop techniques pioneered by Larry Graham and Louis Johnson. But Stanley's biggest claim to fame has been his solo career, which began when jazz-rock fusion was in full swing. He struck paydirt when his 1976 effort *School Days* became a crossover hit, the title track snaring listeners with its unforgettable parallel-fifths bass hook. At that point, Stanley Clarke became almost synonymous with bass virtuosity.

These days Clarke divides his time between his solo career and a lucrative business writing film and TV soundtracks. He spends about 75% of his time doing the latter, having left his musical mark on such major motion pictures as *Boyz N the Hood*, *Passenger 57*, and *What's Love Got to Do with It*. In his Beverly Hills home he's built a state-of-the-art recording facility that employs a crew of support personnel, including a studio engineer, and he writes and arranges full scores for 80-piece orchestras. Not bad for a bass player, huh?

Bleeding Fingers

Stanley was born in North Philadelphia on June 30, 1951, the son of Blanche and Marvin Clarke. His first exposure to music was through his mother, who sang opera. After a brief and "embarrassing" period on accordion, Stanley switched to violin—but as he grew and grew and grew (he's now 6'4") he graduated to cello and then to string bass. Formally trained from the beginning, Clarke began to hone his bass chops on the Simandl method (*New Method for the Double Bass*, Carl Fischer), and by the time he reached the 12th grade he had become a *very* serious student. "I locked myself up," he remembers. "It was almost sickening how serious I was about it—eight hours a day, bleeding fingers, everything. At the time I was in some *very* avant-garde groups that played music by composers like John Cage. We didn't really play what I would call music; it was more like noise. My parents thought I was nuts!"

At age 16, when the "conventional" after-school jobs he was holding down weren't quite working out, Clarke decided to try playing music for money. The first thing he did was buy an electric bass. "It was a Kent hollowbody that cost $29," he remembers. "I didn't even have a case; I used to put it in a bag." Stanley joined a blues combo, a country outfit, and then a Top-40 band, jumping headfirst into the Holiday Inn circuit. Along the way he picked up ideas from guitarists Jimi Hendrix, Jeff Beck, and Eric Clapton as well as bassists Jack Bruce and Noel Redding. Meanwhile, his classical education continued. "I was like Dr. Jekyll and Mr. Hyde—one minute I'd be listening to Hendrix, and then it was Bach, Beethoven, and Wagner. I also started getting into jazz, and I started to check out bassists like Charles

Mingus, Scott LaFaro, and Paul Chambers. I was heavily into rock, classical, *and* jazz—all three." Clarke attended the Philadelphia Academy of Music for three-and-a-half years, studying string bass and composition, but he soon got the itch to leave Philly for New York. Realizing a diploma wasn't going to do him any good anyway, he dropped out. "Leaving Philadelphia was a decision that was absolutely correct," he says.

Alone in the Big Apple with just his Gibson EB-2 and some clothes, Clarke began to root out work. He gigged with pianist Horace Silver, played on TV-commercial dates, and landed some sessions with Aretha Franklin, Carlos Santana, Stan Getz, and Art Blakey.

Fusion Forays

The first major turning point in Clarke's career came in 1971, with the birth of Return To Forever. Stanley had worked with drummer Lenny White and was an acquaintance of keyboardist Chick Corea, who had just left Miles Davis' group. Corea decided to put together an electric band, and he found instant chemistry with Clarke and White. RTF quickly became one of the flagships of the rapidly growing jazz-rock fusion genre. After the first couple RTF records struggled in stores, the band regrouped and made a string of influential and critically acclaimed records, beginning with 1972's highly successful *Hymn of the Seventh Galaxy*.

Clarke is often credited with introducing electric slap bass to jazz. Surprisingly, his introduction to the technique came not from Larry Graham but from Lenny White, who had modified Graham's approach. "Lenny didn't really know what he was doing on the bass, but he had great rhythm," says Stanley. "Since I learned from him, my slapping was a little different." But while Graham and his contemporaries stuck mostly to the key of *E*, Clarke transposed the technique to other keys. "Chick wrote tunes in *A♭, C♯*—everything. I didn't get a chance to slap in *E* until I did my solo stuff, and that was like a release—*whew!*—because it was so much easier."

Another important turning point came in 1973. "We were playing at a San Francisco club, and this guy came up to me and said my playing was great but my sound was atrocious. It was Rick Turner, who was with Alembic at the time. He had a bass with him, so I tried it out. It was like a new bass player was born that night—suddenly I could play anything I heard in my head." That was the beginning of a long relationship with Alembic. Clarke's current collection of Alembics is so big he doesn't know how many he owns.

In the mid '70s Clarke came into his own as a solo artist. Although he had released a 1972 solo album on which he played acoustic exclusively (*Children of Forever*), 1975's *Stanley Clarke* was the first record he considered truly his. With a strong backing band, including drummer Tony Williams and keyboardist Jan Hammer, *Stanley Clarke* established the bassist as a serious contender in fusion. With the smash success of the follow-up, *School Days*, there was little doubt Clarke had arrived. He continued to put out solo albums throughout the '70s and '80s and participated in numerous ensembles, including forays into pop with the Clarke/Duke Project (with keyboardist George Duke) and Animal Logic, a rock group with ex-Police drummer Stewart Copeland and vocalist/keyboardist Deborah Holland. Clarke's trademark staccato soloing and popping has inspired players of many different styles, from Michael Manring to Les Claypool to practically anyone else who's laid thumb to string.

Well-Oiled Chops

In 1985, Clarke took his first steps into the soundtrack world. "I was working with the director of *Pee Wee's Playhouse*, Steve Binder, on something completely unrelated to the show.

He mentioned they were doing an episode on childbirth and said they wanted some slightly unusual music—something a little stranger and heavier than usual—to go along with it. He asked if I was interested, and I said, 'Man, I'm not into that stuff.' But he talked me into it anyway." Clarke went out and bought a Macintosh computer, a MIDI keyboard, and some software, and with a lot of manual-reading he managed to finish the job. "Amazingly," he says, "I got an Emmy nomination for that show. I began thinking, Maybe I should stick with this!" But it wasn't until he tackled an episode of HBO's *Tales from the Crypt* that he really got the scoring bug. "The raw footage they gave me wasn't scary at all. There was this one scene where someone was sawing off a guy's leg, and it looked kind of fake. But as soon as I put a low drone under everything, it was like, *whoa!* Everything changed. It was then I realized the power music can have in a film."

Today Clarke's skills are highly sought-after by film and TV producers, and he loves the work. "When you write for films, you can deal with a lot of dynamics of life you can't get into with records. With pop or jazz, the music is mostly love- or dance-oriented—but with films you can write music that's terrifying, or antagonistic, or serene. For a composer, that's real nice."

Stanley reveals that these days, impressing listeners is his *last* priority. "The older I get the more I learn to put everything into proper perspective. When I recorded my first couple of records I'd worry about what people thought. It's not that I don't care anymore, but after getting many good reviews and many bad reviews, I guess I've become jaded. I appreciate that people have opinions, but I've learned you simply can't control human thought. There are people out there who like what I do, and there are people who hate it—but after all I've been through, I'd be a dead man if I thought too much about it."

Jaco Pastorius: The Rise Of A Legend, 1967–72

By Bill Milkowski

From the moment he burst onto the scene with his incredible 1976 solo debut, Jaco revolutionized the electric bass. The uncanny playing on *Jaco Pastorius* [Epic], with its speed, agility, chordal techniques, improvisational daring, and unprecedented use of harmonics—all delivered with impeccable time and a potent, earthy feel—quickly pushed Jaco to the forefront of the bass world. By 1978 he had attained supernatural status through his virtuosic command of the instrument and his larger-than-life stage presence with Weather Report.

Jaco's first instrument was the drums—his father, Jack, was a drummer—but he switched to bass at age 15 after breaking his wrist. At the time he had been playing drums in a local cover band, Las Olas Brass. Although Jaco had never touched a bass before, he picked one up at a pawnshop and began playing effortlessly right away, as if predestined. His big hands were definitely an advantage, as were his keen ears and strong sense of time. With these gifts and his innate musicality, it wasn't long before Jaco was creating a stir around South Florida. Brother Rory Pastorius remembers Jaco's rapid progress. "By the time he was 16, he was probably the best bass player in South Florida. By the time he was 17 he was definitely the best bass player in the state. Then, just before his 18th birthday, Jaco looked me right in the eye and said, really seriously, 'Rory, I'm the best bass player on earth.' I just looked at him and said, 'I know.'"

Brother Gregory contends that Jaco's development was more a product of hard work than Divine Providence: "We'd be watching TV, and Jaco would practice the entire time, working out patterns on the fingerboard. He had made this mini-amp in shop class at school—he could plug in his bass and a set of headphones—and he'd sit on the couch for hours with that thing, constantly moving his fingers. Jaco became so serious about practicing that he used it as an excuse to get out of household chores. I remember him telling our mom, 'This is what I do now. I can't do dishes anymore because the dishwater softens my calluses.' And she was really supportive of him and went along with it."

Bob Bobbing, a close friend and one of Jaco's biggest fans in those days, has several tapes that document Jaco's career from 1967 through 1975, beginning with the Las Olas Brass, continuing through the bands Woodchuck and Tommy Strand & the Upper Hand, and concluding with his celebrated stint as a member of Wayne Cochran & the C.C. Riders, a 14-piece R&B show band. In assessing Jaco's development Bobbing cites three important early milestones: "Jaco's metamorphosis from an R&B nightclub bass player to a unique stylist really began in 1967, when he and I walked into the She Lounge in Fort Lauderdale to check out a band. Their bass player, Carlos Garcia, was using a muting technique that was really funky. Carlos was able to get cool staccato notes, and Jaco really got off on how funky the bass sounded. He went home and began experimenting with muting techniques.

"The next thing that happened was harmonics. Jaco already knew about open harmonics, but I'm talking about false harmonics, where you extend your finger and pick behind it.

Continuum: A Jaco Chronology

December 1, 1951: John Francis III born in Norristown, PA, to Jack and Stephanie Pastorius.

September 1959: Family moves to Fort Lauderdale, Florida.

September 1963: Begins playing drums with the Sonics, a local combo.

Summer 1966: Joins Las Olas Brass as a drummer.

Summer 1967: Switches to bass guitar.

January 1972: Joins Wayne Cochran & the C.C. Riders.

Spring 1973: Begins teaching part-time at the University of Miami. Students include Mark Egan, Frank Gravas, and Hiram Bullock.

Summer 1974: Records a blues album, *Party Down*, with Little Beaver, and a jazz album with pianist Paul Bley, guitarist Pat Metheny, and drummer Bruce Ditmas.

Continued

1975: Records *Jaco Pastorius*, plays on Pat Metheny's *Bright Size Life*, and two cuts on Weather Report's *Black Market.*

1976: Joins Weather Report, plays and co-produces on *Heavy Weather.* Also appears on Joni Mitchell's *Hejira.*

1979: Joins Joni Mitchell's *Shadows and Light* tour, with Metheny, keyboardist Lyle Mays, saxophonist Michael Brecker, and drummer Don Alias.

1980: Records *Word Of Mouth* in Fort Lauderdale.

1982: Leaves Weather Report and tours with his Word Of Mouth big band.

1983: Warner Bros. releases *Invitation,* a selection of live tracks from '82 concerts in Japan. Tours with a sextet that includes guitarist Mike Stern.

1984: Forms trio with guitarist Hiram Bullock and drummer Kenwood Dennard.

September 1985: Arrested in Philadelphia for trying to break into his father's house. Voluntarily enters a rehabilitation center.

March 1986: Tours with guitarist Bireli Lagrene. Live album, *Stuttgart Aria,* is released on a German label, Jazzpoint.

July 1986: Committed to psychiatric ward of New York's Bellevue Hospital,

A guy named Clay Cropper showed that technique to me, and I passed it along to Jaco. His initial comment was something like, 'Oh, I've seen guitar players do that. I ain't got time for that. I'm too busy learning this other stuff.' But he eventually picked up on it in a big way.

"The third milestone was when Jaco got his first Acoustic 360 bass amp. Before that he had been using a Fender Dual Showman, which didn't have much power. Carlos Garcia had a 360, so Jaco bought two of them. With that amp he had the high end, clarity, and overdrive he needed to *really* rip. He could play chords and project really well. That's what gave Jaco his sound: that amp combined with his Fender Jazz Bass and the muting technique. Later he started using roundwound strings, which gave him a brighter sound and longer notes, and he really got his voice together."

Several of Jaco's intimates from the early years point to the organ trio Woodchuck as a key element in Jaco's evolution. "That was a killer band!" recalls Scott Kirkpatrick. "They had Jaco on bass, Bob Herzog on drums, and a guy on Hammond B-3 named Billy Burke. They had a house gig at Code One in Fort Lauderdale, and all the musicians in town used to drop by to check them out."

Bobbing was equally excited about Woodchuck. "That band really put Jaco on the map in South Florida. They had so much feeling and soul. Las Olas Brass was just a Top 40 cover band—but Woodchuck was *it.* That's where Jaco's funk lines started coming together, and that's when he started to become a performer. He was singing, and he had a lot of charisma onstage. It was the greatest little band in the world."

In 1970 Jaco hooked up with R&B group Tommy Strand & the Upper Hand. Kirkpatrick, who played drums in the band, recalls Jaco as the ultimate groove player, even back then. "I tell you, I've *never* played with anybody since who could groove like Jaco," he recalls. "I don't think there ever will be anybody else with that kind of groove power. With two fingers he was laying down the funkiest, most innovative lines I've ever heard in my life."

Around that time Jaco began to supplement his income by working on the cruise ships that sailed from the Miami. The music was cocktail-lounge jazz standards, but when the ships docked in places like St. Thomas and Nassau, Jaco went ashore to mingle with the local calypso and reggae musicians. He added the Caribbean sounds to his vocabulary, and their influence can be heard readily in the music he made with Weather Report and with his Word Of Mouth big band.

During the summer of 1970 Jaco married his high school sweetheart, Tracy Lee Sexton. Tracy gave birth to a daughter, Mary; Jaco took the responsibility of fatherhood quite seriously and became determined to make it as a musician in order to support his new family. "I remember when Mary was born," says Gregory. "We were looking at her through the glass in the maternity ward, and Jaco said, 'Well, Greg, this is it. Now I gotta be the greatest bass player that ever hit the planet. I gotta make a real living at this and not just play in stupid bars all my life.' He was ready to take on the world."

Early in 1972 Jaco joined Wayne Cochran & the C.C. Riders. "He was playing an hour-and-a-half nonstop, three sets a night, five nights a week or more," says Bobbing. "It was a big horn band with no keyboard, so Jaco could experiment with chords, harmonics, and that soloistic approach he became famous for, all while laying down an incredible groove. Every time the band would break it down, Jaco would be right there cooking, doing all his cool funk turnarounds. That gig was like the oven for Jaco Pastorius."

Charlie Brent, guitarist and musical director of the C.C. Riders, recalls Jaco's audition: "We went to see him when he was playing with Tommy Strand & the Upper Hand. I was

where he is diagnosed as manic depressive and placed on medication.

October 1986: Leaves Bellevue and flies to San Francisco, where he stays with drummer Brian Melvin and records several tracks.

December 1986: Returns to Florida. Begins an exercise program and plays with guitarist Randy Bernsen.

February 1987: Starts to self-destruct, drinking heavily and sleeping in parks. Crashes gigs and demands to sit in.

Summer 1987: Bizarre behavior continues. Arrested for various charges, including drunk and disorderly, driving without a license, and shoplifting. After hearing of the deaths of two childhood friends, goes into a deep depression and stops taking his medication.

September 11, 1987: Jumps onstage during a Santana concert in Fort Lauderdale and is ushered off by stagehands who don't recognize him.

September 12, 1987: Early in the morning, he tries to crash an after-hours club and is beaten senseless. Rushed to Broward County Medical Center, where he lies in a coma.

September 21, 1987: Pronounced dead at 10 PM.

completely floored by what I heard, so I asked Jaco to come up to Fort Lauderdale, where we were playing that week. He showed up one afternoon, and I whipped the book in front of him and counted off the show. He just completely burned it to pieces! Later I put out a new chart I had written for the rehearsal. Jaco told me he couldn't read. I said, 'Then how did you just play our whole book?' And he said, 'Well, I caught the show a couple of weeks ago.' That simply fried me—I mean, the kid had total recall!"

On the road with the C.C. Riders, Brent would sit in the back of the bus with Jaco and quiz him about music theory. "It was a rough grind," says Allyn Robinson, former drummer with the C.C. Riders. "We would do 40 one-nighters in a row, from Chicago to Miami, up the East Coast, over to Chicago, and back down to Miami. On the bus Jaco and Charlie would get into these quiz games. If they weren't doing that, then Jaco would be practicing. Every time I saw him, whether it was on the bus or at the hotel, he'd have a bass in his hands. The guy was so motivated it was inspiring."

The Essential Jaco: 25 Historic Tracks

Jaco's peak recording years lasted just over a decade, from the mid '70s to the mid '80s. During that short span he created startling new approaches to the electric bass. The following selections, listed roughly in chronological order, are his finest recordings, both as a player and as a composer and an arranger. Jaco's 1986 instructional video, *Modern Electric Bass* [DCI], is also an essential work, even though it was made past his prime. While any selected discography is arbitrary and open to debate, hearing one or two phrases from a random track is usually all it takes to appreciate a great artist's gift—and that certainly is the case with John Francis Pastorius III.

1. "Donna Lee," *Jaco Pastorius* [Epic, 1976]: The opening track on his astounding debut. It's still an eye-widening experience to hear his fretless '62 Fender Jazz "Bass of Doom" slither sensuously in and out of the Charlie Parker classic, accompanied only by Don Alias on percussion.

2. "Portrait of Tracy," *Jaco Pastorius*: Named for his first wife, "Portrait" is *the* study in bass harmonics. The angular changes and implied upper-structure chords also reveal Jaco's advanced harmony knowledge.

3. "Come On, Come Over," *Jaco Pastorius*: With its funky horn arrangement and vocals by Sam & Dave, "Come On" exposes Jaco's R&B foundation. It's also a prime example of his now-classic interpretation of the steady 16th-note grooves originated by Tower Of Power legend Francis "Rocco" Prestia.

4. "Continuum," *Jaco Pastorius*: With its gorgeous fretless melody, this tune established the trademark sound that would soon be imitated by a legion of bassists. It was later reprised, with big-band augmentation, on Jaco's third solo album, *Invitation*.

5. "Barbary Coast," Weather Report, *Black Market* [Columbia, 1976]: Jaco's

first track and composition for Weather Report, "Barbary Coast" is memorable for its slippery opening bass melody and slower, funkier version of his 16th-note groove—and for the immediate impact he had on the group.

6. "Round Trip/Broadway Blues," Pat Metheny, *Bright Size Life* [ECM, 1976]: On an album that featured two jazz phenoms—Jaco, 24, and Metheny, 21—no track was hotter than this straightahead Ornette Coleman medley featuring deft interplay, fine solo turns, and dazzling unison melodies.

7. "Coyote," Joni Mitchell, *Hejira* [Asylum, 1976]: The first of Jaco's four-album collaboration with Joni, *Hejira* established the pair's typical format, with Jaco roaming freely through the sparse accompaniment. On "Coyote" the up-front bass is an equal voice to Mitchell's, adding soaring contrapuntal melodies while nailing down the groove and punctuating the phrases with ringing harmonic figures (which expand the tonic C chord into a *Cmaj9* or *G/C*).

8. "Birdland," Weather Report, *Heavy Weather* [Columbia, 1977]; also on the live Weather Report double album *8:30* [Columbia, 1979]: Certainly, playing bass in Weather Report was Jaco's most visible role. *Heavy Weather* captured this edition of Joe Zawinul and company at their peak and may be Jaco's best all-around album. "Birdland," the band's "greatest hit," kicks off with Jaco's immortal false-harmonic melody, performed in two different octaves, and hits full stride during a joyous chorus where he lays down a soulful stomp and sings along, falsetto, with the synth melody. The live version is slightly faster and worth investigating for the swing-shuffle feel after Jaco's opening melody.

9. "A Remark You Made," *Heavy Weather*: This haunting ballad revolves around the alternating interpretations, by Jaco and Wayne Shorter (on tenor sax), of Zawinul's unforgettable theme. Listen also to the ideas each plays in support of the other.

10. "Teentown," *Heavy Weather*; also on *8:30*: Perhaps Jaco's best-known composition and a certified bass anthem. Memorable not only for his smooth, serpentine melody line but also for his crisp drumming. It's fast—and the live version (with Peter Erskine on drums) is even faster!

11. "Havona," *Heavy Weather*: Jaco's finest recorded solo and one of his best compositions. The solo quotes everything from Stravinsky's *Rite of Spring* to a Dial soap jingle; although it was reportedly constructed phrase by phrase in the studio, the magnificent end results justify the means. Equally breathtaking is the stuttering groove, which displays Jaco's Latin/Caribbean roots.

12. "Overture/Cotton Avenue," Joni Mitchell, *Don Juan's Reckless Daughter* [Asylum, 1977]: Listen for the crack of thunder in the "Overture" section: It's Jaco smacking his *E* string, which was tuned down to *C*. Throughout this entire album Jaco experiments with overdubbed bass parts and double-tracked unison lines.

13. "Las Olas," Flora Purim, *Everyday, Everynight* [Warner Bros., 1978]: On an album overlooked by many, this Brazilian-flavored cut captures the full force of Jaco's harmonic mastery and inspires an incredible piano solo by Herbie Hancock. Michel Colombier's moving ballad "The Hope," with Jaco's singing bass doubling Purim's vocal melody, also leaves a lasting impression.

14. "Punk Jazz," Weather Report, *Mr. Gone* [Columbia, 1978]: From the opening crack of Tony Williams's snare, Jaco appears to be setting up the sequel to "Teentown," unleashing frightening free-blowing in typical "Florida Flash" form—but there's a sudden mood swing, and the slower, richly orchestrated two-feel section is reminiscent of Duke Ellington.

15. "Dreamland," *Michel Colombier* [Chrysalis, 1979]: Nowhere is Jaco's gift for melody more evident than in his collaborations with French composer Colombier. "Dreamland," a contender for Jaco's best recorded melody, boasts the sensitive support of guitarist Larry Carlton, drummer Steve Gadd—and the London Philharmonic strings!

16. "Goodbye Pork Pie Hat," Joni Mitchell, *Mingus* [Asylum, 1979]: Joni's expanded version of the classic Mingus ballad comes alive with the pathos and poise from Jaco's array of new and vintage licks. Study this one closely.

17. "Dry Cleaner from Des Moines," *Mingus*; also on the live double album *Shadows and Light* [Asylum, 1980]: One of Jaco's greatest recordings. The uptempo live version concludes on a breathtaking note (literally!): Jaco tosses out increasingly abstract chord substitutions and rhythmic twists, and tenor saxophonist Michael Brecker weaves equally ridiculous lines around them. They push each other higher, chorus by chorus, until Brecker's furious squeals race Jaco's diminished climb to the finish line.

18. "Sweet Sucker Dance," *Mingus*: Mingus' melody guides Jaco into new terrain, where he drapes delicious countermelodies around Mitchell's vocals.

19. "4AM," Herbie Hancock, *Mr. Hands* [Columbia, 1981]: Another little-known track that nevertheless stands as one of Jaco's best recorded 16th-note grooves. Check out the gorgeous ending lick.

20. "3 Views of a Secret," *Word of Mouth* [Warner Bros., 1982]: Jaco's second solo album, *Word of Mouth* documents the ripening of his composing, arranging, and producing skills. The jazz-waltz "3 Views" first appeared with sparse accompaniment on Weather Report's *Night Passage* [Columbia, 1980]. One of Jaco's best.

21. "Liberty City," *Word of Mouth*: Count Basie, Jaco-style. "Liberty City" is one of Jaco's most awesome compositions and the jewel in his arranging crown. Tradition meets vision as Jaco covers the bass and guitar chairs with a vintage two-feel capped by cleverly inverted double-stops.

22. "John and Mary," *Word of Mouth*: With its symphonic theme/development/recap/coda structure, this cut hints at Jaco's sadly unfulfilled musical potential.

23. "Soul Intro/The Chicken," *Invitation* [Warner Bros., 1983]: Recorded live in Japan and adapted from composer Alfred James Ellis, this 16-bar R&B instrumental, which boasts a percolating, constantly developing, 16th-note bass line and a tidy horn arrangement, became a Pastorius standard. A more complete documentation of this concert is captured on two double-album Japanese imports, *Twins I* and *Twins II*.

24. "Amerika," *Invitation*: The live "Amerika" is perhaps Jaco's finest unaccompanied solo: He explores and embellishes "America the Beautiful" with single notes, implied chords, chordal harmonics, false harmonics, and stirring reharmonizations. A gem.

25. "Mood Swings," Mike Stern, *Upside Downside* [Atlantic, 1986]: Many of Jaco's later guest appearances ended up sounding like a compendium of his greatest licks. Here it's like the old days, as he lays down a funk groove complete with high-end chords and subtle phrase variations. There's one truly magical moment, when Jaco—walking an uptempo minor blues behind tenor saxophonist Bob Berg's solo—spontaneously matches Berg's eighth-note lick at the second-chorus turnaround. Even as his life was disintegrating, Jaco's musical instincts were infallible. —***Chris Jisi***

On the gig Brent relied on Jaco's inimitable grooves to drive his charts, and he often stood in awe of the sheer chops and ingenuity he heard on the bandstand. "He always played too much, which made everybody else crazy—but his time was so meticulous it never got in the way," says Brent. "He had perfect meter from the day I met him. There were times when Wayne would send the horns out into the audience and leave us up there vamping for 15 or 20 minutes. And Pastorius would cover both the rhythm guitar and bass parts at the same time while I took solos. That's when he got into playing changes with harmonics, just to fill in while we were up there vamping.

"I remember when he started playing fretless. We were somewhere in the Midwest, and Jaco said, 'Man, I wanna try one of those fretless basses.' So he goes down to the hardware store and buys some alligator pliers and wood compound. He takes those pliers and goes at the bass, tearing all the frets out—I mean, wood was flying. I was going crazy, yelling, 'Don't do this. That's the only axe you got on the road. You ain't gonna be able to play the gig tonight!' But I swear, that night he played better than he'd ever played. He was doing slides and all the other things he couldn't do before.

"One time when we were in Texas, he started hitting the harmonics on the 1st, 2nd, and 3rd frets—doing changes down there at the bottom. I'd never heard anybody do anything like that, but he had such a *touch*. He'd hit different strings with different pressure, do different changes—he could get three different chords at the 2nd fret. When he started doing that stuff, that's when I knew he was the messiah."

Brent roomed with Jaco on the road. "Nobody wants to room with a guy who's running around saying, 'Hey, I'm the greatest bass player in the world.' He kind of clashed with everybody, but he always backed up what he said. I mean, you can't say stuff like that unless you can back it up. Wayne didn't like the way Jaco was always saying he was the greatest, so it was a constant struggle. I was always trying to convince Wayne this kid was so good he was worth the aggravation. But Wayne didn't want to hear it."

Cochran had groomed his band with Vegas in mind, tuxedos and all. But Jaco the bohemian beach bum didn't go for that. "Jaco was a rebel," says Brent. "He wouldn't wear the band uniforms. I remember getting him a long cord so he could sit behind the stage and play. He just didn't believe in that kind of discipline.

"I taught Jaco everything I knew about music," continues Brent, "all about chord voicings and arranging, and then I left him running the band. If it wasn't for his personality, he might still be running that band. But he lasted only a few weeks after I left. He didn't have me to run interference for him, and Wayne just didn't want to put up with him anymore."

Allyn Robinson says that when Jaco joined the C.C. Riders his wardrobe consisted of a pair of tennis shoes, a pair of corduroy pants, and three T-shirts. "That's all he ever wore. He was just an odd bird. He lived on McDonald's fish sandwiches, had that one set of clothes, and carried his bass with him all the time. He checked into hotels as little as possible. He used to sleep on the beach instead—he'd save the money and send it back home to his wife and kids."

Both Brent and Robinson look back at Jaco's ten months in the C.C. Riders as a special time in their lives. "It was just magic," says Robinson. "The most beautiful thing about Jaco's playing wasn't the obvious stuff, like playing fast. It was his phrasing. He knew when to play and when not to play—a lot of times, he would just lay out. The music dictated the way he played, and he always made it say something. Jaco was always true to the style, and anything he put on top of it seemed to fit like it belonged there. No matter what Jaco did, he made it

> ## "Jaco looked me right in the eye and said, 'Rory, I'm the best bass player on earth.'"
>
> **—Rory Pastorius**

fit. And he could do that because his playing never got in the way of the groove. Any one of us could drop out at any time and nothing would be lost. No matter how much facility he had, he loved to groove more than anything else."

Robinson recalls how the C.C. Riders' audiences reacted to Jaco's revolutionary approach, four years before his landmark debut album. "People had never heard the bass being played like that back then. I mean, everything you heard him playing years later with Weather Report, he was playing in Cochran's band. He made it sound so different but so right. Plus, Charlie and I had that New Orleans feel, and we'd make it so greasy, so down and dirty, that people's mouths would be hanging open. I don't know where it came from or how it happened, but when we got together—man!"

"There'll never be another," concludes Robinson. "There's bass before Jaco and there's bass after Jaco. That's just the way it is. His playing was so emotional and so creative, and it wasn't cluttered—busy as his stuff was, it always flowed. It was like a living, breathing thing—and that's what people miss. I mean, this guy was touched by God. There's no way you could duplicate him. All you can do is get a little bit of what he was all about and try to develop on that—try to complement his concept. Let the door that he opened open up doors for you."

Flea: Leading A Thrash-Funk Revolution

By Karl Coryat

A familiar face (and torso) to MTV viewers, Flea is a trend setter and a thrash-funk icon—one whose thumb has infectiously influenced many young bassists. How did he get to the position he's in? "I basically do what I do, and I pay no heed to what other people do," Flea said in 1992. "I can't express things in technical terms. There was a time when I needed some cash, so I decided to give bass lessons. People came over, and when they sat down to play I realized I didn't know what to say! All I could tell them was to go for it—get inside the instrument and do what you do as hard as you can." Flea has a deep spiritual commitment to his instrument and to music as a whole, much of which came from his punk roots. "Most of my influences have been emotional, not technical. As a result, I try to apply all of my spiritual and physical energy to the music and believe in it."

That conviction has been a big part of the Chili Peppers' sound, which has evolved over the years from the raw vibe of their 1984 eponymous debut to the subtlety and sophistication of the '96 disc *One Hot Minute*. Though the thrust of the Chili Peppers' music is still pelvic, it lacks the jock-rock frenzy of their previous efforts. Instead, funk—which has been a seed in the Chili Pepper pod all along—has become the main ingredient in the band's genre-spanning mix. Flea no longer plays a million notes a second, but his playing is heavier, deeper, and richer than before.

To appreciate Flea fully, it helps to hear his rap: where he's coming from, where he's at, and where he's going. Here's what he had to say shortly after the release of the Chili Peppers' 1991 CD, *Blood Sugar Sex Magik*.

Complete Metamorphosis

My playing has always been very physical: a constant *whackita-whackita-whack*. I don't do it to impress people; I just play what's fun. Understand that my roots are in punk, which was all about playing hard, fast, and loud. As the Chili Peppers got more and more funky, it was a natural evolution: The energy of punk translated into the music we felt like writing.

Dynamics are important in music, and everything else—that tension and release. I used to play too many darn notes, and there was no room for them to breathe; it's nice to relax and play some simple things that are really beautiful. On our first albums I didn't have a nice, big tone that sounded good with simple parts. Another big factor was that we toured *so* hard after our last record, *Mother's Milk*; every night I was up there jumping around, sweating my ass off, playing as hard as I could, beating the hell out of my bass. When I got home I was tired, and I wanted to relax. We started playing again a few months later, and it felt good to play simple lines. It's important to remember that anyone who has good technique can, with just one note, imply a billion more. Louis Armstrong never needed to play fast.

I don't know if my playing is more mature now or not; it's hard to keep it in perspective. I guess your playing is mature if you try to play just what's good for the song. These days I don't play anything to prove I'm Mr. Bitchin' Bass Player. I'm sure there will be a time when

I'll want to be a big bassopotomous again—but right now, I just want to be part of the band and make it happen correctly.

Blowing Sucking Hitting Plucking

I was born October 16, 1962, in Melbourne, Australia. I moved to New York when I was four years old. My mom and dad got divorced a few years later, and my mom married Walter Urban, a jazz bassist into hardcore bebop. There were jam sessions at the house all the time, and the people would play music that just blew my mind. As a kid having no preconceptions about music, I thought it was the most beautiful thing I'd ever experienced. These guys would pick up these things and start blowing and sucking and hitting and plucking, and it made me so happy I'd roll around on the floor laughing.

That was the first time I felt the real beauty of music. I'd been exposed to music before, but I never got into it; it was just *there*, and I was into playing ball and stuff. I had never actually seen people play. When I was 11, Walter got me to start learning the trumpet, and I played all through junior high school and high school in the jazz bands and orchestras. I also played in the L.A. Junior Philharmonic and the L.A.C.C. Jazz Band.

Fear & Frying

In high school, I met Hillel Slovak. He had a band, and he asked me if I was interested in playing bass. I had never played bass before, but I went out and bought a Fender Mustang and played my first gig after only two weeks—three sets! Hillel also got me into rock music. Before I met him I was listening to Miles Davis, Freddie Hubbard, Dizzy Gillespie, and other trumpet players. Hillel introduced me to Zeppelin, Rush, and Hendrix—the Hendrix really got me. Then I got into the Bill Bruford Band with Allan Holdsworth and Jeff Berlin, the Dixie Dregs, and other fusion stuff. I was in Hillel's band, What Is This, for a few years. By 1982 I had shaved my head and gotten into taking acid and acting wacky and crazy, and the next thing you know I had quit Hillel's band and joined the punk band Fear. It was a complete turn—all of a sudden I was playing bare-bones, raw-energy punk rock.

The musicians in Fear were great. The drummer, Spit Stix, was a big influence on my musicianship. I had never warmed up before I played; he taught me how to get my blood going before a show, how to be physical, and how to push the music. I really enjoyed being in Fear—but after a while I discovered that what I was listening to was different from what they were into. They wanted the band to go in a metal direction, and I liked the funky feel. Hillel and Anthony [Kiedis, Chili Peppers vocalist] and I were living together at that time, and a friend of ours needed an opening act, so we put together a band without rehearsing. We were billed as Tony Flow & the Miraculously Majestic Masters Of Mayhem. When we got onstage, I started some funk-bass thing, Anthony read a poem, and we just played. At the next show, we were the Red Hot Chili Peppers.

The band was starting to happen and I wanted to leave Fear, but I didn't have the guts to quit. I was sitting there trying to get up the nerve to call, and just as I reached for the phone, it rang: "Hi, Flea, you're fired." It was great! From then on, it was just the Chili Peppers for me. Things went pretty well: We were together for only a few months and people were trying to give us record deals.

Learning To Play Wrong

I *never* played along with records; I learned by jamming with *people*. To this day I'm not one

> ## "Anyone who has good technique can, with just one note, imply a billion more."

of those guys who knows every Rolling Stones song; I don't know anyone else's songs, except those we cover.

I took one lesson when I started playing bass. I was having a great time with the instrument, banging it and hitting it with a cup and everything. I walked into the lesson, and the guy said, "I want you to learn this music." It was "Take It Easy" by the Eagles. I said, "No way!" So I never went back.

In high school I saw some guy slapping on a bass, and I thought, Wow, that's cool. So I started doing it. When I got into punk, the way I slapped wasn't really funky; it was more like WHUM—BACKA—BACKA—BACKA! as hard as I could, just *abusing* the bass. I was really into the punk ethic: Play every note like it's your last! You could be dead tomorrow! Play for today! And when you perform, give every ounce of energy you have. It's not because you're better than anyone else, it's just what you have to do. You do it because you mean it: you're pissed, because things are twisted. And that's beautiful—the punk thing is so honest and sincere. Even though the music and the genre were finished a long time ago, the intensity is still important to me. I don't think of soft songs or slow songs as less intense; a pretty song can be just as intense as a hard, thrashing song.

Going on my own really helped as far as developing my style. My biggest strength as a musician is that I sound like myself, not anybody else. The main point of music is expression, not trying to sound like other people. Being self-taught has its drawbacks, though: I can sight-read classical trumpet music really well, but I can't read a note of bass music. I don't know what it is. Maybe it's the clef—I never figured out the clef thing! And I've never learned to flow through chord changes. When I played in bands, I just *played*—I'd find something that sounded cool and I'd play it. That's all I've ever done. These days, I might ask the guitarist what chords he's playing—not because I know anything about chords, but because I know where a *C* is on the bass. I do know a little bit.

I'm sure I play all wrong, even though I can get around okay. For instance, I don't consciously try to use one finger per fret. Usually, I don't use my left-hand pinkie, so I've been doing some exercises that put it to use. I pluck with my first two right-hand fingers, mostly alternating. I played with a pick when I was in Fear; they told me I had to play all downstrokes. Now I never use a pick, except for once in a while in the studio when we're going for a certain sound, but that's rare. When I slap I slam the strings as hard as I can with my thumb; I use only my middle finger—never my index or ring fingers—to pop. If the part is very intricate, I use mostly a wrist motion, but usually it involves the whole arm. I've seen people slap and hardly move their hand at all, but anyone who's ever seen one of our shows knows that's not me! I believe if I get my whole body into it, I can play better.

Touch-Tone Phone Sex

I used to really, *really* hate drum machines, and I still despise them on the whole. It's very unhealthy for technology to take the place of human emotion. People often use drum machines and sequencers because of a lack of creativity—they can just plug them in, press buttons, and get "music." But these days I'm a lot more open to machines, having heard people such as [Public Enemy producer] Hank Shocklee make creative use of drum machines and sequencers.

Real instruments and computers are in totally different worlds. Would you rather have phone sex or real sex with a beautiful girl you love? But then again, I think the majority of pop music is bull. A lot of rock and metal bands *sound* sequenced—they recycle stuff and put it into specific formats. As long as people treat music as a format or program, it's an uncreative, unhealthy, sad state of affairs.

Spring Ahead

The Chili Peppers never approach any project with plans or preconceptions; we just do what we do. As for myself, I'd love one day to do soundtracks for films; I'm very interested in that. I'd also love to play more with other musicians. In the '60s everybody jammed with everyone else—whoever was around—and people learned from each other. There was communication and a sense of community among musicians. People don't jam like that anymore, but they should.

My goals are to continue learning and to keep a fresh attitude toward music; I hope to continue exploring new things and getting better at what I do. In ten years I want to still enjoy playing. If I can still have a blast playing music, I'll have accomplished what I wanted.

Les Claypool: The Cheese Stands Alone

By Karl Coryat

Fifty thousand U2 fans are about to get a shock. All day long they've been humming glorious anthems like "With or Without You," and they're primed for the concert. A wave of anticipation sweeps through the crowd as the lights dim. Who's that wiry creature silly-walking out to the mike—is it Bono? No. It's Les Claypool, and the band is Primus. As soon as the strident, discordant opening of "Those Damned Blue-Collar Tweekers" blurts from the stage, the entire audience begins to stare blankly, question marks hovering over their heads. For 40 minutes, their bodies will not sway, their arms will stay firmly at their sides, and their newly purchased Bics will remain unflicked.

Leslie Edward Claypool was born in Richmond, California, across the bay from San Francisco. (The hospital has since been converted to a psychiatric facility; Les thinks that's only appropriate.) In 1984 Les put together a band, Primate, which quickly evolved to Primus. They began concocting a unique brand of hyperkinetic, angular, often atonal "freak-out music" that took full advantage of Claypool's over-the-top style, which combines a multitude of techniques and idiosyncrasies, often all packed into a single bar and repeated *ad dementia*. The first Primus record, 1989's *Suck on This*, became a college-radio sensation, inspiring the group to invade the studio for the followup, *Frizzle Fry*.

The '91 sessions for *Sailing the Seas of Cheese* found Les scaling new heights as he made the huge jump from fretted 4-string to fretless 6. The record's breakthrough success led to stints opening for Rush as well as U2 and countless appearances on MTV. He spoke to Bass Player a few months after being voted Bassist Of The Year in the magazine's '92 Readers Poll.

* * *

Primus plays pretty outside stuff. How do you account for the band's widespread success?

People seem to have a love/hate relationship with us. A lot of people listen to us and go, "What the hell *is* that crap?" And there are people who dig us; I don't know why. But if you compare our sound to some of the stuff I listen to, like Fred Frith or the Residents, we're really not all that strange.

Did you approach the stadium shows you've been doing differently than theater shows with your own fans?

In front of our own crowd I always have a good ol' time onstage, unless someone's spitting at me or throwing shoes or something. The stadium concerts were fun as an experience, but as for putting on a show and getting into it, they were a little more difficult. I found I had to hide behind dark glasses onstage because the audience was so far away, and it was a little weird. I definitely wasn't as personable at the mike, either—we pretty much just played the songs and left.

Did you grow up in a musical household?

No, not even slightly—it was an *anti*-musical household. But my mom always had the AM radio on, and I remember her scooting across the kitchen floor on her butt to Herb Alpert and Diana Ross tunes. There was a weird exercise you could do where you sat on the

floor and "walked" using only your butt cheeks. That's my earliest musical memory. We had some record albums; the Beatles' *Abbey Road* was my favorite. I listened to that one zillions of times. There were some others, like Elvis and Sinatra and crap like that, but nobody ever really *listened* to records.

It wasn't until junior high that I decided I really wanted to play an instrument. We'd have school dances, and bands would come and play cover tunes—"Stairway to Heaven," "Round-about," that kind of stuff. At that point I didn't know the difference between guitar and bass; there were just these electric things, drums, and keyboards—which I always called "organ." Some guys who won a school talent show—two guitarists and a drummer—played "Ramblin' Man" through little Fender Champ amps. It came time for the solo, and it was the most god-awful, twangy, high-pitched thing I'd ever heard. I thought, That's not the kind of instrument I want to play—I want to play the big, fat-sounding one. I started to notice that the guitar with only four strings sounded huge and fat and the one with six strings sounded twangy and boring.

In high school I met Kirk Hammett [who became Metallica's lead guitarist]. He was a burnout dude with thick, Coke-bottle glasses. Right in the middle of class he'd say stuff like, [*in burnout-dude accent*] "Hey, Claypool—check it out, man," [*holds chord fingering on right arm*] "G chord, man. I'm gonna make it big." He introduced me to Hendrix, and he also asked me to sing in his band. But I was too embarrassed to sing in front of anyone.

Then I met this guy who was the hottest guitar player around. He had a band called Blind Illusion, and he needed a bass player, so I begged my dad to loan me some money; I had the rest saved up from pulling weeds. Everyone was giving me the old "you're gonna give it up" routine, but I ended up getting a bass anyway: a Memphis P-Bass copy with flatwounds. I didn't know how to play at all; I could play "Smoke on the Water" in the wrong key, and that was about it. But I had a bass, and I was in a band.

Who were you listening to while you were in Blind Illusion?

Rush. Geddy Lee was God; there was nobody better than him.

Were you good at picking his bass lines off records?

No, I never did that. I listened to players and watched them in concert, and I got ideas from that. But I don't think I ever learned a Rush tune all the way through. I'd put on Rush records and play to them, but I didn't have an amp, so I was just moving my fingers around. When I saw my first Rush concert I spent the whole time watching Geddy's hands. There were so many things I didn't know; I didn't even know there were such things as round-wound strings. I'd had that Memphis a year and a half without changing the strings, and here I was trying to sound like Geddy Lee and Chris Squire.

I went back to school after summer vacation, and I heard they needed a bass player in the jazz band. I didn't know how to read music, but I signed up anyway. When the teacher, Mr. Johnson, found out he said, "What? What are you doing in here if you can't read?" So after class, he drew the bass clef on the board and showed me where all the notes were. For the rest of the semester I stayed in and stumbled along; it was mostly quarter-notes, so it was easy.

Later on I got into the school concert band, where I started to learn upright. Some of us also put together a dance band that played swing and big-band charts. We'd borrow white dinner jackets from the drama department and play gigs at the Rod & Gun Club—that kind of thing. Playing swing was one of the most fun things I've ever done; all these old people

were out there dancing around, and they'd look through our folder of charts and say, "You've gotta play this—'String of Pearls'—that's a great one."

How did you discover funk?

One day a friend of mine said, "Geddy Lee is good, but he's nothing compared to Stanley Clarke and Larry Graham." I told him he was crazy, even though I didn't know who those guys were. Then I saw Stanley's *I Want to Play for Ya* in a record store. I bought it—and it blew my mind. I also saw Louis Johnson on [the TV show] *Don Kirshner's Rock Concert*, saw him go *bang-bippety-bip-bang*, and thought, Man, that's the coolest thing! By my junior year I was getting way into all the funk players, and around my senior year I bought an Ibanez Musician EQ bass.

One day I saw a Carl Thompson piccolo bass in a store. I had stared at the photo in *I Want to Play for Ya* where Stanley had all his basses lined up, and a couple of them were Carl Thompsons. I always thought, Man—that sure is an ugly bass. But I picked up the one in the store, and I couldn't believe how easy it was to play. Suddenly there were a lot of things I could play I couldn't play on my Ibanez. I used to test basses by trying to play "Round-about," and it was pretty easy on the Carl Thompson. I went home and pleaded my mom for the rest of the money I needed to buy that bass. She lent me some, and I went back and bought it. It's still my main 4-string.

How did you develop your right-hand dexterity?

When I was starting out I decided to play with three fingers. A lot of guys play with two, so I figured if I played with three I could be faster. When you're young, that's the goal: to be fast. I still use three fingers most of the time—going *ring, middle, index, ring, middle, index*—depending on how sore my fingers are. Sometimes I'll mix it up and favor certain fingers over others.

Where did you pick up the strumming technique?

From Stanley Clarke, because of songs like "School Days." The first time I saw Stanley shoot the ol' chords—he'd start at the top and go *pow!* [*mimes strumming and sliding a chord down the fingerboard*]—I thought that was way cool, and I decided to do it. It hurt like hell when I first started.

Did Stanley also inspire you to start slapping?

Yeah, him and Louis Johnson. Louis's right arm would go way out away from the bass. Stanley, though, used minimal hand movement, and I was always into the minimal hand-movement thing. A friend of mine told me your thumb should just *graze* the string and rest against the next one, as opposed to whapping the string and bouncing off it. My thumb got pretty fast, since I was more into thumbing than plucking.

One thing that helped me a ton was playing with a group called the Tommy Crank Band. The other guys were all in their 20s and 30s, and I was 19. I had been playing fusion, and when I played with them the first time I was like *bloobilla-bloobilla-bloobilla!* They said, "Cool," and I got the gig. I had to learn all these blues and R&B tunes; we played everything from James Brown to John Cougar, everywhere from biker bars to weddings. I had never learned any of these songs, so I just asked what key they were in and did my own interpretations. A lot of the time I overplayed, and everyone was always clamping down on me to mellow out. By playing these tunes four hours a night, three to five nights a week, my groove got really good, and I learned to improvise and pull off songs we hadn't even rehearsed.

What made you decide to form your own band?

I was auditioning for every group I could find; I wanted to make it big, but every band around just *sucked.* At the time I was getting into pretty obscure stuff, like Fred Frith, King Crimson, and Public Image Limited. I had a LinnDrum [drum machine] and a 4-track, so I started writing songs. But I couldn't sing; not only did I not have a voice, I was scared to get up to the mike. But I wrote all these lyrics, and I didn't like the way anybody else sang them.

I decided to go into the studio, record a tape, send it to all these record-company names I had gotten from some magazine, and make it big. I sold my car and made the first Primate demo with a guitarist named Todd Huth and a drummer friend of mine, Perm Parker. One of the songs was "Too Many Puppies," which we still play—although back then it was a double-time, B-52's kind of tune. The tape got some airplay on local radio.

Were you influenced by other rock bass players at that time?

I always wanted to play bass parts *and* rhythm guitar parts. I never really listened to other bass players. To this day people come up and say, "Hey, what do you think of Jaco's blah blah blah," and I'll go, "Never heard it in my life." Or, "You haven't heard Jonas Hellborg?" and I say, "Nope." I feel bad because there are a lot of great players out there I haven't heard. I was just never into "player" records; I'm much more apt to buy a Tom Waits CD instead of one by a bass player. I'm also more apt to get into drummers than bass players. I like to play the drums; it's physical and you can get out your aggressions. It's funny—I enjoy playing drums more than bass, but I'm better at bass.

When did you get your fretless Carl Thompson 6-string?

I was doing a demo at a NAMM show, and this guy came up and whipped out this amazing fretless Carl Thompson 6-string. After that I knew I had to have a 6-string, but I wasn't sure if I wanted a fretless.

I didn't actually get my 6 until just before we started *Sailing the Seas of Cheese*. We were in New York, and I tracked down Carl Thompson and told him I was interested in a 6-string. A little while later he started hearing my name around, so he called me and said he'd start building me a bass. I couldn't decide whether I wanted it to be fretted or fretless. But I was getting bored with my 4-string; I needed something that would just blow things wide open, so I decided to go for the fretless 6.

Carl told me he was going to make the best bass he'd ever built in his life. He basically made a butcher block out of all these different pieces of wood, and then he cut the body shape out of it. He called it the Rainbow Bass, and he finished it on his birthday—the serial number is his date of birth.

When I got the bass I thought, Oh my God—what have I done? It was *so* much more difficult to play. I was used to my 4-string's 32" scale, and all of a sudden I had this big hunk of wood with a 36" scale and no frets. When I tried to play chords they sounded terrible, and I couldn't move around very well. But I kept playing it and playing it—and I'm just now getting to the point where I feel comfortable on it.

Do you ever have trouble playing and singing simultaneously?

Yeah, all the time—especially if I try to do other people's songs. Usually I try to get the playing so solid that I can just sit in front of the TV and not think about it, and *then* I'll start laying down the vocals.

Have you ever fooled around with alternate tunings?

No, and I don't really want to. Maybe I'll do something with them when I'm a little older. I have to get to a point of boredom—when I get bored, something new comes about.

What do you have to say to a young player who wants to be just like you?

Anyone who wants to be just like me is in for a life of boredom! [*Laughs.*] You should always play with as many people as you can. If they're terrible, you'll learn from their mistakes—but it's even better to play with people who are better than you. It's just like anything else; if you skate with people who are better than you, you'll become a better skater. One more thing: Don't pick your blemishes, because you'll get crazy scars on your chin like me.

The Agony & The Ecstasy

By Michael Manring

IF you feel the need to expand the horizons of your creative world, you'll find yourself in the good company of brilliant scientists, artists, and thinkers from throughout history—but you may also find it's not as glamorous a position as you might have imagined. To be unconventional makes you an iconoclast to some extent, and our culture has a love/hate relationship with its iconoclasts. We tend to mythologize those heroic figures who have challenged an unnecessary order and who have, at great personal expense, made the world a little better place to live in. But that's often not done until long after the person's time, when his or her brilliant forethought becomes clear. For some entertaining reading I recommend Nicolas Slonimsky's *Lexicon of Musical Invective* [University of Washington Press], an entire book of really bad contemporary reviews of musical masterpieces of the last 200 years. We're talking the biggies here: Beethoven, Stravinsky, Brahms, Tchaikovsky. Although it's an amusing book, it is disturbing to realize how such brilliant music was so completely misunderstood in its own time.

Like the great classical masters, bassists interested in new and challenging ideas sometimes find themselves hated by intelligent, well-meaning members of the music community. It's easy to dismiss critics as insensitive boneheads, but in fact this often isn't the case. It's often those who have the most in-depth understanding of the state of an art form who feel most threatened by someone who questions the order.

People feel strongly about that which moves them, and we all tend to identify ourselves with the things that matter to us. Bass has traditionally been a conventional instrument, so listeners and other musicians rely on us bassists to play a comfortable, consistent role in music. There is no doubt that there has been, and will continue to be, lots of great music in which the bass plays its familiar role. But I believe it's equally undeniable that there is great music to be made where the bass is participating in different ways, some of which may never have even been imagined.

The challenge, I think, is to know when and how to apply your creativity. Even if you have wonderful ideas, if you insist on forcing them into inappropriate situations, it's likely you'll just end up making enemies—and you may therefore ultimately contribute to the number of people who just don't want to be exposed to *anything* new. While I hope I can continue to encourage you to explore our instrument's many personalities, I believe that unless you develop the ability to edit yourself—to question what is the best and most appropriate idea for any musical situation—then your music will end up sounding trite, and you will make it that much harder for your ideas to be taken seriously.

There's nothing more valuable for musicians interested in expanding boundaries than a deep understanding of the tradition from which they are emerging. If you don't really understand what it means to play good, old-fashioned "meat-and-potatoes" bass, your innovations won't have any historical perspective. I don't think I can overemphasize the importance of having respect for the functional styles of bass playing that have served music so well; no matter how intoxicating some new technique may be, the older, tried-and-true techniques have the tremendous advantage of having been proven effective for many years.

That said, I can think of few things sadder than a beautiful idea that never gets to be explored. There is no reason to edit yourself to the point of blandness; it's an issue of balance. When the proper time comes, I hope you'll be prepared to stick up for your creativity—no matter what the cost. Even if your ideas don't work out, the important thing is to try. Even today's most traditional convention was once somebody's radical, hare-brained concept that came into being only because of the will and determination of its creator. Take comfort in the assurance that any art form that doesn't grow and change becomes stagnant and no longer relevant to its culture; while it may still exist as a museum piece, it loses its immediacy and dialog with contemporary society. So as painful a process as it is, progress is essential in any art form— and by being open to new ideas you will help maintain the vitality of our instrument.

I recommend three things: First, *appropriateness*. There are times when it's appropriate to try out your wild new ideas, and there are times when it will just drive people crazy. It's probably good for everybody if you develop a sensitivity to which is which. This is easier said than done, and developing a mature sense of appropriateness is a lifelong struggle. It's always a good idea to have a reason to want to try something new; newness just for the sake of novelty or as an attention-getting device can be pretty tedious. If you're one of those people who cannot compromise and always feels compelled to challenge *any* dogma (and a great many truly creative people really are obnoxious!), then you should be ready to accept the consequences. It may be wise, for example, to look for a different income source, since you may often find yourself at odds with the establishment. Sure, you could wimp out and quit playing, complaining that the world is unfair. But if you're really a creative person, hang in there and find some outlet for your ideas—that way I can hear them someday!

I'd also like to encourage *tolerance*. If we can learn to accept ideas that are different from our own without fear or prejudice, we might avoid causing tragedies even worse than the famous examples from the past. We might even be able to learn from them. This is not to say you should like every new idea that comes along—but at least you can try to understand them on the basis of their own criteria and allow them the right to exist.

Third, I encourage you always to have *satisfaction* with your music. If your goal is to enjoy and learn from the music-making process, you'll probably be more satisfied than if you try to make music to elicit specific audience responses (such as getting them to pay you lots of money!). Try to see past the hype; ultimately, the person you need to satisfy is yourself.

> **Even today's most traditional convention was once somebody's radical, hare-brained concept.**

A Musical Bibliography: 30 Bass Albums You Must Own

By The BASS PLAYER Staff

Nothing will do more for your bass playing than a steady diet of great bass music. After all, before you deal with the numerous concerns involved in getting your music *out* through your hands, you must first get the music *into* your head and your heart. To put it another way: Having something to say is the biggest motivator for learning to talk.

To come up with our bass bibliography we asked the BASS PLAYER Advisory Board for a list of recordings they felt no bassist should be without—and, of course, the BP editors and former Editor Jim Roberts submitted their own picks. Every record here will make you want to put down what you're doing, pick up a bass, and *say something*. What more could you ask of your fellow bassists?

* * *

Bob Marley & the Wailers

Babylon by Bus [Tuff Gong]
Bassist: Aston "Family Man" Barrett

Aston Barrett is the acknowledged father of reggae bass. His essential one-drop rhythms have infiltrated everything from rave to rock. (Did somebody call the Police?) Recorded live during the Wailers' 1978 world tour, *Babylon by Bus* is driven by Family Man's immense tone and amazing feel. He and his drummer brother, Carlton, laid down some of the skankinest grooves ever; here they connect on several Marley classics, including "Exodus," "Stir It Up," "Is This Love?," and "Jamming." Though the stadium-rockin' Wailers of '78 were a far cry from the bare-bones studio crew that all but invented reggae in the late '60s, the Barretts were never mightier than on *Babylon by Bus*.

This disc is also one of the best-recorded examples of live bass. It's deep, clear, and well placed in the mix—a real subwoofer delight! Throughout the record, Family Man's '70s J-Bass surrounds the audience with a thick throb. Wicked bass, mon.

Duke Ellington

Solos, Duets, and Trios [RCA/Bluebird]
Bassist: Jimmy Blanton

Modern jazz bass starts here. Duke Ellington's landmark 1940 duets with the 21-year-old Jimmy Blanton simply changed everything. The duo's continual swapping of rhythmic, melodic, and harmonic roles throughout "Body and Soul" and "Sophisticated Lady" clearly illustrates Ellington's and Blanton's boundary-breaking bass approach. But the collection's centerpiece is the amazing "Mr. J.B. Blues." Based for the most part on the simplest of 12-bar forms, the piece allows Blanton the freedom to showcase his masterful rhythmic acuity and pizz chops, his left hand's unprecedented expressiveness, and his advanced grasp of extended harmonies.

Still, young Jimmy's greatest jazz-bass contribution is more a matter of feel than technique. His revolutionary ability to imply a steady beat without merely thumping on *one* and *three* provided the model—and the inspiration—for all jazz bassists who followed to continue expanding the instrument's role.

For some seriously in-depth analysis of "Mr. J.B. Blues," along with several other Blanton-era Ellington works, check out Ken Rattenbury's *Duke Ellington, Jazz Composer* [Yale University Press].

Patsy Cline

12 Greatest Hits [MCA]
Bassists: Harold Bradley, Bob Moore
The fine and subtle art of country bass reached an apex with these classic late-'50s/early-'60s recordings. Though producer Owen Bradley may have come up with the idea of doubling the upright with a flatpicked Danelectro six-string bass (ostensibly to render the bass line audible through tiny transistor-radio speakers), much of the credit for the successful implementation of the new "tic-tac" sound (as it came to be called) goes to bassist Bob Moore and Owen's brother, session guitarist Harold.

Moore's stately lines and buoyant rhythms form, on their own, a near-complete study in tasteful country comping. But once Harold started doubling 'em with his Dano, the whole rhythm section achieved an airy lift and a delicate sense of motion few bands have matched since. From the rolling click of "Walkin' After Midnight" to the sweet, relaxed bounce of "She's Got You" to Harold's elemental embellishments of Moore's line on "Crazy," this dynamic duo wrote the book that's still required reading for all Opryland wannabes.

Oscar Peterson Trio

Night Train [Verve]
Bassist: Ray Brown
Ray Brown's name may grace more CDs in your local record mart's jazz section than any other bassist, and his continuing career began over 50 years ago. Just about everyone agrees, though, that Ray was always at his swingin' best when laying it down with the Oscar Peterson Trio.

The key attribute of 1962's *Night Train* is the heady, post-bop energy the trio brings to an Ellington-heavy collection of pre-bop nuggets. Brown's modern yet blues-based lines stir just the right blend of old and new into such Duke standards as "C Jam Blues," "Things Ain't What They Used to Be," and "I Got It Bad and That Ain't Good."

For more of Ray's big, beautiful tone and jaw-dropping time, seek out Verve's two-CD Oscar Peterson collection, *The Will to Swing*.

Cream

Wheels of Fire [Polydor]
Bassist: Jack Bruce
Before Jack Bruce, there were only a few notable electric bassists, headed up by James Jamerson and Paul McCartney—and even they were known primarily for their skill as accompanists. Nobody had ever pushed the bass to the front of the stage and made audiences sit up and listen as Jack Bruce did in the late '60s.

Wheels of Fire is the essential Jack Bruce album simply because it captures both his studio and stage personalities so well. On the studio tracks he's a thoughtful and even economical player who focuses on the groove, and he brings the full range of his abilities as a writer, arranger, singer, and multi-instrumentalist to bear. Live, Jack was (and is) a maniacal improviser, stretching the limits of the songs—and his gear—to the breaking point. The two live tracks on *Wheels of Fire* are classics, but don't forget the great stuff on *Live Cream* and *Goodbye*. And there's loads more to appreciate on Jack's solo albums, from 1969's *Songs for a Tailor* right up through '95's *Monkjack*.

Cachao ey su Ritmo Caliente

Cuban Jam Sessions in Miniature—Descargas, Vol. 2 [Panart] (Available from Descarga Latin Music, 800-377-2647)
Bassist: Israel "Cachao" López
During the 1930s Cachao caused a commotion by bringing Afro-Cuban rhythmic elements to the traditional Cuban dance form called danzón. Two decades later he again revolutionized Cuban music with this historic album, which introduced the descarga jam-session format. Lincoln Goines (see page 84) describes the disc as "a dictionary of Cuban styles over exquisitely performed short tunes and improvisations"; Oscar Stagñaro echoes, "It's the encyclopedia of phrasing, tumbaos, and melody, all in one." Andy González points to the interplay between Cachao, Pata Guinas on congas, and Yito Iglesias on bongos.

For some easier-to-locate Cachao check out 1995's *Master Sessions, Vol. 1 & 2* on Epic/ Crescent Moon.

Miles Davis

Relaxin' with the Miles Davis Quintet [Prestige]
Bassist: Paul Chambers
One look at a resumé that includes Miles Davis' *Kind of Blue* and John Coltrane's *Giant Steps* tells you all you need to know about Paul Chambers' stature in the jazz world. (*Kind of Blue* boasts Paul's bass feature "So What," while *Giant Steps* includes Trane's tribute to the bassist, "Mr. P.C.") Chambers was a New York mainstay from the mid '50s to the early '60s. Although alcohol and heroin abuse led to his death at age 34, he nonetheless burned as brightly as any bassist in this century. On this classic 1956 Davis date with Coltrane, drummer Philly Joe Jones, and pianist Red Garland, Paul's modern, forward-thinking approach is evident via his strong, relentless, melodic walking lines on such tracks as "If I Were a Bell" and "I Could Write a Book," as well as his brief, bluesy, bebop-rooted solo on the Rhythm-changes romp "Oleo." (He was quite an accomplished soloist with the bow, too.)

Stanley Clarke [Epic]

Bassist: Stanley Clarke
Even though Clarke (see page 182) recorded this classic disc in 1974, his squeaky-clean Alembic tone, aggressive snaps, staccato runs, string bends, and nasty harmonics are as fresh today as they were then. This disc, Stanley's second as a leader, contains six songs of sheer bass terror. His band included monster drummer Tony Williams, keyboardist Jan Hammer, and guitarist Bill Connors; here they highlight Stan's electric prowess on such tunes as "Vulcan Princess," "Yesterday Princess," "Lopsy Lu," and "Power"; "Spanish Phases for Strings & Bass," meanwhile, demonstrates Clarke's serious upright skills. Also recommended: *Stanley Clarke Live 1976–1977*.

Primus

Sailing the Seas of Cheese [Interscope]

Bassist: Les Claypool

Love him or hate him, you have to admit Les Claypool (see page 200) forever changed the face of bass. While he may not have perfect technical precision or fretless intonation, Claypool is one of the greats because of his ability to throw slapping, sliding, tapping, and chording into a big, sloppy, hugely quirky melting pot. Throughout this and other Primus discs Les takes a twisted bass line, wraps it with warped lyrics and other general weirdness, and manages to end up with a memorable song. Many have tried, but nobody pulls it off quite like Claypool. For an even stranger effort check out *Riddles Are Abound Tonight* by Claypool's side project, Sausage.

The Stax/Volt Singles, 1959–'68 [Atlantic]

Bassists: Donald "Duck" Dunn and others

Duck Dunn anchored a string of '60s soul-pop hits surpassed only by that of Motown's James Jamerson. As bassist with Booker T. & the MG's, the house band for Memphis' Stax/Volt Records, Dunn plied his trade beneath timeless tunes by Otis Redding, Sam & Dave, Albert King, and many, many others—and this nine-disc set covers it all. Other bassists appear throughout, but the majority of these grooves belong to Duck.

Dunn's approach was earthier—and much simpler—than Jamerson's, but Duck's grooves were every bit as deep. With only a few pinpoint, off-beat eighths here (Eddie Floyd's "Knock on Wood") or some stone-simple unison grooving there (Booker T.'s seminal "Green Onions"), Dunn repeatedly tapped into the very essence of a song's inherent rhythms. This unwavering instinct—along with that definitive P-Bass tone—assures Duck a sacred place in groove history.

Red Hot Chili Peppers

Blood Sugar Sex Magik [Warner Bros.]

Bassist: Flea

For nearly a decade Flea (see page 194) was *the* thrash-funk bassist. Nobody could slap with his speed and power. But he threw everyone a curve with this 1991 disc: Suddenly he was tasty yet supremely funky—but in an old-school rather than flashy way. From the straight-up intensity of "The Power of Equality" and the Meters-influenced "If You Have to Ask" to the Bootsy-drenched, polysaturated phatness of "Sir Psycho Sexy," Flea offers an amazingly complete lexicon of funk, hip-hop, and even reggae. And he does so almost without a single slap. Say what you want about Flea's wild stage presence or even his technique—the man has serious *feel*, and that's one reason why it all came together for the Chili Peppers on this highly satisfying record.

The Best of Larry Graham and Graham Central Station, Vol. 1

[Warner Bros.]

Bassist: Larry Graham

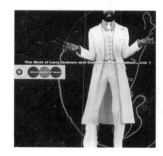

With his seminal work in Sly & the Family Stone and Graham Central Station, Larry Graham (see page 178) became forever established as the Master of Slap. Although any record with Larry manning the bass is cool, highlights of his technique and songwriting can now be found on this choice 11-song collection.

Some of this disc's tunes are a little sappy, but bass lovers will still dig "Hair" and "The Jam," two tunes that fully capture Larry's warm tone, big thumb, and deep groove. Also killin': "Now D-U-Wanta Dance," with its super-slimy Mu-Tron line. If you've never heard the true origins of slap-and-pop, check out this—or any—Larry Graham disc. Funk at its finest.

Charlie Haden & Pat Metheny

Beyond the Missouri Sky (short stories) [Verve]

Bassist: Charlie Haden

Charlie Haden's profound musicality and deep, elemental sound has contributed to so many fine records—from the great early recordings with the Ornette Coleman Quartet (now united in a six-CD box set called *Beauty Is a Rare Thing*) to his groundbreaking albums with the Liberation Music Orchestra to dozens of sessions with such artists as Keith Jarrett, James Cotton, and Rickie Lee Jones. Haden's playing is at its very best in small groups—especially duos. This disc with Metheny is perhaps Haden's best duo outing ever, because it's deeply rooted in his musical heritage and distinguished by inventive and inspired playing throughout. "With every line he plays, with every musical gesture he offers," Metheny has said, "Charlie supports, illuminates, and reveals something about himself and the other musicians he's playing with." There's no better place to hear that than on this album.

Chaka Khan

What Cha' Gonna Do for Me? [Warner Bros.]

Bassist: Anthony Jackson

Among bassists, Anthony Jackson's musical, technical, and sonic innovations have made his name every bit as definitive as "Jaco," "Sting," or "Flea." The inventor of the 6-string contrabass guitar is renowned for his many contributions to seminal pop and jazz recordings. By the time he teamed with drummer Steve Ferrone to record with Chaka Khan, he had already gained notoriety for his legendary pick–and–phaser performance on the O'Jays' "For the Love of Money." But *What Cha' Gonna Do For Me?* captures Anthony just as his various stylistic concepts came together. Given much time and creative freedom by producer Arif Mardin, Jackson mixed spontaneous 16th-note bursts, pick-and-flange forays, and dense, booming low notes, weaving all of them tightly and unobtrusively into the groove. Other essential Anthony examples include Chaka Khan's *The Woman I Am*, Steve Kahn & Eyewitness' *Public Access*, and Michel Camilo's *Rendezvous*.

Hitsville USA: The Motown Singles Collection, 1959–1971

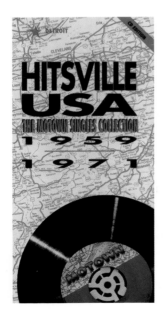

[Motown]

Bassist: James Jamerson and others

If you play electric bass, you owe James Jamerson (see page 164) a tip of your hat. He helped to make the "Fender Bass" a mainstay in pop music and recorded a few classic lines along the way, too. A ton of them can be heard on this four-CD, 104-track box set, which features 36 different Motown artists. (Other bassists heard on various songs include Bob Babbitt, Ron Brown, Wilton Felder, and Carol Kaye.) It's hard to believe Jamerson used only one finger to pluck his funky lines on songs by the Four Tops, the Temptations, Smokey Robinson & the Miracles, Stevie Wonder, and Marvin Gaye. This is *the* box set to own if you're interested in learning bass from pop's undisputed master.

Jamerson students also won't want to miss the book/CD *Standing in the Shadows of*

Motown: The Life and Music of Legendary Bassist James Jamerson by Dr. Licks [published by Hal Leonard]. It's both an award-winning biography and a tribute to Jamerson's style, with recorded examples and comments by dozens of big names from the bass world.

B.B. King

Completely Well [MCA]

Bassist: Jerry Jemmott

One problem with analyzing Jerry Jemmott's transcendent, funk-blues grooves with B.B. King: It's tough to maintain focus while you're shaking your butt. Dig Jerry's two distinctly different takes on one of blues bass' most venerable patterns: the root–octave–♭7th–5th pattern. In "Confessin' the Blues" he plays it relatively straight, but subtly ghosted 16th-notes hint at untapped groove potential. Then, in "Cryin' Won't Help You Now," he fleshes out this tired box pattern with pentatonic passing notes and a dead-funky mix of eighths and 16ths that cooks underneath Herb Lovelle's bare-bones snare. Also highly recommended: *King Curtis Live at the Fillmore* and *Aretha Franklin Live at the Fillmore*. Recorded back-to-back on the same night, these two discs capture more of Jemmott at his sweaty best.

Led Zeppelin II [Atlantic]

Bassist: John Paul Jones

JPJ's bass work on Zep's second record is simply brilliant. His round-sounding lines combine R&B, jazz, and rock into a complex style few bassists have been able to cop. Although the melodic, wandering "Ramble On" line may be one of his most memorable, Jones' big and bold line on "The Lemon Song" simply defines blues rock. And "Heartbreaker" showcases his most extensive use of effects; here he combines distorted grit with Leslie-speaker wobble for one of the best crunch-bass sounds ever. *Led Zeppelin II* is one of the original blueprints for creative bass in a rock setting.

Paul Simon

Graceland [Warner Bros.]

Bassists: Bakithi Kumalo, Lloyd Lelose, Alonzo Johnson, Conrad Lozano

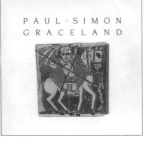

When this 1986 smash album first hit the radio, there probably wasn't a bassist alive whose head wasn't turned by the free-flowing fretless lines of Bakithi Kumalo. The virtually unknown South African lit up such hit tracks as "You Can Call Me Al" and "The Boy in the Bubble," making a positively great album out of what would have been simply an excellent one. Of special interest is "Diamonds on the Soles of Her Shoes"—its sublime bass fills manage to combine busy syncopation and understatement. It's parts like this that made even non-musicians look at the radio and say, "What an amazing bass player!"

Bill Evans Trio

Sunday at the Village Vanguard [Riverside]

Bassist: Scott LaFaro

Like Jimmy Blanton before him, Scott LaFaro forever changed the direction of jazz bass. His early work with such artists as trumpeter Chet Baker and pianist/vibraphonist Victor Feldman hinted at his potential, but it was LaFaro's 1961 recordings with the Bill Evans Trio that showed what could be done with the instrument.

LaFaro didn't just play fast—he brought a whole new dimension of improvisational thinking to the bass. His lines explored and expanded the harmony, and he often carried on a simultaneous "conversation" with both the piano and drums. When Scott soloed he simply exploded up the fingerboard, playing rapid, rhythmically sophisticated phrases—and he always swung, playing with great feeling and passionate commitment. Every jazz bassist since LaFaro has had to deal with his style, either by imitating it or reacting against it.

This must-have CD includes two LaFaro compositions, "Jade Visions" and "Gloria's Step"; seven more can be found on *Waltz for Debby*. All were recorded live on June 25, 1961, only ten days before Scott died in an automobile accident at age 25.

Michael Manring

Drastic Measures [Windham Hill]

Bassist: Michael Manring

Although Manring was already an accomplished veteran of the adventurous New Age Windham Hill label by the time he completed this 1991 disc, *Drastic Measures* marks the culmination of years of pushing the bass-sound envelope. From the opening notes of his "Spirits in the Material World" cover and into "Red Right Returning," the first of four amazing solo bass pieces, it's clear Manring is a composer who approaches the electric bass as an orchestra. *Drastic Measures* also shows that despite the difficulty of his techniques and tunings, Michael's much less interested in flash than pure musicality. So on your second listen, rather than wondering how Manring managed to master so many voices of the bass, note the pure artfulness of his compositions and arrangements, and let that inspire you.

The Beatles

Sgt. Pepper's Lonely Hearts Club Band [EMI]

Bassist: Paul McCartney

Paul McCartney (see page 170) was the first rock bassist to develop a style that completely transcended the instrument's root-bound function. While his style had become fairly well developed by *Rubber Soul* and *Revolver*, it wasn't until *Sgt. Pepper*—aided by the first direct recording of bass and a bottom-friendly mix—that it fully came to fruition. Great feel, articulation, note choices, tone … it's all here, and you'd be hard-pressed to find better bass lines to transcribe and memorize. A close second for Macca is *Abbey Road*, with its unforgettable parts on "Come Together" and "Something." And check out that second verse of "She Came In Through the Bathroom Window"—the quirky syncopation raises the song to an entirely new plane.

Edgar Meyer, Yo-Yo Ma & Mark O'Connor

Appalachia Waltz [Sony Classical]

Bassist: Edgar Meyer

In an era when a musician's ability to authentically play different styles is rare (and too often discouraged), bassist/composer Edgar Meyer brings new meaning to the word "versatility." Called by John Patitucci "the greatest classical bass soloist on the planet," Meyer is equally at home playing bluegrass, country, blues, folk—and pop! More important, he enjoys working on projects that marry divergent styles, such as this hot-selling hybrid of Texas fiddle music, classical, and Celtic forms featuring contemporary violin virtuoso Mark O'Connor and classical cello genius Yo-Yo Ma. For more of Meyer's mongrel mastery check out his 1990 solo disc *Work in Progress*.

Marcus Miller

The Sun Don't Lie [PRA]

Bassist: Marcus Miller

From sideman work with saxman David Sanborn to vocalist Luther Vandross to jazz legend Miles Davis—as well as producing his own vocal R&B albums—Marcus Miller had plenty of time to hone his soulful skills and trademark tone. But 1993's *The Sun Don't Lie* marked the first time he pushed himself to find his solo voice. This broad collection of jazz-funk instrumentals certainly showcases Miller's hot thumb-thumping passages and quick fingerstyle licks. But by sharing the spotlight with other great players—Miles, Sanborn, guitarist Vernon Reid, and others—Miller takes time to lay back in some badass grooves, showing that his sideman role of nailing it down is actually an integral part of his solo voice. And that is groovy indeed.

Charles Mingus

Mingus Ah Um [Columbia]

Bassist: Charles Mingus

Like Miles Davis, Mingus lacks a definitive album—simply because he reinvented, reshaped, and re-attacked his music throughout his career. Still, 1959's *Mingus Ah Um* might be his most *essential* album. He was at his hard-driving, inventive best (cue up "Boogie Stop Shuffle"—no one attacked an upright like Mingus), and his compositional powers were bursting into full bloom. And "Better Git It in Your Soul" and the oft-covered "Goodbye Pork Pie Hat" have come closer to achieving "standard" status than anything else Mingus ever wrote. *Mingus Ah Um* is full of vital links to Charles' recent past; "Better Git It in Your Soul" resurrects a rhythmic riff from the earlier "Wednesday Night Prayer Meeting," and "Open Letter to Duke" evolved directly from 1957's "Nouroog" suite.

Just about any Mingus album will serve as a worthy introduction to the man's genius. Other excellent starting points include *Mingus, Mingus, Mingus, Mingus, Mingus* and *The Black Saint and the Sinner Lady*.

Weather Report

Heavy Weather [Columbia]

Bassist: Jaco Pastorius

Recorded in 1976–77, this gold-selling record captures Jaco Pastorius (see page 186) at his peak and displays a virtual textbook of his dazzling skills. The melodic ballad "A Remark You Made" highlights the gorgeous tone Jaco coaxed from his '62 fretless Jazz Bass. On the flip-side, his high-energy bass anthem "Teentown" showcases unprecedented technical virtuosity. The album's "hit," "Birdland," boasts Jaco's revolutionary use of false and natural harmonics, and—alongside "Palladium"—demonstrates his innate ability to swing while laying down the nastiest of grooves. Don't forget "Havona": Jaco's extensive harmonic knowledge results in one of his finest compositions and arguably his best recorded solo.

The Meters

Funkify Your Life [Rhino]

Bassist: George Porter Jr.

George Porter Jr. is a criminally underrated groover. This two-CD set rescues the Meters' troubled discography from the murky depths of the cut-out bin and shines a bright light on one of groovedom's richest legacies. The way Porter's spare finger funk and rubbery tone blend with super-drummer Zig Modeliste's slinky rhythms defines all Meters music. So is George's insistence on digging into simple, often pentatonic-based countermelodies and then relaxing and grooving tirelessly. What really kills, though, is how he injects an anarchic elasticity into his space-filled lines, allowing them not just to breathe but to pant, moan, and groan. Righteous example: The *E7* intro figure to 1969's "Funky Miracle" can be played with nothing more than open strings and 2nd-fret pull-offs—but you chopmeisters would be hard-pressed to find a more fail-safe funk groove.

Tower Of Power

Tower Of Power [Warner Bros.]

Bassist: Francis "Rocco" Prestia III

True funk should make you feel an irresistible desire to move your head. If you've assumed the position, high on your listening list should be this 1973 classic featuring Rocco Prestia's 16th-note funk barrage. Together with David Garibaldi's busy-but-light drum work, Rocco reached new pocket-playing depths.

Since you might not want to dive right into Prestia's super-fast, carpal-tunnel-inducing approach without a doctor's note, let your ears do the grooving. Later, start mentally deconstructing the groove. Imagine the track without horns or vocals; strip it down to the drums, those powerful bass notes, and the well-placed rhythm guitar. Focus on the instruments' rhythmic interplay, concentrating on which notes Rocco accents. Then focus solely on the space *between* the notes. If such directed listening doesn't affect your playing—and your outlook on life—relax, assume the position, and start over.

Steely Dan

Aja [MCA]

Bassists: Chuck Rainey, Walter Becker

The ultimate in L.A. cool. If some of these other records leave you chops-dizzy, settle into this 1977 disc's smoky grooves. Subtlety is the focus here: Chuck Rainey uses superbly slinky feels, tasty, well-placed fills, and generous space in all the right places. The fabulous ascending slides and double-stops on "Peg" and those ostinatos and fills on "Josie" are relentlessly creative, from the first note to the last. But perhaps even more important than Rainey's notes are his rests. If you could somehow hear everything he *doesn't* play, you'd realize how silence can actually strengthen a bass line, like the mortar in a brick wall.

A runner-up for best Rainey/Dan collaboration is *The Royal Scam*, mostly for Chuck's blazing Jamerson tribute on "Kid Charlemagne"—a line that could keep you in the woodshed for weeks.

Yes

Fragile [Atlantic]

Bassist: Chris Squire

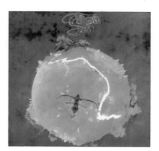

Chris Squire revolutionized both the sound and function of the bass in rock music with his trebly, Clavinet-like Rickenbacker tone and busy but carefully orchestrated lines. He comes out charging with "Roundabout," propelling it with an energy that makes the song sound like it's about to blow apart. On the slower "Long Distance Runaround" Squire still drives the song with aggressive, fragmented riffs that trade off with the vocal. Then there's his composition "The Fish," in which overdubbed bass lines provide melody, harmony, and rhythm parts—well before Jaco, Manring, and Wooten did the same. Every bass line on this 1972 disc is essential to the song's arrangement, a valuable lesson for us all. Wouldn't you rather play parts that are crucial rather than merely ornamental?

Victor Wooten

A Show of Hands [Compass]

Bassist: Victor Wooten

Sure, Victor can slap, tap, double-thumb, open hammer pluck, and wield a few other techniques that probably have even weirder names. But what makes his debut solo effort so worthy is not so much his "show of hands" but his musicality—that all of his technical tools are just that: tools for making music. While *A Show of Hands* might not be ideal for learning how to be supportive in your average rock, blues, or jazz setting, it's great for exploring composition, artistic sensibility, and new approaches to established ideas. Vic nails home the groove in his native funk land—but by managing rhythm and melody parts at the same time, he smoothly sails through everything from jazz standards to Bach-style counterpoint. In fact, so much music comes out of Wooten's 4-string Fodera it's easy to forget this is a solo bass effort.

Index

Contributors

RICH APPLEMAN has appeared in concert with artists ranging from Frankie Avalon to Lionel Hampton to the Boston Pops. A bass teacher since 1972, he is the Chairman of the Bass Department at Berklee College of Music.

TONY BACON co-authored the illustrated history of the bass guitar, *The Bass Book* [Miller Freeman Books].

DAN ERLEWINE is the Technical Director at Stewart-MacDonald's Guitar Shop Supply in Athens, Ohio.

ED FRIEDLAND, a BASS PLAYER contributing editor, has written several Hal Leonard books on jazz, blues, and reggae bass playing.

MIKE HILAND has written numerous bass instructional books for Mel Bay Publications, including *Complete Blues Bass Book* and *You Can Teach Yourself Electric Bass.*

TONY GREEN is a music journalist based in Jacksonville, Florida.

GREGORY ISOLA is BASS PLAYER's managing editor.

CHRIS JISI is a BASS PLAYER contributing editor.

RICHARD JOHNSTON is BASS PLAYER's editor.

DAVE LARUE has played bass with the Dixie Dregs and the Steve Morse Band since 1988.

DR. LICKS, AKA Allan Slutsky, is an arranger, guitarist, and author from Philadelphia, and received the Rolling Stone/BMI Ralph J. Gleason Award for his book *Standing in the Shadows of Motown: The Life and Music of Legendary Bassist James Jamerson.*

SCOTT MALANDRONE is BASS PLAYER's associate editor.

MICHAEL MANRING's adventurous bass approach has been well documented on his solo albums and in his many concert appearances and clinics.

BILL MILKOWSKI is a veteran journalist who wrote the acclaimed biography *Jaco: The Extraordinary and Tragic Life of Jaco Pastorius* [Miller Freeman Books].

TOM MULHERN is *Guitar Player* magazine's former Managing Editor and bass guru.

DAVE POMEROY has played on hundreds of Nashville records with dozens of major artists. He's also a solo artist.

STEVE RABE founded SWR Engineering in 1984. Before that, he worked for Acoustic Control Corp., where he helped design the revolutionary 360 bass amp and personally directed the maintenance of Jaco's Acoustic 360s.

MIKE RICHMOND has performed and recorded with Miles Davis, Stan Getz, Ravi Shankar, Jack DeJohnette, Dizzy Gillespie, Elvin Jones, and Pat Metheny. He is a falculty member at New York University (Teacher of the Year), Rutgers University, and The New School Jazz Department.

JIM ROBERTS was BASS PLAYER's founding Editor and later became the magazine's publisher, eventually becoming Group Publisher of Miller Freeman's Music Group.

STEVE RODBY has played bass with the Pat Metheny Group since 1981.

ALEXIS SKLAREVSKI is a studio musician/ teacher who has toured with Crosby, Stills & Nash. His instructional video, *The Slap Bass Program,* is available from Video Progressions.

JOHN J. SLOG is a columnist for *Vintage Guitar* magazine and owns Guitar Villa in Bethlehem, Pennsylvania, a shop specializ- ing in vintage, used, and new basses and guitars (www.guitar-villa.com).

RICK TURNER was a pioneer of electric-bass design at Alembic in the 1970s, where he helped build instruments for the Grateful Dead and Jefferson Airplane. He now operates Rick Turner Guitars in Santa Cruz, California.

VICTOR WOOTEN is a solo artist and also plays bass for Béla Fleck & the Flecktones.

Photo Credits

BILL ADAMS 154, 160

COURTESY OF BALAFON BOOKS 157, 159

TRIPP BILLINGS 50

JAY BLAKESBERG 195

CLAYTON CALL 9

TOM COPI 187

FRANK DRIGGS 11

TOM ERLEWINE 123, 124

WOLFGANG GONAUS 106

SUSAN GREENBERG 72

PAUL HAGGARD 3, 5, 7, 8, 14, 16, 34, 64, 108, 111, 114, 118, 119, 120, 121, 125, 126, 129, 131, 139, 141, 145, 155, 162, 183, 197, 201, 206

JEAN HANGARTER 31

PHILLIP HIGHT 77

COURTESY OF D. HISCOCK 44, 171

JAY KAHN 32

RICK MALKIN 82

REBECCA MAULEON-SANTANA 84, 87

COURTESY OF BOB McCASKEY 135

COURTESY OF NILE ROGERS 75

MICHAEL SANDY 156, 158

JON SIEVERT 189

COURTESY OF ALEXIS SKLAREVSKI 95

COURTESY OF ALLAN SLUTSKY 165

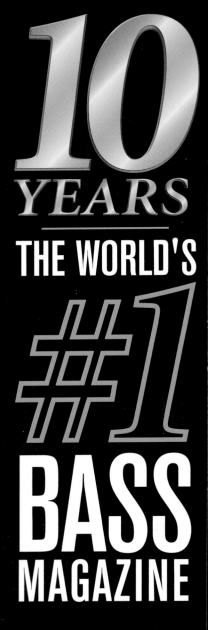